Governmental Controls and the Free Market

Governmental Controls and the Free Market

The U.S. Economy in the 1970's

EDITED BY

SVETOZAR PEJOVICH

TEXAS A&M UNIVERSITY PRESS
College Station and London

Library of Congress Cataloging in Publication Data

Conference on Individual Liberty and Governmental
    Policies in the 1970's, Ohio University, 1975.
    Governmental controls and the free market.

    "Papers presented at the Conference on Individual
Liberty and Governmental Policies in the 1970's held
under the auspices of the Department of Economics,
Ohio University, in June, 1975."
    Includes bibliographical references and index.
    1. United States—Economic policy—Congresses.
2. Laissez-faire—Congresses. I. Pejovich, Svetozar.
II. Ohio University, Athens. Dept. of Economics.
III. Title.
HC103.C735   1975   330.9'73'0924   76-17976
ISBN 0-89096-020-8

Manufactured in the United States of America
FIRST EDITION

Contents

Preface

THIS book contains the papers presented at the Conference on Individual Liberty and Governmental Policies in the 1970's held under the auspices of the Department of Economics, Ohio University, in June, 1975. The purpose of the conference, part of the program of the Liberty Fund, Inc., was to enhance the appreciation of the relationship between individual liberty, the economic problems in the country, and governmental policies in this decade. The Liberty Fund was established to encourage study of the ideal of a society of free and responsible individuals.

The conference was attended by thirty-five economists from all parts of the country; members of the Department of Economics at Ohio University; Helen Schultz, William Fletcher, and Neil McLeod of the Liberty Fund; Don Redekop of the Financial Post, Toronto; Anthony Sullivan of the Earhart Foundation; William Voss of Ohio University; David Williams of the Texas Educational Association; and the conference secretaries Lynn Esque and Lilliana Pejovich. Harry Crewson, president of Ohio University, greeted the participants on behalf of the university.

In preparing the manuscript for publication, I received invaluable help from my colleagues Eirik Furubotn of Texas A&M University; Doug Adie, Ismail Ghazalah, and Lowell Gallaway of Ohio University; and William H. Hutt of the University of Dallas. Kasey Cole and Denise Grassmuck provided excellent typing and clerical services.

Dallas, Texas   SVETOZAR PEJOVICH

Conference Participants

ARMEN ALCHIAN, University of California, Los Angeles
BEN BAACK, Ohio State University
KARL BONUTTI, Cleveland State University
NEIL BROWNE, Bowling Green State University
JAMES BUCHANAN, Virginia Polytechnic Institute
COLIN CAMPBELL, Dartmouth College
ROSEMARY CAMPBELL, Hanover, New Hampshire
ELIZABETH CLAYTON, University of Missouri, Saint Louis
MARILYN FLOWERS, University of Oklahoma
DAVID FRIEDMAN, University of Pennsylvania
EIRIK FURUBOTN, Texas A&M University
DAVID GAY, University of Arkansas
JOHN GIBBENS, Marion College
DAVID HENDERSON, University of California, Los Angeles
WILLIAM H. HUTT, University of Dallas
GERALD KEIM, Texas A&M University
ANTHONY LEE, University of Miami Law School
ROBERT LYNCH, University of Dallas
HELMUT MERKLEIN, University of Dallas
WILLIAM NISKANEN, Ford Motor Company
ANTHONY PETTO, De Paul University
ALAN REYNOLDS, *National Review*
CRAIG ROBERTS, West Georgia State College
TIMOTHY ROTH, University of Texas, El Paso
LARS SANDBERG, Ohio State University
NICOLAS SANCHES, Texas A&M University
MORRIS SILVER, City College, New York
CRAIG STUBBLEBINE, Claremont Men's College
DAVID TEECE, University of Pennsylvania
GEORGE TRIVOLI, University of Missouri, Columbia
GORDON TULLOCK, Virginia Polytechnic Institute
KAREN VAUGHAN, University of Tennessee
WILLIAM WHITE, University of Nevada, Las Vegas
OLIVER WILLIAMSON, University of Pennsylvania
JOSEPH ZIEGLER, University of Arkansas

Governmental Controls and the Free Market

Introduction

SVETOZAR PEJOVICH

SINCE the end of World War II, governmentally directed interferences in the market have grown significantly in the United States. The nation seems to have come to believe that political processes should be relied upon to produce and distribute goods. Today it is difficult to identify a single section of the national economy that is not touched by bureaucratic regulation of some sort. Economic analysis usually treats those regulations as constraints that affect the behavior of decision makers in specific and predictable ways. Recently, however, there has been a quickening of interest in national economic planning that reflects a major qualitative change in the prevailing climate of public opinion concerning the role of government in the national economy. Instead of imposing constraints on the allocation and use of resources, the government proposes to enter, via economic planning, into areas of decision making that have traditionally been the prerogative of ownership. And if the modes of entry into decision making through ownership are circumvented by political controls, then social institutions that define the free enterprise system, such as the right to ownership, the freedom to seek and negotiate mutually beneficial contractual agreements, and limited government, will face a serious crisis.

The Javits-Humphrey Balanced Growth and Economic Planning Act of 1975 is the most serious proposal for comprehensive economic planning ever advanced in the U.S. Congress. It proposes to set up an Office of Balanced Growth and Economic Planning in the Executive Office of the President. The office would consist of a council, a director, a deputy director, and a staff. An advisory committee, balanced to represent "various interests," would also be formed. The planning bill specifies that the national economic plan would analyze the economy industry by industry and sector by sector. It would also determine general objectives for the allocation of resources to various sectors of the economy, for the goods and services produced by those sectors, and for the "quality of life" in the country.

The proposed bill represents a significant step in a powerful movement away from limited government and individual freedom of choice.

Unlike business firms, the government may not only plan—it may also command. While business firms can plan and set goals only for themselves, the government can plan and set goals for others. That is, a national economic plan can be imposed on the people whether they like it or not. While it is true that current proposals for greater governmental controls of the economy are couched in terms of indicative planning, one has to be naïve to believe that a planning bureaucracy will ever allow its influence to be restricted to producing and disseminating information. There should be an appraisal of the relationship between the rewards (including reelection and reappointment) expected by legislators and government officials and the pattern of their behavior. The legislator who does not get reelected and the government official who does not get reappointed are replaced by someone who, in their judgment, is worse.

I do not mean to be critical of our public officials. In fact, it is wrong to think of them either as devious or as virtuous men. What I am saying is that it makes much more sense to base our expectations of the actions that public officials will pursue on the pattern of behavior that the prevailing system of rewards in government generates. Thus, it can be readily predicted that as time goes on, legislators and government officials will produce and market new regulations that in effect will restrict individual freedom of choice. Eventually, the plans of individuals will be subordinated to the common good as understood and defined by the ruling elite.

For all its rich rhetoric about indicative planning, the Javits-Humphrey proposal is an important step toward governmental controls of all economic activities in the country. The fact that the concept of economic planning is now taken seriously suggests that the current challenge to free enterprise and individual liberty in the United States has reached crisis proportions. The system that has given us an abundance of material goods and fed millions of hungry people elsewhere is now facing a fight for its own survival. The prevailing climate of public opinion seems to regard progress as synonymous with expanding the bundle of resources controlled by the government.

It is important to recognize that the case for the free enterprise system does not rest on its productive achievement alone. Neither does it rest on the right of individuals to smoke cigarettes although someone in Washington might feel that cigars are safer, or on the knowledge of individuals that they can always bid resources away from other uses and get what they want, or on the fact that profits must be created in some activities in order to subsidize others. Indeed, the case for free enterprise rests on constitutional guarantees of well-defined individual rights: on the right to ownership, on the individual's freedom to seek contractual partners and negotiate terms of exchange, and on a theory of limited government that is primarily concerned with enforcing constitutional order, protecting contractual partners from breach of contract, and providing public goods. In other words, to be concerned about the consequences of the prevailing climate of public opinion is by no means to be concerned only with economic efficiency. The real concern is with the quality of life generated by the institutions of private property, profit incentives, and social interaction guided by principles of self-responsibility, self-determination, self-interest, and open-market competition.[1]

This book is an enquiry into some more important consequences of the transformation of the American free enterprise system into an overgoverned society. Contributors to the book are recognized scholars in their fields. Their contributions are quite diverse in style, content, and assessment of economic problems, but they are all characterized by a common emphasis on the Western tradition of self-responsibility, self-determination, self-interest, and open-market competition. Thus, the book presents a coherent enquiry into some of the more pressing social issues of our time. Admittedly, this approach has its limitations, some of which arise from the single-approach strategy, yet such a critical assessment of the direction in which public policy is moving is certainly needed.

ECONOMIC ACTIVITY AND INSTITUTIONAL CHANGE

Economic activity involves social interaction at two levels. The first level involves the development, specification, and modification of institutions by which the community seeks to resolve social problems that find their source in scarcity. (Those institutions are defined as arrangements, widely sanctioned and tolerated, that specify the relationships among men that arise from the existence of scarce goods and pertain to their use.) The prevailing set of institutions defines the general character of economic life in the community. Traditionally, economic analysis has treated prevailing institutions as exogenous to the economic system. Recently, some important studies have suggested, indeed, quite strongly,

---

[1] See an excellent book by James Buchanan, *The Limits of Liberty* (Chicago: University of Chicago Press, 1975).

that the development and specification of social institutions are, to a considerable degree, endogenous to the system.[2] Clearly, the implications are that economic reasoning is capable of explaining changes in the social structure.

The second level of social interaction involves decision-making processes, individual choices, the content of contractual agreements, and activities within the set of opportunity choices defined by the prevailing institutions. Traditionally, economic theory has been primarily concerned with the analysis of social interactions at this level of economic activity—that is, with the analysis of equilibrium solutions within a given institutional framework. And if this framework is considered invariant, economic efficiency becomes the end objective instead of an instrument to be relied upon in attaining other social objectives. Then, disappointment with economic expectations is capable of turning the tide of public opinion against the entire social order.

The development and specification of institutional structure in a community depends on economic conditions of life and a host of other factors such as tradition, religion, culture, education, work ethic, the ruling elite's taste for power, and so on. Together, these factors form the prevailing climate of public opinion. Their relative importance in shaping the character of economic life differs from one community to another. For example, the importance of tradition in determining the social structure has been much stronger in India than in Western Europe. Yet the influence of various factors on the development and specification of institutions does not operate on an all-or-nothing basis. The prevailing institutions in a community can be taken to represent some sort of trade-off among all the various sources of influence.

It can be asserted that a change in the prevailing climate of public opinion might translate into institutional restructuring. In that case, a change in the prevailing institutions is likely to affect the allocation and use of resources in specific and predictable ways.[3] Let us now raise an

2 See Douglass North and R. Thomas, *The Rise of the Western World: A New Economic History* (Cambridge: Cambridge University Press, 1973); Harold Demsetz, "Toward a Theory of Property Rights," *American Economic Review* 57 (May, 1964): 347–359; Svetozar Pejovich, "Toward an Economic Theory of the Creation and Specification of Property Rights," *Review of Social Economy* 30 (Sept., 1972): 309–325.

3 See Eirik Furubotn and Svetozar Pejovich, "Property Rights and Economic Theory: A Survey of Recent Literature," *Journal of Economic Literature* 10 (Dec., 1972): 1137–1162.

important question: why has the climate of public opinion in the United States turned against the free enterprise system?

The free enterprise system rests on the right to ownership in resources. That is, the mode of entry into decision making is through ownership. The behavioral principles of self-interest, self-determination, self-responsibility, and price competition mentioned above, which determine the character of social life in a free enterprise economy, stem directly from the institution of private property.

However, even though the right to ownership is an exclusive right, it is not an unrestricted right. It is exclusive in the sense that it is limited only by those restrictions that are explicitly stated in the law. Of course, those restrictions are coercive; they define things that an individual cannot do. But there is no such thing as a completely coercive or a completely free society. All societies employ some degree of coercion to protect the stability of social order. The point is that the free enterprise system, through the linkage between ownership and decision making, minimizes the right of one individual to coerce another into doing something that the coerced would rather not do. It also minimizes the coercive power of the state by restricting the role of government to that of enforcing constitutional order and of providing public goods.

Restrictions on individual liberty in the free enterprise system can then be treated as a kind of exchange. Individuals trade some of their particular rights for more efficient (lower-cost) protection of other rights. Thus, "social order [emerges] contractually from the rational utility-maximation of individuals, social order that would embody a definition of assignments of individual rights, and the establishment of a political structure charged with enforcing rules of personal behavior with respect to these assigned rights."[4]

The important result that economic analysis attributes to the free enterprise system is that the allocation of resources satisfies the equi-marginal principle. That is, open-market competition and the right of ownership combine to perform two functions. Competition identifies alternative uses for each resource (a piece of land can be used to build a home, a plant, or a parking lot, or to grow food or flowers), while transferability of ownership (coupled with self-interest) ensures that the most valuable alternative is chosen—that is, that the land is allocated

[4] Buchanan, *The Limits of Liberty*, p. 74.

to the highest-valued use. It is in open market that the incompetent and the crooks and cheaters lose out in the long run to other competitors, that efficiency and foresight about other people's desires are rewarded, and that a reputation for honest dealing becomes an economic asset that yields return to the owner.

In my judgment we should distinguish between two types of change in public attitude concerning the role of government in the American economy. First, the government was called on to improve the performance of the national economy within the framework of free enterprise. Then, in the late 1960's, the climate of opinion turned against free enterprise. Today, we witness many incidences of public pressure to replace the market-oriented allocation of resources with political controls in areas of decision making that traditionally have been the prerogative of ownership, either directly or through hired representatives. What is under attack today is the mode of entry into decision making with respect to the allocation and use of scarce resources.

I believe that externalities (the fact that not all the costs of a decision are borne by the decision maker) and unemployment provided an efficient cause for a change in the climate of public opinion concerning the role of government in the national economy. They gave support to those social groups in our society that stood to benefit from a shift away from limited government toward collective control of economic activities. In some sense the standard theory of production and exchange, which has traditionally assumed that all resources are privately owned and that transaction costs are zero, made a contribution to this change in the climate of public opinion. On the basis of these two assumptions, economic theory was able to demonstrate that in a private-property, free-market economy, all costs of a decision are borne by the decision maker, and the allocation and use of resources tend to be consistent with the equimarginal principle. While this conception of the environment permits useful analysis, it does narrow the range of real-world events that can be explained. Transaction costs are never zero, *all* resources are never privately owned, and the right to ownership is frequently attenuated (subject to various legal restraints). Thus, the allocation and use of resources often result in market solutions that are inconsistent with the equimarginal principle. In consequence, the idea of producing a "socially optimal" output mix through the political process has gained public support.

Most economists recognize that the market should not be faulted for the existence of all externalities, nor should all externalities be eliminated. Demsetz's zero-priced parking example is a case in point. He says that the cost of selling parking space at a shopping center could easily exceed the value of the good: "We may end up by allocating more resources to the provision and control of parking than had we allowed free parking because of the resources needed to conduct transactions."[5]

The optimal solution in the political process requires a careful balancing of the marginal social costs and benefits. Unfortunately, public recognition of the need to reduce some externalities through the political process has been slowly but steadily converted into a fantastic array of government regulations of business activity. For example, California licenses dog trainers, while Florida is about to license lawn sprinkler installers. Clearly, these and similar regulations have little to do with private/social divergences.[6] The implication is that we cannot trust the market to have displaced and to continue to displace those who do not perform to the consumer's satisfaction.

Similarly, the market should not be blamed for all unemployment. However, the problem of unemployment gave rise to the popular belief that the market mechanism cannot maintain the level of economic activity at a full employment level. The U.S. Congress responded to this change in the climate of public opinion and charged the government with maintaining the level of aggregate demand consistent with full employment. This congressional action has resulted in an ever-increasing level of public spending and not much change in the rate of unemployment.

In the late 1960's, the climate of public opinion concerning the free enterprise system experienced a major change. While the demand for government spending and regulation of business activity continued to grow, a remarkable change occurred in the public attitude toward private property, profit incentives, and the principles of self-responsibility, self-determination, self-interest, and price competition. What we witness today in the United States is an attack on the very foundations of the

[5] Harold Demsetz, "The Exchange and Enforcement of Property Rights," *Journal of Law and Economics* 7 (Oct., 1964): 14.

[6] Henry Manne, *Government Control of Business: Popular Myths and Economic Reality* (Miami: Center of Studies in Law and Economics, University of Miami, n.d.), p. 2.

free enterprise system. Interestingly enough, the most outspoken advocates of replacing the free enterprise system with economic planning are often the same people who are the most zealous defenders of non-economic individual freedoms—as if these two aspects of freedom were not mutually interdependent. What *are* some of those factors that have affected the climate of public opinion toward the free enterprise system?

It would not be difficult to demonstrate that free-enterprise-oriented teachers in institutions of higher learning are relatively few. It is only logical to assume that the same situation exists in secondary schools, since their instructors are are products of our universities. And these people are retailers of ideas to our youth. Many high school teachers object to economics as a discipline because they find economic analysis "cold" and "inhuman"—something that prevents the young from wholehearted involvement in social affairs. It is doubtful if it is often said in classrooms that most corporations got to be large by selling things that people wanted and by producing them more efficiently than other firms, that corporate profits are the rewards for serving the public, that economic profits are a powerful, perhaps necessary guide for the efficient allocation of resources. Professor R. M. Hartwell of Oxford University summarized the effects of education on the youths' attitude toward capitalism in a 1972 Mont Pelerin lecture in Montreux as follows:

> Much of the study of literature . . . has moved from analyses of the universals of artistic expression to the sociology of literature, in terms of the artist's reaction to "relevant" problems; the worth of a writer is now often measured in terms of his reaction to the social problems of his day. . . . Economics . . . is more often concerned with the efficiency of government intervention, with how to make socialism work better, than with challenging the interventionist philosophy. Basic to much teaching of economics is the assumption that market economy is not working because it cannot work, rather than objective analysis of the thesis that market economy does not work because it is not allowed to work. And what formal education in its various subjects propagates, social institutions reinforce: the social teaching of the Christian churches is anti-market and interventionist in spirit; the mass media maintain a constant barrage of criticism of liberalism and over-dramatise the ills of industrial society; creative art caters too often for irresponsible and destructive views of society. . . . It is not surprising, therefore, that so many young people grow up to accept the need for government intervention to solve all society's ills, and to believe that conditions are only as good as they are because of government, or that conditions are as bad as they are because

of the failure of government. Thus they see no paradox in accepting the goods of market economy at the same time as believing that the system which produces them is both inefficient and immoral.

Our business community, which has succeeded so well in providing us with goods and services, has completely failed to identify our affluence with the existence of capitalist free enterprise, profit incentives, and competition. Moreover, in the field of advertising, many companies are in fact promoting antimarket sentiments in response to emotionally charged calls for "social responsibility." Little or nothing is being said by our business leaders about the relationship between the right to seek and capture more profits on the one hand and the associated improvements in social welfare on the other. Thus, the public is left to regard profits as things that are left over from the operation of business and are not really needed—things that can be reduced without harm. The point is frequently left unsaid that profits earned in various lines of business activity reveal our preferences from the output mix, that they guide the flow of resources among various uses, that they motivate the profit-seeking producer to produce more and spur someone else to develop a substitute.

M. A. Wright, chief executive of Exxon, has said that it is up to the business community to make a wholehearted effort to ensure that Congress does not kill the golden geese.[7] Unfortunately, but predictably, individual business leaders find it less costly to go along with the tide of public opinion than to put up strong resistance. A chief executive may harm his own stockholders if he supports a cause that would be advantageous to all stockholders of all business firms collectively. Vigorous bucking of public opinion is simply too costly to a single firm and its management.

Yet the greatest opposition to the free enterprise system comes from our legislators, government officials, media, and intellectuals in general. In fact, their behavior is quite predictable. Legislators and public officials capture rewards by increasing resources under their control. Irving Kristol named this group a "new class" and predicted that our future will be marked by a struggle between the public sector, striving for control, and the private sector, fighting to retain its identity. His explanation of the factors that motivate the behavior of this new class is quite succinct:

[7] M. A. Wright, "The Assault on Private Enterprise" (address to the 26th Annual Business Conference, New Brunswick, N.J., May 31, 1974).

Today there is a new class hostile to business in general, and especially to large corporations. As a group, you find them mainly in the very large and growing public sector and in the media. This new class consists of well educated and intelligent professionals who work in all levels of government: public officials, civil servants, bureaucrats, doctors, lawyers, and engineers in some form of public service; teachers and school administrators; psychologists, sociologists, and environmentalists; members of the media; foundation managers (who are not in the public sector, but think that way), and more. No one knows how large this group is, but it could amount to as much as 15 per cent of our population. Those people are smart and articulate. They share a disinterest in personal wealth, a dislike for the free market economy, and a conviction that society may best be improved through greater governmental participation in the country's economic life. As a result of technical, economic, and social developments, this group has become terribly influential. They *are* the media. They are the educational system. Their dislike for the free market economy originates in their inability to exercise much influence over it so as to produce change. In its place they would prefer a system in which there is a very large political component. This is because the new class has a great deal of influence in politics. Thus, through politics, they can exercise a direct and immediate influence on the shape of our society and the direction of national affairs.[8]

Kristol's eloquence is fully matched by his perceptions. It is not surprising at all that the "new class" is soft to the left and hard to the right.

SUMMARIES OF THE CHAPTERS

If the modes of entry into decision making in business activity are to be controlled by some sort of political determination, their restriction must have significant social and economic consequences. This book examines some of the more crucial consequences of the direction in which the tide of public opinion is moving in the United States. Contributions to the volume are divided into three parts: "Economic Problems in the 1970's," "Governmental Policies in the 1970's," and "The Modern Corporation and Its Critics in the 1970's."

The first part examines the problems of inflation, unemployment, and poverty in the United States. In the mid-1970's the country experienced the highest rate of inflation and unemployment since the end of

[8] Irving Kristol, "The Question of Liberty in America," interview in *Exxon* 14 (Fall, 1975): 9.

World War II. Those are the real economic problems facing the nation. Poverty, however, is a political issue that finds its origin in income inequalities that are allegedly biased against minority groups.

The prevailing public opinion either attributes the problems of inflation, unemployment, and poverty to the market or considers the market to be incapable of resolving them. The public seems to have become convinced that "something has gone wrong" with the free enterprise system and that "something should be done." This conviction produced the proposals for more government controls. Price controls, more government spending, various types of transfer payments, and, finally, economic planning are but a few of the results. Chapters 1 and 2 question these widely held beliefs concerning the causes of inflation, unemployment, and poverty.

In chapter 1, Alchian uses the tools of modern economic theory to relate inflation to the prevailing system of incentives in the public sector. He shows that inflation financing of government activities is a "convenient" form of taxation that can be easily hidden from the general public. Therefore, we can expect government-produced inflation to continue, with business corporations and organized labor bearing the burden of public displeasure. Gallaway's chapter 2 contains more quantitative data and some startling findings concerning the effects of government programs on unemployment and poverty in the United States. In addition, Gallaway finds no significant differences in the distribution of income between the United States, on the one hand, and Sweden and the Soviet Union on the other. In summary, Alchian and Gallaway find no reason to attribute our major economic problems to malfunctioning of the market.

The second part of the volume has four chapters. They analyze three important topics: the nature of political processes, the content of government regulation of business activity, and the effects of transfer payments on the level and character of economic activity in the country. In chapter 3, Niskanen questions the conventional prescription for good government that consists of selecting wise and honest men for public office and giving them the power to translate what they think the public interest is into public outcomes. Instead, he treats political processes as purposeful actions serving quite private interests. Niskanen's analysis shows that public policy can effectively be analyzed in terms of how the institutions of government are organized to harness private purposes to public outcomes.

The rising cost of the social security system in the United States is the subject of Campbell's analysis in chapter 4. Expenditures and revenue for social security are now major items in the federal budget. Thus, the question of how well this expensive system works is important. Campbell finds that it is not working well. His analysis suggests that the lack of a close relationship between the cost of the program and the benefits one can expect to receive from it aggravates disincentive effects that the social security system seems to have on labor participation, saving, capital formation, and economic growth.

The analysis of the effects of governmental transfer payments continues in chapter 5. Buchanan is concerned with a relative reduction in productive outlays and an increase in transfer outlays that has occurred in the composition of the public sector share in the GNP. The transfer share of federal spending increased from 5.6 percent of the GNP in 1960 to about 10 percent of the GNP in 1974. He finds that the redistribution of income via transfer payments tends to reduce the rate of private saving, private capital formation, and work effort and to increase one's taste for nonpecuniary sources of utility.

In chapter 6, Tullock turns to an important question of what are the factors that determine the content of various regulations. He reviews some alternative explanations of the regulating process and concludes that the only approach that seems capable of yielding testable implications is the one that is based on the personal advantages and disadvantages of the members of the regulatory board. The formal problem emerges as one of maximizing the commission member's utility subject to the constraints imposed by the opportunity set. Tullock then proceeds to identify some important consequences of granting decision-making powers to individuals who bear no responsibilities that are associated with ownership in scarce resources.

The last part of the book examines the role of the modern corporation in the American economy today. Of course, that institution is a primary target of the critics of free enterprise. One group of critics claims that the modern corporation is an inefficient instrument for resource allocation. The contention is that the "separation of ownership from control" has diluted the economic consequences which economic theory derives from the fact of ownership. In addition, the alleged market power of the modern corporation implies the existence of monopoly profits. Thus, the managers of corporate firms supposedly are in the position to determine the level and character of economic life in the nation. Williamson confronts this contention in chapter 7 and shows that the modern corporation is an efficient instrument for mitigating frictions that are associated with the operation of labor and capital markets. An interesting conclusion that Williamson deduces is that the conglomerate is not an anticompetitive structure. Therefore, he suggests a more sympathetic posture on the part of the antitrust enforcement agencies toward conglomerates.

An emerging school of radical political economists forms another group of critics of the modern corporation. The question of efficiency of the modern corporation vis-a-vis some other forms of business organization is of no interest to that group of writers. They are hostile to the fundamental structure of free enterprise, most specifically to the right to ownership. They assert that private property is a vehicle by which the ruling class secures gains at the expense of the mass of exploited workers. In chapter 8, Furubotn examines some of the more important contentions and arguments advanced by the radical writers. He finds them emotional in tone and poor in logic. Most importantly, he examines that dominant thesis of the radical left, worker alienation, and its proposed cure, the labor-managed firm. He finds that the labor-managed firm is much less effective in reducing worker alienation than its capitalist counterpart. Furubotn ends his contribution to the volume by a word of warning to those who would destroy an effective economic system in the blind pursuit of an illusion. Thus, his analysis forms an appropriate conclusion to this book.

PART I
Economic Problems in the 1970's

Chapter 1

Problems of Rising Prices

ARMEN ALCHIAN

I believe inflation is inevitable as a long-run trend, with transient, decade-long interruptions of stable or falling prices. That forecast reflects my view of government. Inflation is a tax on money. Like any tax, it will be used. The more subtle, the less detected, and the less avoidable the tax, the better it is for those with predominant political power and the more surely it will be used. I join Keynes in at least part of the following: "progressive deterioration in the value of money through history is not an accident, and has had behind it two great driving forces—the impecuniosity of governments and the superior political influence of the debtor class."[1]

Since Keynes has been dead wrong in interpreting the effects of inflation, I cite him for eloquence, not authority. Furthermore, the "superior political influence of the debtor class" is not clearly significant. But impecuniosity of governments, that is, their desire to spend more and their ability to do so by creating money, is, I believe, irresistible for any government. And when we add the recent priestly dogma that increasing the money stock is a means of assuring high employment, there is no doubt that inflation at a transient varying rate is a way of life.

By inflation I mean either a single-shot rise in the price level or a continuing rising price level. Thus, I can interpret a rising price level as a sequence of factors, possibly overlapping, causing single-shot rises, though possibly so overlapping that one is unable to distinguish their putt-putt forces from a continuous jet stream.

SOURCES OF INFLATION

I turn first to sources of inflation. Two already have been mentioned

[1] J. M. Keynes, *Tract on Monetary Reform* (London, 1923; reprint New York: St. Martin's Press, 1971), p. 12. Is it a definition of government to say that any possessor of the dominant military power and monopoly of the base money is a government?

—the ability to print money and the dogma that more *should* be printed to reduce unemployment. As causes of inflation, two factors should be distinguished: (1) changes in the ratio of money supply to money demand, and (2) factors that induce changes in that ratio—that is, that induce us to embark on an inflationary policy. An increased supply of money relative to demand creates higher prices. But the factor that persuaded the money suppliers to increase the supply of money is what induced us to embark on a monetary policy that creates inflation. Monetary policy is a *means* of creating inflation; the objective of the policy is the *reason* for resorting to inflation. Both are often called "causes." The increased money stock relative to demand creates inflation, whatever the reason ("cause") for embarking on the inflationary increase in the supply of money. Unless we keep those things distinct, we aren't going to get anywhere.

The supply of money can increase in a variety of ways. Gold or silver discoveries, development of new, more efficient forms of money (bank demand deposits) used along with the existing money, or the simple printing of more money by the official money printer for the "impecunious" government all are increases.

Certain interesting factors, events, or goals induce the government to spend more than its explicit tax income. To identify them, ask, "What do governments do?" The answer is, "More than before." That reply is especially valid when the costs can be spread over a wide range of people and their impact can thereby be attenuated below the individual's costs of preventing them. A larger fraction of national income will be taxed, and the larger that fraction, the greater the extent to which the printing press will be used to "balance the budget." That is the Keynesian "impecuniosity."

In addition, it has recently become respectable to create money by twisting the Keynesian doctrine that government should increase the money supply to counter major monetary contractions. That original Keynesian monetary prescription has been twisted particularly by political aspirants, for whom it is a congenial way to enhance their political status or use of government power. The new dogma is that employment is to be maintained—or, more accurately, efforts are to be exerted to try to maintain it—above that level maintainable in a free, liberal society in which people not assigned to jobs could investigate and choose those they themselves deem best. In other words, each person has the right to refuse to work for wages he, and he alone, deems unacceptable because of opportunities he believes to be discoverable elsewhere or available later. If we announce that action will be taken to assure current jobs at wages greater than those acceptable to both parties, we are announcing a policy of trying to maintain an impossibly low average rate of unemployment by assuring jobs and incomes to people whose services consumers think are not worth their asking price. The policy is to induce employers to buy their employees' services by increasing the employer's demand for their services and in turn by increasing the demand for that employer's products. This is not the desirable policy of avoiding monetary contractions; instead, monetary expansion is recommended for *any* reduction in actual employment.

The source of the (erroneous) belief that monetary expansion would assure such jobs—that is, that it would hold unemployment below that rate consistent with changed demands and with costs of getting information about new opportunities and costs for entrepreneurs to ascertain to what other tasks or outputs they should convert their productive facilities (I shall return to this point later)—is a result of confused analysis and misread empirical evidence. The employment acts in the United States and Britain simply assumed that we could somehow keep employment at that natural "full employment" rate, presumably by pure fiscal policy. But transient shifts in demand among firms and industries and products will induce higher rates of unemployment in some and lower rates in others. To prevent all unemployment increases in every sector is to attempt the impossible in a free, liberal society—a fact that still seems to escape most people. That doctrine was given an aura of respectability by the delusion of the Phillips curve.

In sum, at least two forces for inflationary monetary policy are present: "impecuniosity" of governments, and the attempt to assure full employment by money expansion (whether through government expenditures or otherwise). The former force regards money increases as regrettable but necessary, because we just "can't" balance the budget. The latter regards them as desirable. Who can beat a combination like that?

There are other policies intended to aid high employment and rapid adaptability to changing demands and supply conditions that do not involve monetary expansion. These policies attempt to lower that natural unemployment rate by, for example, cheapening the costs of ascertaining the best unexploited opportunities or by trying to avoid downward, transient shocks in the system caused by misguided, politically motivated monetary policy keyed to interest rates, balance of payments, and fixed exchange rates.

IRRELEVANCY OF MONOPOLY

Anyone, unions, business firms, or a single person, can set and persist in a price too high for his full employment or output. The belief that unions or large corporations have monopoly power and thus push up prices and cause inflation is a fallacious analysis and is wrong in fact. Any union or business or seller that pushes prices above its wealth-maximizing level will lose business and reduce employment. Resources will be released for use elsewhere, and prices elsewhere will have to be lower than they otherwise would be. The price level is not changed; relative prices are changed. Once a monopoly has set its best price, it will not raise prices higher, and not even a union, which some people think wants higher wages for the fewer and fewer remaining members who retain jobs at those higher wages, would raise the price level if it raised prices higher than its best price. The unemployed in that occupation would have to work elsewhere, lowering wages. Despite this analysis and empirical studies, some people (for example, Galbraith) try to incriminate corporations for driving up prices, while others (for example, Haberler) condemn the unions. Neither accusation is correct.

What is necessary is a will by the government to increase the stock of money to assure employment to anyone who raises his wage above the market clearing wage or price. To blame unions or corporations is to misdirect attention from the critical factor at work—the will to inflate the money supply to assure employment at whatever wages or prices people may ask. Anyone who raises his prices, be he college professor, gardener, or machinist, and to whom the government responds quickly in assuring full employment, can be said to "cause" inflation. But as we said earlier, the term *cause* is so ambiguous that we should avoid putting the proposition that way. We can say that the money supply increase creates inflation—that the money supply increase occurs as the government implements its promises of full employment assurance, revising expenditures when it observes unemployment (of some degree someplace). We could say that the particular people whose unemployment is the most important to the government policy makers will be the "more important" inducers of inflation, but I don't know who they are. Nor is it conducive to clarity of analysis to try to attach the concept of "cause" to any one of those stages of the process.

The amount of verbiage in the literature arguing whether to call the inflation cost-push, demand-pull, monopoly-union, monopoly-corporate, full-employment-assurance, or money-supply-increase inflation is dismaying. One is reminded of the scandalous literature on the equality of savings and investment by the writings on the cause of inflation. Indeed, some people have even proposed trying to test which is *the* operating cause! I suppose we might interpret that to mean they are proposing to test whether the government has a full-employment assurance policy, whether it has increased the quantity of money, or whether anyone ever raises his wages or prices to a height which creates less than market clearing employment or output for him. As for myself, I perhaps foolishly was willing to take each of those factors for granted with casual though extensive evidence. An inquiry that does appear interesting to me is this: Given all the above, to whose unemployment is government most responsive?

We cannot wholly abandon the monopoly element in inflation. One monopoly, the government monopoly of the supply of legal base money, does indeed permit inflation. Without that monopoly, with open competition in the creation of separate, identifiable brands of money, it can be argued very cogently and persuasively that inflation would be avoided. Suppliers of money, each producing a different brand of money, would compete to produce the best money—a noninflating one. However, this possibility will remain purely hypothetical and therefore is given no attention.[2]

Money is more than a lower-cost substitute for simple barter. It also is a store of value, a measure of debt in generalized goods. Instead of expressing or settling all debts or expressing them in single goods, a general package in terms of the exchange value of a medium of exchange is an economically useful institution. But while money may perform its function as a medium of exchange (because of easy portability, recognizability, and divisibility), its storability, or economic value of such

---

[2] For the two best discussions of which I am aware, see B. Klein, "The Competitive Supply of Money," *Journal of Money, Credit and Banking* 6, no. 4 (Nov., 1974), and E. Thompson, "The Theory of Money and Income Consistent with Orthodox Value Theory," in *Trade, Stability and Macroeconomics: Essays in Honor of Lloyd A. Metzler* (New York: Academic Press, 1974), pp. 427–453.

future claims, is more uncertain. Furthermore, variations in its rate of inflation make the value more variable. Money loses the predictability of its value. One of our great social institutions, money, is damaged, and our wealth is subjected to greater variations, which we all can justifiably regard as unjustifiable.

Disposable also is the excuse that inflation is a world-wide phenomenon, like some disease that infects us all. Such error hardly merits notice, except that sometimes we are careless and think fixed exchange rates tying all countries' monies together are a cause of inflation, a mistake that confuses covariation with inflation. The world-wide deflation of the 1930's was a result of fixed exchange rates. Fixed exchange rates imply a similarity in price level movements, not necessarily inflation or deflation. Indeed, if exchange rates are allowed to respond to free, open-market forces, I know of no basis on which to predict whether countries would inflate faster or less fast, though I would bet on less correlation and faster inflation simply because the government is released from a restraint on the rate at which it can inflate.

A PROCESS OF PRICING IN INFLATION

How do expectations operate in inflation? That process is, I believe, widely misunderstood, which means that my understanding of it differs from that of most other people. I believe an analysis along the following pattern is valid. When speaking of expected price, I mean, and economic analysis refers to (or should refer to), the price (1) that a person initially (now) sets (in other words, will accept) for his services or goods, and (2) at which he believes he will sell the amount he chooses to offer at that price. For example, a producer hopes, plans, or expects to sell some amount of product at a price. He sets that price and then soon begins to learn whether he gets the amount of demand he anticipated. If he does, that price (his expectation of his market clearing price) was correct. It was the price that did permit him to sell what he offered at that price. That actual price is the one he expected to be or believed would be the market clearing price. If it is not, he will sell less than he offers or he will find more demanded than he offers. He will learn whether it is an equilibrating price. Before asking how he learns that, if he does, let me emphasize in the strongest way that I know there is reason to assume the price he asks (his "expectation") is just as solidly, firmly, or confidently held if it is a higher price than yesterday's, by, say,

10 percent, as if it were the same price. In each case, that price is an actual price *and* a prediction of what the market clearing price is. It is asked (set) and it is not withdrawn at the instant sales deviate.

As I have argued elsewhere, price inflexibility is not a silly, uneconomic thing. Nor does price firmness mean unchanged price over time. It means unchanging price in the face of only *transient* reversible deviations of sales or production around what is believed to be a market clearing rate. Noncontinuous varying sales rates are not responded to by instant changes of prices. Production and inventories are among the adjusting variables.

A price that may turn out not to be an equilibrium price is just as slow to adjust in the face of new developing information if (1) it was set higher today in response to (erroneous) beliefs that the market clearing price was higher, or (2) it is the same as yesterday's price when no inflation was (erroneously) expected. If the price is wrong, in each case correct adjustment to the new equilibrating price is equally uncertain, costly, and time-consuming and is preceded, or accompanied, by changes in output or sales. Nor is information about all other market options and opportunities provided instantly and costlessly. The new market clearing price vector can not be discovered instantly. Actual prices "lag" behind the market clearing vector. That information lag is the pertinent lag, an "error" in forecast.

A price today that is the same as a past price is no more natural than a rising sequence of prices. It all depends upon what current demands will sustain.[3] So long as demand does not sustain the price (as a market clearing price), and so long as the parties do not know the new best price vector, the search for the new best prices and best alternative activities is no simple task. Nor are the processes and implications of the search well understood. It is no less complex during stable price expectations than during rising demands with rising price expectations. (Add to this complexity the long-term commitments or arrangements emphasized by D. Gordon in explaining why wages do not fall quickly enough to permit hiring of the unemployed, even though those who retain their jobs still receive higher wages than the unemployed are asking. Gordon's

---

[3] There is no inconsistency between this analysis and the Martingale property of prices. The interest rate reflects that average belief about future price levels. Hence, the *average* equilibrating price expectation for tomorrow is today's price plus the interest rate—the usual Martingale property. Cf. A. Alchian, "Information, Martingales and Prices," *Swedish Journal of Economics* 76 (1974): 3–11.

analysis also is consistent with the proposition that one should not expect rising demand to be synonymous with demand rising *above* the prices people expect to be appropriate for clearing the market.)[4] Whatever people believe is today's market clearing price is asked (or bid) and persists until they are convinced of their error. Then they have to search for more appropriate price, product, rate of output, and investment. An increased nominal demand—but not sufficient to exceed or match the increased current price—is as contractionary as a falling demand with constant prices. Demand for a good is relative not only to various other goods; it is relative also to an expected market demand for the good at the currently charged prices.

In the usual jargon, the preceding discussion is translated into terms of anticipations or expectations of inflation not matching "actual" inflation. I prefer to identify prices now being set as the prices that are expected to be the present market clearing prices. These prices are actual prices—not "expected" prices. What is expected is that they will be market clearing.

Can the adjustment process be reversed? Can the "latest," unknown, equilibrium price vector be revised toward actual prices? This is the reverse of the common insistence on adjusting actual prices to the new, but unknown, market clearing vector. For example, many economists in the thirties strongly recommended monetary re-expansion to restore that market clearing nominal price vector up toward actual prices, rather than await the process of search, discovery, and convergence of actual prices with the low market clearing price vector to which actual prices have to be adjusted. How can the market clearing nominal vector be inflated to match current prices?

1. New money may be sprinkled from the skies, with all demands increasing until the formerly underpriced, over-demanded goods rise in price relative to the formerly over-priced goods. This plan will increase the average price in the clearing vector, and if we assume greater upward price adjustments in response to increased demand for goods that were more fully employed at existing prices, we *might* ease and quicken the convergence of the clearing vector and actual prices. Old money will be taxed (or depreciated) by the price rise, and initial recipients of the new money from the skies will gain wealth. If new money

---

[4] D. F. Gordon, "A Neo-Classical Theory of Unemployment," *Economic Inquiry* 12, no. 4 (Dec., 1974): 431–459.

is given in exact proportion to the old money holdings of each person, there is no net interpersonal wealth transfer of money.

2. New money may be initially spent directly in the excessively priced vector, increasing demand there. In this case, the tax on moneyholders finances the intentionally increased relative demand in the "depressed" sector and brings a rise in the equilibrium market clearing price for that sector, thereby bringing it closer to the actual price. The equilibrium (absolute and relative) price structure over the whole economy approaches the actual prices. Increased demand relative to newly posited prices (which are the objective aspects of "expectations") increases output and employment. Sales exceed the expected sales at the prices that are believed to be market clearing prices. No lag of any actual prices behind any other prices (no relative price change) is involved. The pertinent lag is the lag of adjustment of actual nominal prices to the market clearing vector, for which search must be made. That informational lag is critical. It creates what we call the natural rate of unemployment, it is always present—during unanticipated inflation, unanticipated deflation, anticipated inflation, and anticipated deflation—as long as the future (that is, the market clearing vector) is not costlessly, correctly perceived by everyone.

The excessively priced sector may require a greater increase in demand relative to the rest of the economy than can be financed by the inflation tax on money—and there is a limit to how much real wealth can be taxed by an inflation. In such a case inflation simply cannot finance the required shift. It will not restore full employment in that sector if that sector insists on, and is assured of, a higher real wage relative to other sectors. Expenditures financed by a direct tax on other forms of wealth or income must be used to shift relative demands sufficiently. But if these excessive prices are "assured" in enough sectors, it will be impossible to "assure" the excessive real demands, since the price vector would more than exhaust the social product at full employment.

Political assurance of full employment has the terrible problem of ascertaining whether current prices assured politically to everyone are compatible with physical production possibilities—a problem the free enterprise price system escapes because no one can have any assurance of profits or employment at whatever real income or price he deems "right." But we have politically made that commitment—or we act as if we have made that commitment—and now we naïvely wonder why we have inflation or more and more controls by government. Whatever other reasons are increasing the role of government, that desire for full employment certainly is.

A "puzzle" disposed by the preceding analysis is the so-called paradox of inflation and unemployment, or inflation and recession. The puzzle arises only if one assumes that a zero inflation rate is the basis on which people are making price commitments. If people expect the equilibrating, market clearing prices to be higher today than in the past, and yet if today the higher actual prices are not maintainable with full employment, what is adjusted? I know of no reason to expect prices to give way under that situation any more than when market clearing prices were incorrectly expected to be the same today as yesterday (incorrect because of a deflation).

Deflation? Does a reduced growth of the money stock and market demand below the anticipated inflation rate produce a less severe, shorter recession than does an equal-sized difference in money growth below a formerly constant price level? If so, ability to break a recent inflation without causing a long, severe depression would be enhanced. But I have no evidence for or against that possibility.

Irrelevancy of cost push and demand pull. This analysis does not say that demand increases and then prices go up. Nor is it a cost-push view either. Nor is monopoly power involved. If people believe and forecast that market clearing prices will be higher, they will enter the market with higher prices which they believe are market clearing prices. If demand has increased less than that forecast, people will not instantly revise their prices downward. The erroneous belief that they will instantly bid prices down assumes costless discovery of information about the state of market demand here and about opportunities elsewhere. If prices are too high, what will happen? Unemployment and recession will be the result; indeed, they are the process of the search for the new equilibrating price vector and wealth maximizing activities (if prices were too high initially).

This analysis of the stimulation of employment does not rely on the hoary, falsified dogma that wages lag behind prices. That phenomenon *does not* occur. There is no other conclusion that can be drawn from the extensive empirical analysis or from economic analysis.[5]

---

[5] M. Friedman, "The Role of Monetary Policy," *American Economic Review* 58 (Mar., 1968): 10. Even so careful an economist as Friedman slipped into the "lag of wages behind prices" error in his presidential address of December, 1967. Scores of economists, in trying to understand the relation between inflation and employment,

THE PACE OF INFLATION

How fast will inflation occur? It depends upon the expectations and commitments. Whatever the forecast inflation, the government will have to validate a higher rate of inflation if it attempts to maintain employment at every price asked by a seller. Once we have embarked on the policy of validating whatever price vector exists and however rapidly anyone wants more, there is no limit to the speed of inflation.

It is commonly believed that inflation is fed by insatiable desires and attempts of people to beat each other out, and that if only we would restrain our demands or prices, inflation would not occur. That is simply wrong. (Did we all become less greedy in the Great Deflation of the thirties?) What counts are *forecasts* of the equilibrium prices. Hence, even if we all miraculously, in saintly fashion, asked for lower real incomes, but had at the same time done so on the basis of too high a forecast of the market clearing price vector, inflation would be induced *if the government were to stand ready to assure full employment by monetary methods.*

The motivation for resorting to an inflationary policy is the political policy of validating whatever prices the public asks in order to "assure" employment by government action. That is what is implied by a full employment assurance policy. Then in this case the public, or that portion of it that asks for the greatest increases in price, sets the rate at which inflation must be created. The governmental monetary authorities will have shirked the responsibility that belongs to a monopolist in charge of the money stock. If any monopoly is to be blamed for inflation, it is clearly the government monopoly over the money stock, not any of unions or business, that is responsible.

It does not make any difference whether only one group asks for more than is sustainable at an equilibrium price vector with existing relative demands, or whether the whole economy asks for greater real income than can be produced if full employment promises are believed and attempted. The price level will explode at whatever rate a portion of the public asks for prices above the equilibrium. There will be an

---

chased him down that alley but haven't yet understood that they are as much in error in taking that path. They accept that premise and then try to find the flaw someplace else. If one accepts that error, the negative-sloped Phillips curve is hard to dismiss, but if one grasps the error, the vertical Phillips curve for correctly anticipated inflation is obvious, as is avoidance of propositions about real wage changes supposedly inherent in the process.

explosion, determined not by choice of some inflation rate but by how fast the public thinks the government will respond to any unemployment.

What would stop the explosion? Obviously and forlornly, we should never have started the policy of full employment assurance by monetary expansion, however much that expansion is done in the name of "fiscal" policy. Equally forlornly, we can now stop inflating the money stock and disappoint those who seek higher employment than is maintainable at their currently requested prices. That action would, aside from resulting in transient recession, amount to reverting to price controls by market competition, not by political power, the kind of market competition that says if you raise your price above the full employment level acceptable to buyers you will be quickly and surely punished by loss of sales or employment—a penalty imposed by consumers, not by some government agent. Or we could try to reduce the natural rate of unemployment by lowering costs of search, discovery, and transfer to new, best alternative tasks.

THE EFFECTS OF INFLATION

Wealth Redistribution Effects. The wealth transfer effects of inflation depend on whether it was under- or over-anticipated—except for the tax on non-interest-bearing money, usually the base money of the economy. Other forms of money usually pay implicit interest (for example, bank services), and it is difficult to know whether holders of bank demand deposits lose from an inflation of, say, 10 percent a year. Services rendered as checking services are not trivial.

For under-anticipated inflation a wealth transfer from net monetary creditors to net monetary debtors is implied and well established. Usually associated with the inflation is a shift in relative demands, which the inflationary increase in money stock was created to facilitate, possibly toward the borrowing sector or any other that happens to be politically strong. (To illustrate these demands, an example of a five-person economy is given in the appendix to this chapter.) The main moral is: distinguish between the inflation and the relative demand shifts for which the inflationary money increase may have been initiated and financed by the inflation tax on existing money.

If the inflation is anticipated correctly by every participant with complete confidence, the interest rate will have an adjustment factor and all wealth transfers from net monetary creditors or net monetary debtors will cease except for a monetary asset or liability that does not pay interest (would cash and currency be an example?). Demand deposits would pay interest explicitly or implicitly. All monetary asset claims will be indexed (though by what index, I do not know). I suspect the short-term rate will dominate most interest rate contracts. If the adjustment is made in interest rate, the term of the loan is essentially shortened, as the interest rate includes adjustment for loss of capital value due to the rising price level. Capital is repaid earlier because the constant nominal amount due always represents the falling real amount of principal still due on the longer-term loan. This means the life length or term of the loan will depend on the rate of inflation that results or is forecast during the interim. A speeding up of the rate will result in higher interest rates being placed on the loan—if it is a long-term, floating-interest-rate loan —and a shortening of the average maturity of the loan.

Resource Use Distortions. If *everyone* zeroed in on the forecast with no greater uncertainty in their minds than for forecasts during zero rates of inflation, the effects of error of anticipated inflation would be no different than during deviations around stable prices. But that is not our world. Not everyone will have the same forecast, though the average of their beliefs could create exactly the right market interest rate. Therefore, even if the market interest rate did correctly anticipate the inflation, two effects are significant: (1) more people are disappointed, and some are pleasantly surprised, by the wealth transfers that do or do not occur because of the incorrect forecasts by different people, and (2) the capital structure is changed.

Two extremes are instructive. One person believes that the nominal rate is the real rate, with zero expected price-level rise. He invests only up to the point at which the real and nominal return on investments equals that high real rate. He later discovers that the price level rose while the real rate was lower. He has underinvested in real capital. Another person believes the real rate is low, say 1 percent, with the rest of the nominal rate reflecting expected price-level changes. He invests heavily in real investment but suffers a loss in real terms because the real rate was higher.

The noise and random alteration of investment results imply less efficient use of investible resources and also cause disappointment and annoyance. Confidence in the economic system and the monetary system as not having an excessive incidence of socially useless, "unjustified" gains and losses provokes attempts to alter the system by giving aid to each person who believes he has been abused.

The variance of outcomes to which we are exposed increases. We are forced to play a game with a larger, more "random" variance of outcomes—one larger than with a zero price level. That is another cause for dissatisfaction. Appeals to government to compensate for the large "unjustified" changes in wealth enlarge government. Even without price controls and appeals to government to force others to compensate us for those changes, the increased insecurity and inability to know how much our wealth will be worth later tends to reduce the willingness to save and invest. The belief that price controls are then necessary (along with mandatory allocations, "compensatory" taxes, and subsidies) increases the scope of government regulation of economic action.

There is more. Normally shifting relative demands and costs cause "unemployment," a process of seeking the new best available activities (whether of employees detecting best jobs or of producers trying to detect new most profitable products, investments, or output rates). That task is hard enough during stable price levels. With a price level more subject to larger, variable rates of increase, each person now has demand for his service affected by nominal changes as well as by relative changes. A new source of noise is added. With inflation at an unpredictable rate, a new source of confusion arises. Are the shifts real (relative to others) or nominal? If all shifts that were nominal impinged on each person equally on the demand side and the cost, or input, side and were of the same proportion in each, at least the relative shifts would be less confused. But that is not the way events are understood or news is transmitted. Sales rates change, then prices change—at least in some sectors. But in others, prices change faster, with sales rates not changing (especially if buffer inventories are more expensive). Prices do not all respond at the same rate, because, for one reason at least, information about what underlying factors have changed is not freely and instantly available to everyone.

The increase in noise because of the variable and imperfectly predictable increases in rates of inflationary demand makes detection of the shifting (if it is) market clearing activity and price vector more difficult and slower. Activities are less efficiently coordinated and directed.

This inefficiency may show up as overemployment, but it may induce higher quit rates if people believe options elsewhere are increasing faster than in their present jobs. I know of no theory to rely on to derive unambiguous implications. One could get a positive-sloped Phillips curve. As an aside, I believe that a trade-off between inflation and unemployment is misinterpreted. It confuses the recovery of prices from a recession and longer-run inflation. Increased rates of inflation over the expected rate may reduce the full-employment rate of unemployment, but that is not demonstrably a desirable thing. The choices of people in jobs are distorted toward accepting less than the best available job, because they are misled into accepting jobs at lower wages than they would have obtained with more search. This stricture applies to full-employment rates of unemployment. I conjecture that inflationary increases in demand that are faster than anticipated lead to too small unemployment—too little search for the better market clearing vector of prices and activities by all people, employees, employers, equipment owners, and so on. In real terms, output value is smaller.

The higher the inflation, the greater is its component of noise—or so I believe. Please do not ask me for hard evidence or proof. I "believe" a higher inflation rate will have a higher (in basis points, at least) variance. I cannot imagine a country with a 5 percent rate experiencing the same variance around that rate, or into the near or distant future, as one now experiencing a 40 percent rate.

Implicit in the preceding argument is a presumption that beliefs of price-level stability around zero percent average change are more accurate than around high rates of inflation. A belief, faith, goal, objective, or commitment to a money that does not depreciate or appreciate relative to most other goods is a characteristic of a preferred money. I believe a zero average rate is a more clearly identified and "agreed-upon" rate than is 1 or 2 or 3 percent—any of the other infinite alternatives. But once belief in a departure from zero as a goal or criterion occurs, I know of no way to identify or produce agreement on an alternative. Do higher rates of inflation create greater interpersonal dispersions of predicted rates by different people? B. Klein seems to have demonstrated that the higher the rate, the larger the variance and the less likely are differences in successive price-level changes to be negatively correlated.[6] The variance and error for a given interval—say, a five-year span—will be larger because of the more highly positively correlated first differences. The

---

[6] B. Klein, "The Social Costs of the Recent Inflation and Our New Monetary Standard: The Mirage of Steady 'Anticipated' Inflation," unpublished manuscript (Apr., 1974).

available evidence, though it is not overpowering, is sufficiently strong to command serious consideration.

If we can identify factors that induce an inflationary monetary policy, are there reasons to conclude that when those factors make us resort to higher rates of inflation then they are also more variable? Do factors that induce inflation tend to be quickly reversing, independent, or positively correlated? We do not have sufficient evidence, but I conjecture increased variance at higher rates. My colleague E. Thompson suggested one explanation that would imply higher inflation and higher variation *across countries.* Assume, in argument, that poor countries have less efficient direct taxing systems and use inflation more as part of their general tax structure. Assume also that the poor countries have less developed, more expensive capital markets in which governments (or anyone else) can borrow funds. Then any fluctuations in government expenditures will be financed less by equivalent variations in borrowing and more by the remaining buffer source of finance: creation of new money by the government. Given those assumptions, we find that poorer countries will have higher inflation and greater variation in that rate. If that sounds like a weak proposition (and it does not sound weak to me) try conjuring up your own explanations of why higher inflations have higher temporal variance and less predictability of future price levels or rate of rise—if they do.

The problem of rising prices is not only the "random" wealth redistributions of inflation or the increased natural rate of unemployment caused by higher rates of inflation. It is, in my weighing of cultural and economic effects, the consequent increased power of government in our daily cultural, social, and economic life—an increase aided by inflation. First, inflation financing is a "convenient" form of taxation by the government—at least until the money stock is replaced with a new money that the government "promises" will be stable for who knows how long. Neat and beautiful is the inflation money tax that can be hidden from public awareness. Second, it induces more government activity. The random changes in wealth create disaffection with (or may I say "alienation" from?) the economic system. The public's attitude toward a stable currency is not one relying on any legislative law that the money unit will be stable, but rather on a deeper, more pervasive "common law" that a stable money is a characteristic of a good economic and political system. That the instability of money values is a result of political power instead of an economic system resting on private property rights must be news to many people. Indeed, even many economists get cheap publicity by blaming unions, corporations, wars, businessmen, oil embargoes, middlemen, and greedy people (who else is there?) for inflation. The public demands correction of the random "unjust" wealth redistributions. Any ailment that befalls them during inflation is blamed on the inflation. But since the reasons for the inflation are unfathomed, they demand government correction of their idiosyncratic ills. Such demands enlarge the scope of government and are not resisted by the politically strong or aspiring. Third, direct attacks on the symptoms known to flow from inflation are politically convenient. As inflation occurs, politicians and the public blame businessmen and producers for raising prices and mulcting the public. It is even fallaciously announced by government officials that of the one-thousand-dollar rise in average annual incomes over the past year, 80 percent is eroded away by inflation. The stamp of official doctrine is established that inflation reduces real incomes, when in fact it does not. The obvious response is to call for price controls. They provoke shortages; there obviously must be government action to set matters aright. The markets have failed; the economic system has failed.

The so-called shortage of gasoline and energy in the United States was *precisely* and *only* such a political attack. It could not have been brought about more cleverly and deceitfully even if the politically ambitious had explicitly written the script. Inflate the money stock; when prices rise, impose price controls to correct the situation. These controls lead to shortages which "require" government intervention to assure appropriate use of the limited supply and to allocate it and even to control and nationalize the production of energy. The powers of political authorities are increased; the open society is suppressed.

That is, in my opinion, the problem of inflation. Those are the results of inflation that frighten me. Those are the consequences that I cannot help but attribute as a goal of those who argue that inflation is really not so serious if it is announced and anticipated and that the unemployment it "avoids" is a very small price.

In fact, there is no lasting trade-off at all. There is only a transient effect from an acceleration or deceleration, while the lasting effects are those of greater political power. Incomes policies, wage and price controls, allocations, and nationalization are politically administered, with power and wealth going to those to perform those tasks, at least until they are forced by competition into the increased costs of achieving those powers. Inflation increases government power and growth. *That* is the problem of rising prices. I see no escape.

APPENDIX

Let us suppose that the government—which we shall arbitrarily use as our source of inflation—decides to shift its relative demands. People for whose services or goods there has been a relative increase in demand will experience an increase in income and wealth. These demand-revision effects neither cause nor are caused by the effects of inflation on net monetary status. The gross effect is a sum of both inflation and demand-shift effects, as can be illustrated by the following numerical illustration. Suppose that the government wishes to obtain wealth by printing fiat money. Assume that it creates and spends new money for services rather than for existing capital goods (although this spending does not affect the wealth transfer process). Furthermore, let the creation of money and the resulting inflation be a one-shot operation. Let the individuals in a community be typified by five individuals whose wealth and income positions are summarized in Table 1–1.

TABLE 1–1
Pre-inflation Wealth, Debts, and Incomes of Individuals

Persons	Wealth	Cash	Goods	Interpersonal Debts (−) or Credits (+)	Income
A	15.15	2.40	12.75	0	2.25
B	9.85	.85	9.00	0	1.00
C	16.10	.60	14.25	1.25	.75
D	4.65	.40	4.75	− .50	.25
E	4.25	.75	4.25	− .75	.75
	50.00	5.00	45.00	0	5.00
Government	10.00	1.00	9.00	0	1.00
Total	60.00	6.00	54.00	0	6.00

All sorts of assumptions are possible about the ratio of income from capital assets and from labor. Assume, for simplicity, that the total income flow per period from labor and capital is equal to 10 percent of the community's capital and that all income is consumed. Capital goods can be used up if consumption is to be changed. For the redistributive process, that assumption would make no difference. Only the numerical results would be modified. In equilibrium, assume that the community jointly (but not severally) holds 10 percent of the total wealth (including money) in the form of money ($6 of the money equals 10 percent of the community's wealth of $54 + $6 = $60). Let the government inflate the money supply by $1.20 of fiat money and spend $1.00 of it—all for the services of individual B.[7] When $1.00 per period of increased money demand impinges on B, the price of his service is assumed to double (his income was formerly $1.00 per period). The government gets only half of B's services, since the private sector was offered $1.00 for all of B's services before the government's additional demand of $1.00. None of this increased demand goes to anyone except B in the first stage. The rise in service prices is reflected in capital goods prices.

Looking at each individual, we see what this implies. A's balance sheet initially is:

A (before inflation and demand revision)

Cash	$ 2.40	Equity	$15.15
Goods	12.75		
	$15.15		

In the first period, his income stays at $2.25, while the price level of services rises to, say, $1.20. If he spends all his income, his consumption in real terms falls to $2.25 ($= 1.20 \times \$1.875$), a decline of $0.375 in original-price units. In the next period he receives a larger income, $2.70, as B spends part of his increased earnings. A has the choice of spending $2.70 or saving part of it to restore some of his wealth. If he spends it all in order to maintain his consumption at its original level, his balance sheet will be:

A (no saving)

Cash	$ 2.40	Equity	$17.70
Goods	15.30		
	$17.70		

His equity, in original-price units, would be $17.70 ÷ 1.20 = $14.75, a decline in wealth of $0.40 (from $15.15). He experienced a decline in real income in the first period of $0.375. The wealth loss, $0.40, is

---

[7] By the time the government has spent $1.00, prices will be 1.20 of the former level. At this price level the government, given its propensity for liquidity, will want to hold larger cash balances, because the demand for cash is in part a function of one's level of nominal wealth. If prices have risen by 20 percent, we shall suppose the government wants to hold $1.20 in money. The upshot is that only $1.00 of the new money is spent.

his wealth redistribution loss due to the inflation, and his second loss is the loss of income consequent to the *demand revision* as relative demand is shifted towards B. In fact, no matter what the demand shift, the inflationary loss is unaffected. Only if the degree of demand shift is tied to the degree of inflation are the two effects related, but this tie is a policy correlation, completely independent of the fact of inflation.

Suppose that A decides to save the increment of money income in order to increase his stock of money. His balance sheet would now appear:

A (saving all his increased money income)

Cash	$ 2.85	Equity	$18.15
Goods	15.30		
	$18.15		

In real terms his equity is $18.15 ÷ 1.20 = $15.125, a decline of $0.025 from the original level. He has to save still more if he wants to restore his equity to its original real level. Although he can choose any level of saving and resultant equity, he will have suffered the same loss of $0.40 in wealth because of the inflation and the reduced real income of $0.375 consequent to the demand revision. How he chooses to bear these two separate losses, that is, whether he will maintain consumption by eating up his wealth, restore his wealth by saving, or not save at all, is entirely up to his discretion. He is forced into no particular way, but he is forced into making a choice among them—a choice forced on him by both the inflationary wealth redistribution and the revised demand effect on income and asset values.

In the same manner, B's experience can be examined. Initially, his balance sheet is:

B (before inflation and before demand changes)

Cash	$0.85	Equity	$9.85
Goods	9.00		
	$9.85		

During the first period he has received $2.00 of income and has spent $1.00. With the higher prices, his real income is $2.00 ÷ 1.20 or $1.666, an increase of $0.666 in original-price units. He has lost wealth by being a net monetary creditor; the real value of his money stock falls to $0.85 ÷ 1.20 = $0.70833, a decline of $0.1416—exactly the same loss as if there were no demand shift. He can choose any combination of saving and consequent level of wealth that he wishes. If he saves all of his increase in real income, $0.666, this will more than offset the inflationary loss of wealth of $0.1416. He will have a net increase in wealth of $0.525. If, instead, he saves, say, only $0.20, his balance sheet will be:

B (after restoring cash ratio)

Cash	$ 1.05	Equity	$11.85
Goods	10.80		
	$11.85		

His equity (in original-price units) is now $11.85 ÷ 1.20 = $9.875, an increase of $0.025. This increase is the result of his voluntary decision to save $0.20. In summary, he loses $0.1416 (original-price-level units) by being a net monetary creditor during the inflation, and he gains a transistory one-period increase of $0.666 in income by the demand shift. He chose to save $0.20 of that increase in income ($0.1666 in original-price-level units), so his wealth increased by $0.1666 − $0.1416 = $0.025. The rest of the increased real income, in original-price-level units, $0.666 − $0.1666 = $0.50, is devoted to increasing his consumption. Similar analysis for C, D, and E yields the results given in the appropriate rows of Table 1–2. Columns (1) and (3), when summed, give column (4).

Table 1–2 shows that all of the income gain, $0.666, accruing to B is at the expense of the rest of the community (proportionate to their income) and not from inflation. Also, the net wealth redistribution due to inflation is independent to the degree of demand revision. With the demand revision, income revision has occurred, as shown in the second column, whereas the inflation wealth redistribution went from the moneyholders to the government and from private net creditors to private net debtors. In this particular example, the amount of savings increments was simply assumed to be just sufficient to restore the private community's stock of real wealth. Under different assumptions about the desire to hold cash and to save, the numerical results would be different. The government could get the services without at the same time inducing the rest of the community to do any saving or dissaving. Or the community could insist on maintaining its consumption rate (and consume some wealth). In our example the community saved enough to restore its wealth to the pre-inflation level. But in any event, the inflation effect is one thing, the shift in relative demand another, and the resultant saving decision still another.

TABLE 1–2

Summary of Effects of Inflation and Demand
Shifts on Income and Wealth
(all in original-price-level units)

	(1) Net Wealth Redistribution from Inflation	(2) Income Change Caused by Demand Revision: One Period of Income	(3) Voluntary Savings Increments	(4) Net Changes in Wealth of Private Sector
A	−$0.4000	−$0.3750	$0.3750	−$0.025
B	− .1416	.6666	.1666	.025
C	− .3083	− .1250	.1250	− .1833
D	.0166	− .0416	.0416	.0583
E	.0000	− .1250	.1250	.1250
	−$0.833 (to government)	0	$0.8333	0

Chapter 2

The Folklore of Unemployment
and Poverty

Lowell Gallaway

AS we reach the fourth quarter of the twentieth century, it is clear that a very substantial folklore concerning economic affairs has been created in the United States. This folklore is especially evident when the subjects of unemployment and poverty are considered. In particular, I would suggest that there are at least five propositions that qualify as being a part of the contemporary folklore of unemployment and poverty:

1. Over the long run it is possible to meaningfully reduce the typical unemployment rate in the American economy through the use of macroeconomic policy.

2. The distribution of personal income in the United States is highly unequal.

3. A major source of inequality in the American income distribution is the unequal distribution of income derived from property sources.

4. Equalization of educational accomplishment will lead to greater equality in the overall income distribution.

5. Racial discrimination in American economic institutions contributes substantially to the inequality of income distribution.

Note that none of the propositions I have listed explicitly refers to the problem of poverty. However, as the poverty question is currently treated in many circles it becomes essentially a matter of the degree of inequality in the personal income distribution. Thus, the poverty issue is subsumed under the statements referring to the nature of the distribution of income in the United States.

CONTROL OVER THE UNEMPLOYMENT RATE

The first of our five propositions, that the unemployment rate can be significantly reduced in the long run through the use of macroeconomic policy, has acquired widespread acceptance, particularly among legislators and economic policy advisers. Over the past quarter-century or more this notion has been expressed in the contention that appropriately selected monetary and/or fiscal policies are capable of reducing overall levels of unemployment, which is a goal that acquired the status of public policy with the passage of the Employment Act of 1946. At the time that legislation was enacted, the memories of the Great Depression of the 1930's were still quite fresh, and the consensus among professional economists was that the post–World War II era would be a reprise of the 1930's. Thus, faced with what they thought was the prospect of a return to the relatively high unemployment of the 1930's, our legislators reacted predictably and passed a law against that possibility by mandating a governmental effort to achieve "full employment," although they did not attempt to define that concept with any precision. Once the commitment to maintain something called full employment had been made, it was almost taken for granted that it could be achieved, albeit with temporary falls from grace.

Probably the high point of confidence in the ability to reduce the aggregate unemployment rate by the monetary-fiscal policy route was reached in the mid-1960's, when, armed with the concept of the Phillips curve and ignoring the additional injunction of the Employment Act of 1946 that the objective should be full employment consistent with price stability, policy makers and their advisers tended to view the unemployment rate issue as a simple matter of choosing the optimal unemployment-inflation combination from among a stable opportunity set (defined by the Phillips curve). Perhaps the classic example of the optimism of that period was a statement by Secretary of Labor Willard Wirtz, who, as the unemployment rate approached the 3.5 percent level, issued a proclamation calling for reducing it even further to the level of 1.5 percent. Allowing even for the political license one normally grants a secretary of labor, this statement must qualify for some award for excessive expectations regarding the efficacy of macroeconomic policy tools.

In all fairness, there was not universal acceptance of the doctrine that the unemployment rate could be controlled through the use of monetary-fiscal policy in a fashion that would enable us to maintain it at some predetermined relatively low level as long as we were willing to pay the "cost" in terms of a certain amount of price inflation. However, the dissenters, with Milton Friedman being the best known, were generally regarded as just that, dissenters, and nothing more. And the empirical evidence during the decade of the 1960's certainly seemed to support the notion that systematic control of the unemployment rate was possible. From 1961 through 1969 the unemployment rate fell from 6.7 percent to 3.5 percent while the annual rate of inflation in the prices of privately produced product rose from 0.9 percent to 4.5 percent.[1] Interestingly, in his 1968 presidential address to the American Economic Association, Friedman issued a warning to the effect that the notion of a stable trade-off between unemployment and the rate of price inflation was illusory.[2]

The events following 1969 substantially confirmed Friedman's prophecy. In 1970 the level of unemployment averaged 4.9 percent, and through 1974 the annual average of the monthly unemployment rates varied from 4.9 to 5.9 percent. Meanwhile, the rate of price inflation actually accelerated, reaching a peak of 10.6 percent in 1974. Over the five-year period 1970–1974 unemployment averaged 5.4 percent, and the average rate of price inflation soared to 5.6 percent.

What happened? The scenario is a simple one. From 1961 to 1965 compensation per man-hour in the private sector of the economy rose by 18.8 percent while the value of privately produced output per man-hour increased by 22.3 percent.[3] The net effect of these increases was to lower the real wage rate (adjusted for productivity increases) and increase both profit and employment opportunities. Of course, what is involved here is the operation of a money illusion effect in labor markets. Over the interval 1961–1965 workers received real wage-rate increases that were less than the increase in productivity per unit of labor in the economy. As a result, the profit share of national income rose from 11.77 percent in 1961 to 13.49 percent in 1965.

After 1965, however, money illusion ceased to operate. In fact, it appears that workers were attempting to "make up" for the period 1961–1965. Compensation per man-hour rose by 31.0 percent in the interval 1965–1969 while the value of output per man-hour only increased by 25.3 percent. Predictably, the profit share of national income fell to 10.42 percent, and finally the long upward swing in the business cycle

[1] This is based on the implicit price deflator for the private sector of the economy. Using the consumer price index, the rate of price inflation rose from 1.2 percent a year to 5.4 percent.

[2] Milton Friedman, "The Role of Monetary Policy," *American Economic Review* 58 (Mar., 1968): 1–17.

[3] The index of output per man-hour rose by 16.6 percent while the implicit price deflator in the private sector rose by 4.9 percent.

that began in 1962 came to an end and unemployment rose sharply in 1970 and 1971.

If that had been the end of the adjustment process, the tale told here might be quite brief. However, workers had apparently become attuned to the phenomenon of inflation, and they continued the catching-up process beyond 1969. Between 1969 and 1974 compensation per man-hour increased by another 44.1 percent, but the value of private output per man-hour rose by almost the same amount (43.3 percent). The major source of the increase in the value of private output was an increase in prices (31.0 percent), while productivity per man-hour rose very modestly (9.4 percent). By contrast, during the period 1961–1965 productivity increases accounted for a 16.6 percent increase in the value of output per man-hour while price rises led to a 4.9 percent increase. The mix between productivity and price increases shifted between 1965 and 1969 toward more emphasis on price increases (14.2 percent) and less on productivity (9.7 percent). Very simply, after the downturn of 1961, reductions in unemployment occurred because real wages rose less rapidly than would have been expected on the basis of increases in productivity. However, after the downturn of 1970–1971, the same phenomenon did not occur. As a consequence, we have witnessed in the 1970's the simultaneous occurrence of a relatively high rate of price inflation and unemployment levels that have been consistently in the vicinity of 5 percent or more.

The intriguing question is whether this difference in the labor-market behavior of workers can be explained. In short, why did workers behave differently in the early 1970's than they did in the early 1960's? The answer lies in the previously mentioned phenomenon of becoming attuned to the presence of inflationary pressures in the late 1960's. As the makers of public policy behaved as if there were a stable trade-off between inflation and unemployment and attempted to keep the economy operating at low levels of unemployment, the ensuing consistent inflationary forces led workers to anticipate inflation in their wage demands. Furthermore, competitive labor-market pressures on employers participating in relatively tight labor markets induced them to offer wage rates high enough to erode away the advantage they had achieved through the operation of money illusion in the early 1960's. After all, what had really happened in the early 1960's was this: money-wage-labor demand curves shifted to the right more rapidly than did money-wage-labor supply curves (money illusion slows the shift in the money-wage-labor supply curves). The effect of this difference was to increase employment without having real wage rates rise as rapidly as productivity per man-hour. However, the real wage rate under these conditions is at less than equilibrium unless money illusion remains in effect. As money illusion weakened in the late 1960's, the quantity demanded of labor simply exceeded the quantity supplied at existing wage rates, and employers began bidding up wage rates toward the equilibrium level. Since the relatively high employment and low unemployment of the late 1960's was triggered by the less than equilibrium level of real wage rates, inevitably this process led to the downturn of 1970–1971. However, the persistence with which policy makers had pursued low levels of unemployment in the 1960's had created a very strong set of expectations concerning inflation. These expectations apparently carried over into the 1970's with a vengeance. As a consequence, workers continue to anticipate inflation, as is reflected in the fact that after 1969 compensation per man-hour rose at an average rate of almost 8 percent a year while productivity increased by less than 2 percent. The result was a rise in unit labor cost and prices of almost 6 percent a year. Obviously, this increase results in a reinforcement of the expectation of inflation. In fact, under these circumstances the expectation of inflation becomes a self-fulfilling prophecy as long as governmental policy makers pursue courses of action that accommodate the general rise in money wages and prices. Such has been the case in recent years in the United States. For example, when money wage rates began to increase more rapidly than productivity between 1965 and 1969, the federal government responded by running an average deficit of $8.3 billion for 1966–1969 compared to an average of $4.6 billion for 1961–1965. Similarly, the money supply (currency plus demand deposits) increased by 21.8 percent between 1965 and 1969 compared to an increase of 15.2 percent in the previous four years. But this was only a preview of things to come. When the rise in unemployment did come in 1970 and 1971, the response was vigorous. Between December, 1970, and December, 1973, the money supply increased by 22.6 percent, and for the three years 1971–1973 the federal deficit averaged $20.2 billion per year. This strong intervention inflated the value of private output per man-hour by increasing prices, but its impact on employment levels was largely vitiated by the previously noted reinforcement of inflationary expectations and the resultant continuation of the high rate of increase in compensation per man-hour. Also, of course, it set the stage for the disaster of 1974, when we witnessed an 8.7 percent rise in compensation per man-hour, a decline of 2.7 percent in output per man-hour, and a 10.6 percent rise in the prices of private product, the so-called double-digit inflation.

There would seem to be no end to the cycle of inflationary expectations as long as the central authorities are cooperative with their monetary-fiscal policies. This is precisely the case, and once the cycle is set in motion, what is needed to break it is a disappointment of expectations. To create this disappointment, some constraint, such as a restrictive monetary and/or fiscal policy that will not permit prices to continue to rise, must be allowed to operate. However, given the presence of deep-rooted inflationary expectations, restraining price increases through monetary-fiscal policy will necessarily produce the negative output and employment effects and increases in the unemployment rate that were so vigorously resisted from 1971 through 1973. This situation seems to be exactly what we witnessed in 1975. The only question that remains is whether we will have sufficient will and fortitude to maintain this posture until the cycle of inflationary expectations is broken. Based on the past behavior of the federal government and the central monetary authorities, I must admit to a fair amount of skepticism in this regard. Certainly, the prospect of monetizing a substantial portion of a federal deficit of over $60 billion is not a reassuring one.

If my explanatory sketch of the events of recent years is accepted, the question that now arises is: What is to be learned from this experience? The basic thrust of the argument I have presented is that our current difficulties are primarily the result of the buildup of inflationary expectations that was triggered in the 1960's by a concerted effort to hold the unemployment rate permanently below what is apparently the equilibrium rate for the American economy. This situation has something to say about the idea that it is possible to effect a permanent reduction in the typical unemployment rate in the American economy through the use of a proper mix of macroeconomic policies. Clearly, it suggests that this notion is an ill-advised one and that attempts to pursue it will be at best ineffective and at worst counterproductive. For an example of the latter, I remind the reader that the relatively high current unemployment rates are directly traceable to the arbitrarily low rates that existed during the late 1960's and the attempt of 1971–1973 to avoid paying the price for those earlier low rates.

Quite obviously, what has been argued here is that there is an equilibrium unemployment rate in the American economy which tends to prevail over the long run.[4] It is this rate which Friedman refers to as the "natural" rate of unemployment. From the standpoint of historical perspective, the conclusion that there is an equilibrium or natural rate of unemployment in the American economy should not come as a surprise. An examination of the data we have on unemployment indicates that before 1947 (the first full year after the passage of the Employment Act of 1946) the median rate of unemployment in the United States was 4.8 percent (the interval covered is 1900–1946). On the other hand, in the period 1947–1974 the median rate of unemployment was 4.9 percent. A more careful examination of the data reveals that in the period before the existence of the Council of Economic Advisers, the only significant difference in our unemployment experience was the extremely high rate of the 1930's. But that takes us to another matter—the contribution to economic stability of our other great macroeconomic experiment, the Federal Reserve System.

The Federal Reserve System was created in 1913, and it is interesting to note that the American economy has been much more unstable since its inception than before. In the 60 years from 1914 through 1975 the mean monthly change in the level of economic activity (adjusted for secular trend) has been almost 20 percent greater than it was in the 124 years from 1790 through 1913.[5] A very good argument can be made that the severity of the Great Depression of the 1930's can be attributed in large part to the destabilizing impact of the Federal Reserve System. After all, the agency presumably charged with stabilizing monetary conditions did permit the money supply to fall by about one-third in the early 1930's. Abstracting from the destabilizing influence of the Federal Reserve System, it is very difficult to make a case that the record on unemployment after the Employment Act of 1946 represents any significant improvement over previous experience.

DISTRIBUTION OF AMERICAN INCOME

One frequently finds the second of our five bits of folklore, that

[4] The equilibrium unemployment rate is determined by the institutional structure of labor markets. Thus, it is a function of such things as the availability of labor-market information, the presence of trade unions, and governmental regulations such as minimum wage laws.

[5] The month-to-month changes in economic activity were calculated from the Cleveland Trust Company's analysis of historical data pertaining to levels of economic activity in the United States.

there is great inequality in the distribution of American income, advanced almost without challenge. For example, in her Ely lecture at the 1974 meetings of the American Economic Association, Alice Rivlin pondered why so few have so much and so many so little in the United States.[6] Taken at face value, a statement such as that one constitutes something of an indictment of the American economy. However, it cannot be taken at face value, for it raises more questions than it provides answers. To begin with, when an income distribution is described as being "highly unequal," one is entitled to ask what that distribution is being compared to. Unfortunately, there is no purely objective standard for determining whether a given amount of income inequality is high or low. The most generally accepted measure of income inequality is the Gini coefficient, which may vary from zero (perfect equality) to unity (perfect inequality). For the United States that coefficient is approximately .33, but to describe that fraction as indicating a great amount of inequality involves a very substantial value judgment.

There is no simple way to avoid this problem, but we can obtain some insight into the relative amount of inequality in the American income distribution by comparing it to income distributions in certain other countries. First, let us look at Sweden. I choose Sweden because it is generally taken for granted in liberal intellectual circles in the United States that Sweden is something of a model as far as equality of income distribution is concerned.

Data describing the Swedish distribution of income that are comparable with American data are not very readily available.[7] However, by adjusting some basic estimates developed by Martin Järnek for the impact of the value-added tax in Sweden and the American data derived from the Bureau of Economic Analysis of the Commerce Department for the effect of the tax system,[8] the after-tax and government-transfer-payment family income distributions shown in Table 2–1 appear to be

[6] Alice M. Rivlin, "Income Distribution—Can Economists Help?" *American Economic Review* 65, no. 2 (May, 1975): 1–15.

[7] One such source is Martin Schnitzer, *Income Distribution* (New York: Praeger Publishers, 1974), which contains information on the Swedish income distribution. However, the income concept is not that of the family unit, and the adjustment for taxes and transfers is incomplete.

[8] I am making an implicit assumption that the incidence of a value-added tax is borne by the consumers who purchase the final product. The tax adjustment for the United States is based on Roger A. Herriot and Herman P. Miller, "The Taxes We Pay," *Conference Board Record*, May, 1971, p. 4.

TABLE 2–1

Shares of Personal Income, by Quintile, of Families in Sweden,
1964, and the United States, 1971

Income Quintile	Share of Income (percent)	
	Sweden*	United States
Lowest	7.7	6.9
Second	⎱ 23.1	12.4
Third	⎰	17.2
Fourth	⎱ 33.4	22.9
Highest	⎰ 35.9	40.6
Top 5 percent	12.9	15.9
Gini coefficient	0.27	0.32

SOURCES: Martin Järnek, *Studier i hushållens inkomstförhållanden 1925–1964* (Lund, 1971); Daniel B. Radner and John C. Hinrichs, "Size Distribution of Income in 1964, 1970, and 1971," *Survey of Current Business*, Oct., 1974, pp. 19–31.

* For Sweden the data are not available by quintile between the twenty-first and eightieth percentiles. The two income groups are given, the twenty-first through the fiftieth percentiles, and the fifty-first through the eightieth.

reasonably accurate representations of the patterns of income distribution in the two countries. The Gini coefficients for these distributions indicate greater equality in the Swedish case, but how much greater? For purposes of evaluating the significance of the difference, it may be useful to keep in mind that between 1947 and 1968 the Gini coefficient for the American family income distribution fell by .03, and most commentators on the American income distribution passed this off as a "negligible" change in the degree of equality. If their judgment on this matter is accepted, it becomes difficult to claim that there is a substantial difference between the Swedish and American income distributions.

I suspect that there will be some inclination for people to be suspicious of these data. After all, the high degree of progressivity in the Swedish tax system is itself a bit of folklore in the United States. However, there are some widespread misconceptions in this regard. To illustrate, I have provided in Table 2–2 a comparison of effective tax rates for families in the United States and Sweden by income level.[9]

[9] The median level of Swedish family income about 1970 was about Kr 20,000, compared to about $10,000 in the United States. Consequently, I have attempted to compare the income levels at which the Swedish level in kroner is twice that of the United States in dollars. If an exchange rate were used to convert the currencies into a common measure, it would appear that the conversion factor should be substantially higher than two.

These rates include transfer payments for the United States and children's allowances for a family with two children in the case of Sweden, but exclude the impact of the Swedish value-added tax. For the very high

TABLE 2–2

Comparative Effective Tax Rates by Income Level,
United States and Sweden

United States Income Level (dollars)	Tax Rate (percent)	Swedish Income Level (kroner)	Tax Rate (percent)
Less than 2,000	−56.5		
2,000–4,000	−13.9	6,000	−44.0
4,000–6,000	11.4	10,000	−26.4
6,000–8,000	21.5	15,000	− 5.9
8,000–10,000	23.7	20,000	4.5
10,000–15,000	25.9	30,000	17.8
15,000–25,000	27.0	50,000	35.0
25,000–50,000	32.8		
50,000 and over	44.7	100,000	51.1

SOURCES: Roger A. Herriot and Herman P. Miller, "The Taxes We Pay," *Conference Board Record*, May, 1971, p. 40: and *The Swedish Budget, 1973/74* (Stockholm: Ministry of Finance, 1973), p. 134.

and very low income levels there appears to be little difference in the effective tax rates.[10] However, in the middle-income range the American income recipient is much more heavily taxed than his Swedish counterpart. This is consistent with the income distributions of Table 2–1, which indicate a more substantial share of Swedish income going to the middle three quintiles than is the case with the United States. Thus, it appears that relative to Sweden the American middle class bears a more substantial tax burden.

A comparison of the pattern of income distribution in the United States with that of the Soviet Union is also illuminating. The Soviet data are admittedly fragmentary, but Table 2–3 shows a distribution for the nonagricultural portion of the population of one area within the Soviet Union. Income is defined on an annual basis in terms of rubles per family member. Assuming an absolute minimum of two hundred rubles

[10] It is worth remembering that the maximum marginal tax rate at the federal level in the United States is 70 percent, while it is only 54 percent in Sweden. However, there is also the Swedish local income tax of about 25 percent. Adding in state and local taxes in the United States produces maximum marginal tax rates in the two countries that are fairly similar.

per family member,[11] a Gini coefficient for this distribution was estimated and found to be about .29, that is, intermediate between the
Swedish and American distributions. Also, estimates of the income

TABLE 2–3
Personal Income per Annum in Rubles per Person,
Non-kolkhoz Population of a Selected
Area of the Soviet Union

Income (rubles)	Percentage of Persons
Less than 600	32.6
601–900	31.2
901–1,200	17.7
1,201–1,500	9.1
1,501–2,100	7.1
2,100 and over	2.3

SOURCE: *Osnovnyye,* 1971, p. 112, reported in *Soviet Economic Prospects for the
Seventies: A Compendium of Papers Submitted to the Joint Economic Committee, Congress of the United States* (Washington, D.C.: Government Printing Office, June 27,
1973), p. 110.

shares by quintile can be calculated, and Table 2–4 shows a simple comparison of those shares in the United States, Sweden, and the Soviet
Union. A reasonable interpretation of the data in Table 2–4 would seem

TABLE 2–4
Estimated Shares of Personal Income, by Quintile, in the
United States, Sweden, and Soviet Union*

Income Quintile	Share of Income (percent)		
	United States	Sweden	Soviet Union
Lowest	6.9	7.7	7.5
Second through fourth	52.5	56.5	55.0
Highest	40.6	35.9	37.5
Top 5 percent	15.9	12.9	14.0

SOURCE: Tables II and IV.
    * As nearly as possible, the income concept is an after-tax and transfer-payment
one.

to be that the differences in the degree of inequality in the respective
distributions are relatively minor. Consequently, if one follows the line
of thinking of Alice Rivlin's statement above, one is entitled to speculate

11 This is based on a minimum wage of 70 rubles per month and a family of four.

why so few have so much and so many so little in the Soviet Union, Sweden, and the United States.[12] Of course, there is always the alternative possibility that perhaps the degree of inequality in the American income distribution has been overstated by commentators like Rivlin.

My personal view is that the amount of inequality in the American income distribution is not nearly as great as is commonly believed, particularly if *lifetime* levels of income are considered. This lifetime level would seem to be the appropriate magnitude on which to focus, since the critical aspect of inequality in the distribution of income is its impact on the total lifetime experience of people. When lifetime levels of income are the focus of attention, two critical considerations arise, both of which operate to reduce the degree of lifetime inequality in the personal income distribution below that observed at any single point in time. These considerations are (1) the impact of the life cycle in income on the distribution of income at a point in time and (2) the effect of movements of people between income classes over time on lifetime levels of income. The first of these I call "senescent" inequality in the observed income distribution; its impact can be measured by assuming a steady-state world in which the existing life cycle in income is unchanged over time, there is no growth in the average level of income, and the distribution of income within every age class is perfectly equal. Under these conditions, which would lead to perfect equality in the distribution of lifetime income, the Gini coefficient that would be observed at any point in time would be slightly over 30 percent as large as the coefficient now observed.[13] Thus, for the distributions reported earlier for the United States, the Gini coefficient would be about .10, assuming perfect equality of distribution within each age class. This means that the effective Gini coefficient, after controlling for "senescent" inequality, is about .24.[14]

The second source of overstatement in the extent of income inequality in the United States, the failure to take account of the impact of mobility between income classes over time, is somewhat harder to

[12] In this respect we might also add the United Kingdom and West Germany. After taxes in the United Kingdom, the lowest quintile of the income distribution has 7.1 percent of all income. In West Germany, the percentage is 5.9 percent. See Schnitzer, *Income Distribution*, chaps. 4 and 6.

[13] The actual Gini coefficient in the income distribution used is about .40, while that which would result from our assumptions is about .13.

[14] This is calculated from the expression $(G - G_s)/(1 - G_s)$, where G is the observed Gini coefficient and G_s is the Gini coefficient calculated on the basis of our assumption of perfect equality of income distribution within age groups.

measure. However, on the basis of a comparison of the behavior of wage levels of a cohort of workers over a five-year period, it appears that the Gini coefficient ought to be reduced by perhaps as much as another 25 percent.[15] This reduction would move it below the .20 level. Now, if we are cautious and simply adjust the Gini coefficient downward to .20, we might ask what an income distribution would look like that would yield such a Gini coefficient. A sample distribution is shown in Table 2–5. How realistic is that distribution? Well, consider that by itself the adjustment to the lowest quintile's share that is warranted on the basis of the "senescent" factor alone would increase that share by 23 percent, which would raise it by about 1.5 percentage points or to about 8.5 percent. If the mobility factor produced a similar change, we would have approximately the income share shown in Table 2–5. Therefore, the distribution would not seem to be unreasonable.

TABLE 2–5
Hypothetical Income Shares, by Quintile, for an
Income Distribution with a Gini
Coefficient of .20

Quintile	Income Share (percent)
Lowest	10.0
Second	16.0
Third	21.0
Fourth	21.0
Highest	32.0
Top 5 percent	12.0

What generally can we conclude at this point? First, while we cannot assert that there is great equality in the American income distribution, we can say that there is not as much difference as there is conventionally assumed to be between the distribution of income in the United States and that of other countries that commonly are viewed to have much greater equality in their income distributions, for example, Sweden and the Soviet Union. This finding tends to give the lie to the conventional wisdom that full-blown central planning or some form of modified socialism, a la Sweden, leads to drastic reductions in the degree

---

[15] These data are from the Social Security Administration's Continuous Work History Sample for the period 1955–1959. The Gini coefficient for five years of wage earnings within an age group is about 75 percent of that for a single year's earnings.

of inequality of personal income distribution. Our second major finding is that once corrections are made for the impact of the life cycle in income and mobility between income classes, the actual degree of income inequality in the United States over the course of one's lifetime is substantially less than that observed at any single point in time. Consequently, it would appear reasonable to argue that much of the conventional wisdom about the degree of the inequality in the American income distribution ought to be viewed with great caution.

PROPERTY SOURCES AND INCOME INEQUALITY

The third piece of economic folklore, the assertion that inequality in the distribution of property income is a major source of inequality in American income distribution, can be dealt with rather quickly and directly. Recent data are available which can be manipulated to estimate the impact of any one type of income on overall income inequality.[16] The data are for 1972, and the particular income distribution used is shown in Table 2–6 and has a Gini coefficient of .342. (In this case we have to carry the calculation of the Gini coefficient to three decimal places.)

TABLE 2–6

Personal Income Distributions, Adjusted and
Unadjusted, for Impact of Property
Income, United States, 1972

Income Class (dollars)	Percentage of Units	Percentage of All Income	Percentage of All Income Less Property Income
0–4,999	16.6	4.06	4.05
5,000–6,999	10.2	4.83	4.84
7,000–9,999	16.8	11.20	11.28
10,000–14,999	26.1	25.35	25.72
15,000–24,999	23.0	33.89	34.18
25,000 and over	7.3	20.67	19.93

SOURCE: U.S. Bureau of the Census, *Current Population Reports*, Series P-60, no. 90.

[16] We can only estimate the impact, since the ordering of income units is based on all income and not on all income less the source being evaluated. The estimates will err in the direction of overstating the contribution to inequality if the income source in question produces greater inequality and in the direction of understating the contribution to equality if the income source has an equalizing impact.

Now, if we remove all income of a property nature (dividends, interests, and rents) from the income distribution, we obtain an adjusted distribution which is also shown in Table 2–6. A brief examination of the original and adjusted distributions seems to indicate that there is very little difference between them, an impression that is confirmed when the Gini coefficient is calculated for the adjusted distribution. It is .338, about 1 percent less than the coefficient for the unadjusted distribution. In fact, if we round to two decimal places, the coefficients are identical.

To avoid erring in the direction of understating the impact of property income on inequality, we should note that there is a tendency for this type of income to be under-reported in the data source that is used here. The under-reporting is substantial, with something less than 50 percent of property income being incorporated in the data. If this unreported property income were included in the overall distribution of income, it would increase the Gini coefficient for that distribution to something in excess of .34. How much the increase would be depends on where (in which income class) the under-reporting occurs. If all under-reporting occurred among those with incomes of $25,000 and over, the Gini coefficient for the overall income distribution would rise to about .37. On the other hand, if the degree of under-reporting were proportionally the same in all income classes, the Gini coefficient would rise to only .35. The first possibility represents a maximum impact, and the second probably a minimum. Consequently, it seems reasonable to conclude that the impact of property income on the equality of income distribution in the United States is to increase the Gini coefficient by from .01 to .03, with the latter being undoubtedly an unrealistically high maximum impact.

Again, the natural question would seem to be: How can this be the case? After all, everyone knows how unequally property income is distributed. Three remarks are in order here. First, while property income is generally more unequally distributed than all income, the difference is not as large as most people assume. Table 2–7 shows the distribution of both all income and property income by income class. The greatest disparities between the two distributions lie above the $7,000 income level. From $7,000 to $25,000, property income is less than all income, and for the class $25,000 and over, it is greater. To gauge the difference in the two distributions, we can calculate a Gini coefficient for property income using the ordering of income units based on all income. It is .47,

TABLE 2–7
Percentage Distribution of All Income and Property
Income by Level of All Income,
United States, 1972

Income Class (dollars)	Percentage of All Income	Percentage of Property Income
0–4,999	4.1	4.3
5,000–6,999	4.8	4.7
7,000–9,999	11.2	9.0
10,000–14,999	25.3	15.6
15,000–24,999	34.9	26.6
25,000 and over	20.7	39.8

SOURCE: U.S. Bureau of the Census, *Current Population Reports*, Series P-60, no. 90.

and while it is not a true Gini coefficient, it does provide some insight into why property income has less of an impact in producing income inequality than is commonly thought.

Second, the relative importance of property income in the overall income distribution is very frequently overstated. It is remarkable how much ignorance there is in this respect. Allowing for under-reporting and the like, property income accounts for less than 10 percent of total income. Thus, its weight in the overall income distribution is remarkably small. In fact, if all property income (including that unreported) were given to those families with incomes of $25,000 or more, the Gini coefficient for the entire income distribution would only be raised from .34 to .39.

Finally, what is most frequently overlooked in discussions of the American income distribution is the relatively great amount of inequality in the distribution of earnings-related income (wages, salaries, and self-employment). If one views an overall income distribution with a Gini coefficient of .34 as having substantial inequality, what about the distribution of earnings income for which the Gini coefficient approaches .40? To provide some perspective in this respect, simply consider that whereas families in the $25,000-and-over income class receive about five times as much total income as those in the under-$5,000 class, they receive almost eleven times as much earnings income.[17] An illuminating comparison in this respect is given by Table 2–8, which shows the distri-

[17] Remember that much of the income of the under-$5,000 income class is of the transfer payment variety.

bution of both earnings and nonearnings income by income class. These distributions rather clearly indicate that the true origin of what income inequality there is in the United States is to be found in the pattern of

TABLE 2–8
Percentage Distribution of Earnings and
Nonearnings Income by Level of All
Income, United States, 1972

Income Class (dollars)	Percentage of Earnings Income	Percentage of Nonearnings Income
0–4,999	2.0	18.9
5,000–6,999	3.8	12.4
7,000–9,999	10.7	14.8
10,000–14,999	26.4	17.7
15,000–24,999	35.9	19.3
25,000 and over	21.2	16.9

SOURCE: U.S. Bureau of the Census, *Current Population Reports*, Series P-60, no. 90.

distribution of earnings-related income, a source that accounts for almost seven-eighths of the income reported in this distribution.

The dominance of the earnings component in the income distribution is shown by the information in Table 2–9, which indicates that the

TABLE 2–9
Gini Coefficients for Different Combinations of
Sources of Personal Income,
United States, 1972

Income Source	Gini Coefficient
All Income	.34
Less social security payments	.37
Less public assistance payments	.35
Less unemployment compensation	.35
Less private pensions	.35

SOURCE: U.S. Bureau of the Census, *Current Population Reports*, Series P-60, no. 90.

other sources of income, such as Social Security payments, public assistance, private pensions, and unemployment compensation benefits, have only marginal impacts on the Gini coefficient. In fact, collectively, all of these sources of income only reduce the Gini coefficient from .39 to .34. The message is clear: if one is unhappy with the amount of inequality in the American income distribution, the villain is not property income. Rather, it is the unequal distribution of earnings-related income.

EDUCATION AS THE GREAT EQUALIZER

I turn now to the fourth bit of economic folklore detailed earlier, the notion that in some fashion making educational opportunity more readily available to individuals in the society will tend to equalize economic opportunity and status. A number of arguments seem to lead in this direction. In fact, this is one of the few propositions on which most economists generally will agree. Admittedly, at one extreme the argument is frequently couched in terms of normative judgments about equality of educational opportunity, while at the other the emphasis is on investment in human capital, but the underlying premise is the same, namely, that there is a substantial positive return to individuals that accrues to them when they receive additional amounts of education.

A seemingly obvious corollary to this proposition would appear to be that equalizing the amount of educational accomplishment of people would tend to produce an equalization of economic rewards, that is, income, and a more equal distribution of income. Some very simple data are shown in Table 2–10 which seem to support such a notion. They

TABLE 2–10
Educational Accomplishment of Those in Lowest
Quintile of Family Personal Income
Distribution, United States, 1964

Educational Accomplishment	Percentage
Elementary only	49.1
High school not completed	17.7
High school, completed	12.2
College, less than four years	5.9
College, four years	6.6
Graduate school	8.5

SOURCE: Daniel B. Radner and John C. Hinrichs, "Size Distribution of Income in 1964, 1970, and 1971," *Survey of Current Business*, Oct., 1974, table 13.

show that about 50 percent of the heads of consumer units in the bottom quintile of the 1964 Bureau of Economic Analysis family personal income distribution had only elementary levels of education compared to about 30 percent for the total income distribution. The instinctive response to such data among those concerned with the degree of inequality in the income distribution is to argue that inequality could be reduced by increasing the educational qualifications of those in the bottom quintile of the income distribution.

Unfortunately, life is not that simple. To illustrate, let us assume that (1) the average level and distribution of abilities of those with elementary education are the same as those of individuals with four years of college education, and (2) if provided with an opportunity to acquire four years of college education, the level and distribution of income of individuals presently with an elementary education would be identical to those of people with four years of college.[18] The question now is how much of a reduction in inequality in the income distribution would be produced by these assumptions? Surprisingly, the answer is, "Very little!" Table 2–11 shows the actual 1964 distribution of family personal

TABLE 2–11

Actual Distribution of Personal Income and
Hypothetical Distribution Assuming Those
with Only Elementary Education Had
Four Years of College,
United States, 1964

Income Quintile	Actual Distribution (percent)	Hypothetical Distribution (percent)
Lowest	4.2	4.9
Second	10.6	11.2
Third	16.4	16.1
Fourth	23.2	22.0
Highest	25.5	24.8
Top 5 percent	20.0	21.0
Gini coefficient	.40	.39

SOURCE: Daniel B. Radner and John C. Hinrichs, "Size Distribution of Income in 1964, 1970, and 1971," *Survey of Current Business*, Oct., 1974, table 11.

income by quintile as well as what the distribution would look like if our assumptions were realized. The Gini coefficient for the hypothetical distribution is .39, while that for the actual distribution is .40.

The problem now is how to account for this remarkable finding, and I am not certain that I can. However, some interesting possibilities come to mind. Suppose that formal educational achievement beyond the

[18] These assumptions will produce the maximum impact in terms of reducing inequality in the overall income distribution.

level of acquiring basic literacy skills has relatively little to do with levels of personal income. Rather, imagine a world in which the primary determinant of economic success is some form of innate or genetic capacity which is also a significant factor in one's ability to absorb formal education. Further, assume that this innate ability is normally distributed in the population. In such a world, within any particular educational class, there will exist a distribution of ability which is a microcosmic slice of the distribution for the entire population. Under such circumstances, it would not be surprising to find that the distribution of income within any particular educational class roughly mirrored (in terms of equality) the distribution for the entire society. This is what seems to be the case in the United States. A brief look at Table 2–12 indicates that there is

TABLE 2–12

Gini Coefficients for Family Personal Income
Distribution by Educational Accomplishment,
United States, 1964

Educational Accomplishment	Gini Coefficient
Elementary only	.39
High school, not completed	.36
High school, completed	.33
College, less than four years	.36
College, four years	.39
Graduate school	.40

SOURCE: Daniel B. Radner and John C. Hinrichs, "Size Distribution of Income in 1964, 1970, and 1971," *Survey of Current Business*, Oct., 1974, table 13.

substantial uniformity in the Gini coefficient by educational class. The closest thing to a deviation from the pattern of uniformity is among those with four full years of high school education. Among this group the Gini coefficient is .33. Other than this exception, the Gini measures range from .36 to .40.

The possibility of the pattern of personal income distribution being dominated by ability differentials is reasonably consistent with some recent investigations, particularly that of Taubman and Wales.[19] Thus, it is not without empirical support. However, it does run contrary to the

[19] Paul Taubman and Terence Wales, "Higher Education, Mental Ability, and Screening," *Journal of Political Economy*, Jan.–Feb., 1973, p. 35. They conclude that "it is almost certain that for those who are at least high school graduates, ability is a more important determinant of the range of income distribution than is education."

general trend of much thinking, which tends to minimize the importance of genetic differences among people. After all, assigning a significant role to genetic differences in determining individual economic achievement limits the extent to which environmental factors (such as education) are important in this respect. Besides, it tends to imply the decidedly unpopular position that the poor may be poor not because of lack of opportunity but for want of ability.

At the level of the society as a whole, our analysis has substantial implications. Specifically, it undermines the idea that educational policy can be a significant tool in shaping and controlling the economic and social structure of America. In our contemporary world this notion is virtually a sacred cow. Tremendous social investments in education have been undertaken, frequently with the avowed purpose of creating a more egalitarian society. The arguments presented here suggest quite strongly that whatever we do in the educational area will have little impact in an egalitarian sense. In fact, there is almost a suggestion of something analogous to the idea of a "natural" rate of unemployment, namely, a "natural" degree of inequality in the income distribution. To be sure, it is not as unmodifiable as the "natural" rate of unemployment. For example, it is well known that there has been a substantial decrease in income inequality in this century in the United States. However, the "natural" level of inequality may impose a limit to reductions in inequality beyond which we cannot go without substantial confiscation and redistribution of earnings-related income (actually, we do this to a very sizable extent already). Remember, the fundamental source of income inequality in the United States is inequality in the distribution of earnings income, and if that distribution is apparently not capable of being significantly modified by educational investment and the like, one has to admit to there being some lower limit to the Gini measure of inequality that can only be breached through the use of the power to tax away and redistribute the earnings-related income of individuals.

DISCRIMINATION AND INCOME INEQUALITY

Our last subject for discussion, the impact of alleged discrimination based on ethnic and/or racial origins in creating income inequality, is potentially the most controversial of the subjects I have chosen to discuss. Again, serious questions arise concerning the validity of the conventional wisdom, that is, that something called discrimination is so dominant in

American life that ethnic and racial minority groups receive decidedly inferior treatment at the hands of the white majority. And, of course, it is further argued that this discrimination contributes to greater economic inequality in the society. Let us deal with that proposition first before moving on to the more complex issues.

Table 2–13 shows the 1964 Bureau of Economic Analysis income

TABLE 2–13
Shares of Family Personal Income by Income
Quintile and Race, United States, 1964

Income	Percentage of Income	
Quintile	White	Nonwhite
Lowest	4.4	4.4
Second	11.0	10.6
Third	16.6	16.3
Fourth	23.0	23.8
Highest	45.0	44.9
Top 5 percent	19.9	17.1
Gini coefficient	.39	.40

SOURCE: Daniel B. Radner and John C. Hinrichs, "Size Distribution of Income in 1964, 1970, and 1971," *Survey of Current Business*, Oct., 1974, table 13.

distributions for both whites and nonwhites in the United States. Clearly there is little difference between these distributions in terms of the shares of income received by quintile. In fact, the Gini coefficients are .40 for nonwhites and .39 for whites, while the Gini measure for the two groups combined is intermediate between those for the two radical groups. What this means is that giving nonwhites exactly the same level and distribution of income as whites would result in almost no change in the Gini coefficient for the American income distribution. Thus, racial differences in income levels cannot be viewed as a source of overall income inequality in the United States.

This point still leaves unresolved the issue of whether differences in racial income levels constitute a basic inequity in American society. The answer to that question depends on how one chooses to explain such differentials. The standard analysis focuses on overt discrimination, which, in its simplest form, means either paying white workers more than equally productive nonwhite workers or excluding qualified nonwhites from employment. This is what was originally meant by the term *discrimination.*

In recent years, though, it has become increasingly difficult to document the existence of overt discrimination. In particular, pressures from governmental agencies charged with enforcing equal employment opportunity have been substantial and, in many cases, have pushed into the area of "affirmative action," even going so far as to provoke court cases alleging "reverse" discrimination. Yet, the white/nonwhite income differential has been naggingly persistent, as is shown in Table 2–14. This fact is somewhat puzzling, for accompanying the drive for equal

TABLE 2–14
Ratio of Median Family Income of Nonwhites to Whites,
Selected Years, United States, 1950–1973

Year	Ratio of Nonwhite to White Income
1950	.54
1955	.56
1960	.55
1965	.55
1966	.60
1967	.62
1968	.63
1969	.63
1970	.64
1971	.63
1972	.62
1973	.60

SOURCE: U.S. Bureau of the Census, *Current Population Reports*, Series P-60, no. 98.

employment opportunity has been a marked closing of the white/non-white educational differential, the most obvious form of societal discrimination against nonwhites. At first glance, the data of Table 2–14 might seem to reflect adversely on the discrimination hypothesis. However, this interpretation is to ignore the fact that in recent years the content of the term *discrimination* has been altered to encompass the impact of what is called "institutionalized racism."

What is meant by "institutionalized racism"? As nearly as I can tell, it encompasses any facet of the social, political, and economic fabric of present society that adversely affects nonwhites. And what is the evidence for its existence? That is simple: in the economic sphere, the very fact that there is a white/nonwhite income differential is sufficient to demonstrate the operation of institutionalized racism. Now, notice the change this factor introduces into the treatment of white/nonwhite economic differentials. Whereas previously discrimination was offered as an explanation for racial economic differentials, the differentials themselves are now offered as proof of discrimination. Thus, the reasoning process has become somewhat circular.

The circularity of this reasoning has substantial implications for the analysis of racial economic differentials. I will illustrate. Some of my remarks on the previous topic suggested that there was a tendency to underestimate the contribution of differences in inherent ability when attempting to explain inequality in the distribution of personal income. Transferred into the realm of racial economic differentials, this suggestion might imply the possibility that these differentials are the product of variations by race in the average level of endowment with certain types of inherent abilities that are important determinants of both economic productivity and the associated incomes that such productivity generates. However, in the world of institutionalized racism, the existence of differential endowments, by race, with what I prefer to call "genetic" human capital is not only denied but, more importantly, there is virtually no evidence that can possibly refute this contention. For example, there are data that are consistent with the hypothesis that systematic white/nonwhite productivity differences are capable of explaining the white/nonwhite income differential.[20] This evidence, though, is irrelevant in an intellectual milieu that accepts the principle of institutionalized racism, for the productivity differential is explained away as being itself a product of discrimination. Similarly, almost any hypothesis for explaining the white/nonwhite income differential that is an alternative to the discrimination notion can be rendered consistent with the discrimination thesis by introducing the concept of institutionalized racism.

The perplexing thing about the question of discrimination and its economic impact is the tendency for most people to overlook and ignore data that are inconsistent with the discrimination thesis. In its most virulent form, the discrimination hypothesis maintains that the majority

[20] Lowell E. Gallaway and Gerald W. Scully, "An Economic Analysis of Minority Group Discrimination in the United States" (paper presented to the Midwest Economic Association, Chicago, Ill., Apr., 1969). The results contained in that paper are reported in Gallaway, *Manpower Economics* (Homewood, Ill.: Richard D. Irwin, Inc.), chap. 11.

in America is so obsessed with its white Anglo-Saxon Protestant heritage that it either consciously or unconsciously suppresses and maltreats all ethnic and minority groups such as Jews, Negroes, Orientals, Chicanos, Puerto Ricans, Filipinos, Poles, Catholics, and others. Of course, in the economic realm this discrimination has the effect of creating systematic income differentials. Therefore, we have a picture of the white Anglo-Saxon Protestant sitting at the top of the heap, so to speak, exploiting everyone else for his own benefit. Complete data describing income levels by race and ethnic group are not available, but some simple statistics from the 1970 census are shown in Table 2–15. They are fasci-

TABLE 2–15
Median Family Income Level by Racial or Ethnic
Group, United States, 1969

Racial or Ethnic Group	Median Family Income (dollars)
Japanese	12,515
Chinese	10,610
White	9,957
Filipino	9,318
Cuban	8,529
Mexican	6,962
Puerto Rican	6,165
Negro	6,063

SOURCE: U.S. Bureau of the Census, *Decennial Census of 1970.*

nating, and reconciling them with the straightforward discrimination thesis requires some intricate cerebral machinations.

To begin, we note that among the groups included in Table 2–15 whites *do not* have the highest income levels. At the top of the list are those of Japanese descent, whose median family income level is some 25 percent higher than that of whites. They are followed by the Chinese-Americans, with 6 percent higher incomes. Below whites on the list are those of Filipino descent, with 6 percent less incomes. The list ends with Negroes, who have income levels that are about 40 percent less than those of whites.

This distribution would seem to require some explanation. In the case of the Japanese-Americans one possibility is that they are more heavily concentrated in relatively high income areas, particularly Hawaii.

However, an examination of the data at the regional level (Table 2–16) reveals that the pattern of higher Japanese-American incomes is quite general. Interestingly, the Chinese-American data show a similar pattern.

TABLE 2–16

Median Family Income by Racial or Ethnic
Group and Region, United States, 1969

			Income (dollars)			
Region	Japanese	Chinese	White	Filipino	Spanish Heritage	Negro
Northeast	10,992	8,752	10,721	10,859	6,020	7,327
North Central	11,683	10,769	10,298	12,012	9,151	7,764
South	7,470	10,684	8,721	7,628	6,653	4,900
West	12,847	11,415	10,374	9,144	8,268	7,379
California	12,393	10,915	10,969	9,124	8,791	7,484
Hawaii	13,542	14,179	10,508	9,289	9,028*	6,699

SOURCE: U.S. Bureau of the Census, *Decennial Census of 1970.*
   * Spanish language in Hawaii.

What should be made of these data? At the very least they require either (1) a substantial effort to render them consistent with the discrimination hypothesis for explaining racial income differentials or (2) recognition of the fact that they contradict the discrimination thesis. I will assume, I hope without objection, that everyone will reject the explanation that these differentials reflect the dominance of American political, social, and economic life by a small, elite clique of Orientals. No, some other explanation must be found. One possibility is the relatively small number of Oriental families. On statistical grounds this is no problem, since beyond a relatively small number of observations statistical reliability improves only marginally with increases in the size of the population sample (I am assuming that the minority group populations in the United States are samples of their respective parent populations).

Another aspect of relative smallness is the possibility that there might be some threshold level of relative size of a minority population before discrimination manifests itself. This would not seem to be a viable proposition, particularly in the case of Orientals. For one thing, there are states in which the Negro minority is as small relatively as the Japanese minority in California, and yet the black-white income differential in those states is similar to that for the entire nation.[21] Second, there is

[21] Simply examine the income differential for Negroes vis-a-vis those for other races in Hawaii. See Table 2–16.

presumably a long historical record of American antipathy toward Orientals. Remember the Chinese exclusion legislation of the late nineteenth century, the spectre of the Yellow Peril, and, of course, World War II and its associated anti-Japanese feelings. It simply boggles the mind to suggest that the Japanese, for example, have gone relatively unnoticed in areas such as California.

A more appealing alternative explanation is that there is something unique about the subset of Orientals living in the United States. Perhaps, for example, the Japanese-American and Chinese-American cultures encourage industriousness and the like. However, one is entitled to ask how such cultures manage to overcome the alleged all-pervasiveness of institutionalized racism. Another possibility is that Orientals living in America are unique among Japanese and Chinese in terms of their inherent genetic abilities. But that presents problems, for it suggests that those abilities are an important factor in shaping income levels of individuals, and, as we have seen, this explanation runs contrary to the conventional wisdom that tends to ascribe differential economic achievement to environmental influences such as discrimination rather than to genetic differences.

Where does this leave us? Frankly, it seems that whichever way we turn, the standard discrimination hypothesis comes apart at the seams. Actually, this is not a completely novel development. For some time there have been indications that the conventional policy recommendations that flow rather naturally from the usual explanations of racial economic differences have failed to appreciably alter the relative economic status of our major minority group, Negroes. A variety of approaches has been employed—compensatory education at an early age, equalization of expenditures on schooling as well as busing of students at the public school level, preferential admission policies in higher education, equal employment opportunity legislation and affirmative action programs in the labor market—and we still have Negro income levels that are approximately 60 percent of those of whites. In fact, the seeming permanence of the white/Negro income differential is truly remarkable, considering the massive social effort that has been directed at its elimination—so remarkable that one wonders why there has not been serious questioning of the philosophical basis of that social effort, namely, the discrimination syndrome.

But, you may ask, what is the alternative to the discrimination hypothesis? One hesitates to mention an almost obvious possibility in this respect, one that is consistent with our previous remarks concerning the possible importance of differences in inherent genetic ability, that is, genetic human capital, in determining economic success. Of course, the alternative hypothesis I refer to is the possibility that racial economic differentials are the product of variations in the average endowment of genetic human capital possessed by the various ethnic and racial groups. There is sufficient evidence available on this point to warrant serious scholarly consideration of this alternative hypothesis.[22] Unfortunately, though, for the most part intellectual America has shown almost no disposition to engage in investigations that might substantiate or, by implication, refute such a hypothesis.[23] This is indeed unfortunate, for given the obvious failures of the standard discrimination hypothesis as an explanation of racial economic differentials, we can ill afford the luxury of discarding a hypothesis simply because it is potentially unpopular.

CONCLUDING REMARKS

After a lengthy discussion of five different topics, the reader is entitled to ask for some integration of them. Actually, there is a rather compelling common theme that runs through the positions I have advanced here. Put succinctly, it is that an adequate understanding of the contemporary problems of unemployment and poverty requires recognition of the possibility that there are "natural" constraints operative in the American economy which impose limitations on our ability to control economic affairs. Among those which ought to be recognized are the natural rate of unemployment, the natural degree of inequality in the personal income distribution that results from the unequal distribution of genetic human capital among people, and, *possibly*, a natural set of

[22] For example, data describing performance of children on standardized mental ability tests for which socioeconomic class is controlled predict almost exactly the relative economic position of Chinese, Puerto Ricans, and Negroes. For the data, see Gerald S. Lesser, Gordon Fifer, and Donald H. Clark, *Mental Abilities of Children from Different Social Class and Cultural Groups*, Monographs of the Society for Research in Child Development, Vol. 30 (Chicago: University of Chicago Press, 1965). The interpretation of these data is mine and not that of the authors of the study cited. Space limitations prevent a detailed exposition of the argument for the consideration of this alternative hypothesis. For a more complete discussion of this question, see chapters 5 and 6 of my *Poverty in America* (Columbus, Ohio: Grid, Inc., 1973).

[23] For example, at a meeting of the National Academy of Sciences at Dartmouth College in Sept., 1969, a letter was read stating the National Academy's decision not to support recommendations urging the study of the link between intelligence and genetic factors.

racial economic differences that can be traced to variations in racial endowments of genetic human capital.

In these times arguing for the existence of natural constraints in social and economic affairs is a somewhat heretical position. Basically, it runs counter to the dominant philosophic bent of the twentieth century, which takes as its point of departure the position that individual attitudes, behavior, and abilities are largely shaped and determined by the social, political, and economic institutions that constitute the social environment. Since these institutions have been created by the collectivity known as society, it would seem to follow quite logically that they are subject to modification at the wish of that group. And, of course, this implies that they could be changed in a fashion that would influence and alter the behavior patterns of individuals.

Within the context of this line of thought there is little or no room for the concept of the natural constraint. Why is this? In part, I suspect, because to many people the notion of natural constraints seems to imply a certainty of knowledge that is inconsistent with the primal thrust of the contemporary philosophy of science that dominates the social sciences, that is, the argument that we can only "know" something imperfectly. Most of us, excepting any Misean-style praxeologists, would probably agree on that point. However, our inability to perceive and identify in an exact fashion the existence of natural constraints in operation does not mean they are not there. In short, it does not follow that because there is nothing we can know with complete certainty, there is nothing to be known.

Ultimately, though, the primary source of opposition to natural constraints is the threat they seem to pose to the basic belief that all human actions are susceptible to social control and direction. To many, this is an intuitively attractive proposition, for it suggests a degree of control over the human condition that will permit its being moved in the direction of some utopian perfection. While this view may be appealing, we should be wary lest we find ourselves attempting to alter the circumstances of our economic life in a manner that is incompatible with the "natural" constraints we face. If we consistently attempt to act in defiance of those natural constraints, we are likely to be exceedingly frustrated at our apparent inability to control our circumstances. And, unfortunately, this frustration may lead us toward even stronger control measures, especially if we persist in failing to recognize why our attempts at control have failed.

PART II
Governmental Policies in the 1970's

Chapter 3

Public Policy and the
Political Process

WILLIAM A. NISKANEN

> . . . social functions are usually the by-products, and private
> ambitions the ends, of human action.
> > ANTHONY DOWNS, *An Economic Theory of Democracy*

> . . . good law is a public good. That is why it is not produced.
> > DAVID FRIEDMAN, *The Machinery of Freedom*

PERSPECTIVES ON POLICY ANALYSIS[1]

A specter is haunting policy analysis—the specter of the Decision Maker. In the "ideal" form of the conventional myth, the policy analyst is portrayed as a modern Machiavelli advising some Pareto-optimizing Prince. The decision maker is assumed to be beneficent, omnipotent, and all but omniscient—lacking only the specialized information that no one but the policy analyst can provide. All that stands between existing conditions and a state of bliss is the heroic art of placing the right analysis before the right decision maker. In the "realistic" form of the conventional myth, any perceived failure of public policy is explained in terms of personal attributes of the decision maker: he is evil or stupid, he lacks sufficient authority, or he lacks sufficient information. The conventional prescription for good government is to select good men for public office and to give them the power and knowledge to do what they believe is in the public interest.

This summary, of course, is a caricature of the conventional view. This description exaggerates but efficiently illustrates the dominant themes of public administration literature from Confucius and Plato to Woodrow Wilson and McGeorge Bundy that are now enshrined in the

[1] This introductory section is developed from an earlier article. See William A. Niskanen, "The Political Economy of Policy Analysis," *Beleidsanalyse*, Jan., 1975.

policy research foundations and other institutional fortresses of the conventional wisdom. The conventional prescription for policy analysis is to identify the objective function of the decision maker, estimate the relation between action and outcome, and apply the calculus of efficiency. It is all very neat.

An alternative perspective is developing from the harsh lessons of recent history and a rediscovery of another intellectual tradition. For the moment, there is a widespread sense of public failure. Although there are some who maintain a "devil" theory of public failure, many others have come to recognize that good men do not assure good government, high purpose does not assure good law, and good analysis does not assure good policy. This perspective, building on the critical insight of Adam Smith, explains public outcome as the by-products of actions serving quite private purposes, as organized through the institutions and processes of government. Public failure is thus explained in terms of flaws in the institutions and processes that harness private purpose to public outcomes.

A theory of public outcomes must be based on the distinguishing characteristics of the structure of a specific government. A useful start is to exorcise the specter of the Decision Maker. For any policy issue, even in the most authoritarian government, there is more than one decision maker. And the set of decision makers are seldom a "team" in the sense that they have common objectives; there may be as many private purposes as the number of decision makers. No one of the decision makers may have the least personal concern about efficiency or the general welfare (whatever that means), particularly if achievement of these conditions requires any personal diligence and effort. As with businessmen, these conditions may be the consequences of his personal behavior, but they are not the purpose of his behavior. The demand for and use of policy analysis depends on how it serves the private purposes of the set of decision makers. And any social function served by policy analysis depends on how the institutions of government are organized to harness these private ends. If the structure of government has serious flaws, one should expect good analysis to have about the same effect as informing a polluter about external costs or arguing with a thief about the inefficiency of theft as a procedure for allocating resources. Many years ago, Madison warned us, "If the impulse and the opportunity [for the pursuit of private interests at a cost to others] be suffered to coincide, we well know that neither moral nor religious motives can be relied on as an adequate control. They are not found to be such on the injustice and violence of individuals, and lose their efficacy in proportion to the number combined together, that is, in proportion as their efficiency becomes needful."[2] The conventional model of government decision making and the role of the policy analyst fail to account for the structure of any actual government. The decision maker as a Pareto Prince is just not consistent with the facts.

A useful next step is to recognize that economists generally use different professional tools and perform different professional roles when they address government services than when the same economists analyze private goods and services. The characteristic approach to the analysis of government services is to focus on conditions specific to the producing unit. What is the demand for the service as revealed by the political system? What is the production function for the service? What are the budgetary costs of factors used to produce the service? Some constrained maximization technique is then used to calculate the set of factors and activities that minimizes the budgetary cost of meeting a given demand for the service. In this role, the economist is an estimator and a calculator, that is, a "systems analyst" for the producing unit, taking as given the process by which demands and budgetary costs are established and government decisions are made.

The characteristic approach to the analysis of private goods and services, in contrast, is to focus on the market; that is, on conditions *external* to the producing unit: Are there any Pareto-relevant external benefits or costs to the production or use of these products? Are there any taxes, subsidies, or price controls that distort product and factor prices? Are there any barriers to entry in the product and factor markets? Are any such barriers to entry the result of economies of scale relative to the size of the market, collusion among firms or factor owners, or government restrictions? Analysis of these conditions usually leads an economist to recommend government policies to change those market conditions: generalize property rights or use taxes or subsidies to internalize Pareto-relevant externalities; set prices for any related government services at marginal cost; remove the taxes, subsidies, and price controls that distort product and factor prices; reduce barriers to entry by penalizing collusion, reducing tariffs, and removing government entry controls;

[2] Alexander Hamilton et al., *Federalist Papers*, ed. Clinton Rossiter (New York: New American Library, 1961), p. 81.

and so on. In this role an economist is a social scientist and leaves the systems analysis task to the consumers and producers.

The main argument of this chapter is that economists have a better opportunity to improve public policy by focusing on the political process instead of on specific policies—by asking the same type of questions and using the same type of professional tools that they bring to the analysis of private decisions. The body of this chapter summarizes my perception of those current characteristics of our political processes that most distort the decisions on public policy, given the best possible analyses of specific policies. My main conclusion is that changes in the market for government services in the United States, some quite recent, have substantially weakened the relationship between the personal interests of government officials and the shared concerns of the American population.

POLITICS AND POLICY

My personal perspectives on the major imperfections in the market for government services in the United States are summarized in this section. These perspectives are based on the developing economic theory of public choice, some scattered empirical evidence, and personal reflection. After two centuries of our grand experiment with constitutional government, our contemporary political institutions do not seem to serve us very well, and the prospects for the near future are even less encouraging. We seem to be in the early stages of "the English disease." Although the facts are not complete, a preliminary diagnosis is more valuable than an autopsy.

THE FEDERAL GOVERNMENT

The "Economic Constitution." A political constitution, above all, is a set of rules that limit the nature and extent of decisions that may be made by government officials without widespread popular consent on a change in these rules. Some of these rules may be defined in a formal written constitution. Others that reflect the same extent of popular consent may be defined only in the form of an "implicit constitution." Three important rules in our "economic constitution" have been substantially changed, most rapidly during the last decade, without any formal process of constitutional change: (1) the rule of the enumerated powers and the tenth amendment, (2) the fiscal rule, and (3) the monetary rule. In each case the actual process of change is clear: these three rules have collapsed under the weight of a massive assault by the intellectual community and the self-interest of government officials. For several decades most American intellectuals—and economists are the most culpable—have been iconoclasts.[3] A correct observation that such rules are not always optimal, given full information and benevolent officials, has led to an incorrect conclusion that such rules are unnecessary in a world of imperfect information and self-serving officials. And no new rules have been suggested that reflect the consensus for the old rules. Government officials have always had an incentive to break the rules. The intellectual assault on the "economic constitution," however, provided the necessary opportunity.

Our formal Constitution (Art. 1, sec. 8) enumerates a small set of powers (or functions) that the federal government may perform. Madison forcefully summarized the sense of the constitutional convention concerning these powers:

> The powers delegated by the proposed Constitution to the Federal government are few and defined. Those which are to remain in the State governments are numerous and indefinite. The former will be exercised principally on external objects, as war, peace negotiation, and foreign commerce, with which last the power of taxation will, for the most part, be connected. The powers reserved to the several States will extend to all the objects which, in the ordinary course of affairs, concern the lives, liberties, and properties of the people, and the internal order, improvement, and prosperity of the State.[4]

Article Ten of the Bill of Rights, added later as a condition for approval of the Constitution, strengthens the limit on the federal powers: "The powers not delegated to the United States by the Constitution, nor prohibited by it to the States, are reserved to the States respectively, or the people." The nature and intent of these limits could hardly be clearer. And no subsequent amendment has added to the enumerated federal spending powers.

Today, however, most federal spending programs and many regulatory activities have no formal constitutional basis. Our implicit constitution has been changed to read: "All powers not formally prohibited to it by the Constitution are reserved to the federal government." More-

---

[3] My dictionary defines this term as "a breaker of icons, or images . . . one who attacks cherished beliefs as shams."

[4] Hamilton et al., *Federalist Papers*, pp. 292–293.

over, this change has been rapid and recent. Although there was some erosion in the Tenth Amendment from the earliest years, total domestic spending by the federal government seldom exceeded 1 percent of national income through the 1920's. The New Deal, of course, was the first massive breach of this rule. It was rationalized as a temporary necessity in an economic crisis, and in fact many New Deal laws, programs, and agencies expired with the end of the depression. The few new federal functions introduced from World War II through the early 1960's were at least rationalized in terms of the enumerated powers: the interstate highway program and the first federal education programs were labeled and advertised as national security programs. The Great Society began the first massive breach of this rule in a noncrisis period. The flood of domestic legislation since 1965 does not even pay lip service to the enumerated powers. The Tenth Amendment, alas, is a dead letter.

Federal spending data reflect a massive change in the federal role in the postwar period. From fiscal year 1947 through fiscal year 1976, total federal spending for national defense, international affairs, veterans, and interest increased at an annual rate of about 6 percent. Total federal spending for all other functions increased at an annual rate of about 13 percent. Federal spending for these other functions increased from about 17 percent of total federal outlays to about 58 percent of the current budget. Most of this current federal spending does not have an explicit constitutional basis in the enumerated powers. Moreover, these spending data do not reflect the recent large federal lending program or the addition of federal regulatory powers affecting product and occupational safety and uses of the environment. For this paper, my argument is not that these new federal functions are unworthy, but that the federal government has assumed these functions by an extraconstitutional process of constitutional change.

For most of American history, except during intermittent wars and economic crises, the federal budget had a small surplus. A fiscal rule that federal spending should normally be slightly less than tax revenues, I contend, was part of our implicit constitution through the early 1960's. For the first twenty years following World War II, a period that included a war and several minor recessions, the federal budget had a surplus in eleven years and a cumulative surplus over the period.

After several decades of assault on the balanced budget rule by the economics community, however, a skeptical president endorsed the "new economics." A tax reduction was approved in 1964, a prosperous year that, maybe not coincidentally, was also an election year. The murmur of self-congratulation among economists was enough to disguise the fact that the new economics does not suggest a new fiscal rule. Once the nexus between federal spending and revenues was broken, no consensus developed on any other rule to constrain the level of spending and the deficit. In the following eleven years through fiscal year 1976, a period that also included a war and two recessions, the federal budget had a surplus in one year and a huge cumulative deficit over the period, and no balanced budget is in prospect. Some recent evidence confirms the politicians' perception that voters are more averse to tax increases than to deficits.[5] In that case, one should expect a positive relation between the increase in federal spending and the size of the deficit, and federal spending patterns are consistent with this relation. From fiscal year 1947 through fiscal year 1965, a balanced budget period, total federal spending increased at an average annual rate of about 8 percent. In the later "new economics" period through fiscal year 1976, federal spending increased at an average annual rate of about 11 percent. The 1975 tax reduction will probably trigger a new round of demands for federal spending. A tax *increase*, however, by increasing the perceived tax price of federal services, may be a necessary part of a strategy to constrain total federal spending.

For most of American history, federal monetary authorities were constrained to maintain the money supply in some relation to the commodity reserves or, since the 1930's, to maintain the value of the dollar relative to major foreign currencies. These rules, I contend, were also part of our implicit constitution until very recent years. And these rules, however flawed, were usually effective. Price stability was the norm, and inflation was only a wartime condition.

A continuous assault on these rules, again by the economics community, led to a final rupture in 1971, when the dollar was devalued and later floated. Although some of the advocates of floating exchange rates have long promoted a rule of slow, steady monetary growth, there is no consensus on a new rule and apparently no incentive for the monetary authorities to follow a steady-growth rule. Again, the consequences of replacing an imperfect rule with no rule have been dramatic: in the

[5] William A. Niskanen, "Economic and Fiscal Effects on the Popular Vote for President," Working Paper No. 25 (Berkeley: University of California Graduate School of Public Policy, May, 1974).

period from 1947 through 1971, a period that included two wars, consumer prices increased at an average annual rate of 2.5 percent. In the three years after 1971, a period in which the ending of a war and a subsequent recession should have reduced inflationary pressures, consumer prices increased at an average annual rate of 6.5 percent. For the last several years, the alternative acceleration and braking of the monetary base have destroyed the stability of expectations that is a necessary condition for sustained economic growth. In a world of imperfect information and fallible authorities, any one of several old or new rules would perform better than no rule. A major criterion for choosing among these rules should be a broad consensus for the rule, and for this reason some old rule (such as maintaining exchange rates) may be preferred.

The Presidency. The American presidency is a unique institution. In general, I believe, the presidency has served us rather well. Several developing conditions, however, appear to be reducing the responsiveness of the president to the interests of the population. In recent years, several political historians have rediscovered "the imperial presidency," as if this condition were unnatural or specific to some recent incumbents. Such concerns usually fail to distinguish between the power of the presidency and the conditions affecting the use of power. The presidency was *designed* to be a powerful institution, and any significant reduction of the power of this office would require a restructuring of our whole political system. Several developing changes in the system for selecting candidates and electing presidents, I contend, are responsible for most of the perceived abuses of presidential power.

Our national parties perform only one important function—to select presidential candidates and to organize the campaign to elect a president. The incentives and constraints facing individual party members, the relative role of the parties and other constitutions, and the "market structure" of parties will determine how well this function is performed.

Some years ago Anthony Downs demonstrated that a system of two parties, *both* of which are motivated *only* by the rewards of office, will select candidates and implement policies that reflect the preferences of the median voter on every issue.[6] Both parties must be nonideological; that is, they must select candidates and policies to maximize votes. If the

---

[6] Anthony Downs, *An Economic Theory of Democracy* (Ann Arbor: University of Michigan Press, 1957), p. 29.

entry costs to a third party are high, this system breaks down if one party is an ideological party and the other party acts to maximize votes. (The 1964 and 1972 elections are examples of such a condition.) If both parties maintain their respective ideological and vote-maximizing behavior, the vote-maximizing party will continue to win by policies that more nearly reflect the position of the ideological party than that of the median voter. The necessary conditions for restoring responsiveness to the median voter are the abandonment of ideology by the opposition party, a revision to ideology by the governing party, and/or the establishment of a major third party.

More recently, Donald Wittman demonstrated that a system of two parties, both of which are concerned only about governmental outcomes, will select candidates and policies that serve only the interests of party members.[7] The governing party selects a policy that maximizes the minimum benefits to its members, given a benefit-maximizing strategy by the opposition. The opposition, knowing the position of the governing party, selects a policy that maximizes the benefits to its members. This game is played in front of, and with the nominal participation of, other voters, but all of the benefits accrue to members of the two parties. This disturbing result is possible only if the entry costs to a third party are prohibitive.

A critical test of the Downs and Wittman models of party government has not been performed. A few observations, however, are suggestive. In the Downs model, the Republican party could assure a Democratic victory and Republican policies by choosing an ideological candidate and platform. In 1964, however, this Republican strategy led to the Great Society. In 1972 a similar strategy by the Democrats led to a Republican victory and Democratic policies, an outcome more consistent with the Downs model. The important point to explain is why recent presidents of both parties promote the policies of the Democratic party. The Wittman model suggests that these policies—a rapid growth of federal spending, special-interest programs, regulation, and deficits— serve the interests of the officials of both parties, and recent history seems to be more consistent with this model. The current move to establish a third party on the right, for example, suggests that both major parties are identified with policies to the left of the median voter. A

[7] Donald Wittman, "Parties as Utility Maximizers," *American Political Science Review*, June, 1973.

perspective that arises from both models is that the responsiveness of party government is critically dependent on either (1) conditions that would lead *both* major parties to pursue vote-maximizing strategies or (2) low entry costs for a third party.

Several evolving conditions, I contend, have led to an erosion of a responsive two-party system. One such condition is the increase in the number of presidential primaries. At present, roughly one-half of the states hold presidential primaries, and for many years the winner of these primaries has won a first-ballot victory at the party conventions. This system strengthens the ideologues in both parties and reduces the opportunity for either party to select vote-maximizing candidates and policies. A second condition is the decline in patronage and the associated growth of the civil service. This change has both reduced the number of people for whom winning the election is very important and increased the number for whom the level of government spending is very important. A candidate cannot now afford to confront the civil service voting bloc on employment and salary issues because he cannot promise jobs to a comparable number of voters on the condition that he wins. These two twentieth-century "good government" reforms appear both to have reduced the opportunities and the incentives for the major parties to maximize votes and to have increased the incentives to maximize the benefits to government outcomes, whoever wins the election. A reduction in the number of presidential primaries and the number of government positions filled by civil servants may be essential to assure a responsive presidency.

In the absence of a detailed study, I sense that the entry costs to a third party have always been high. The recent laws requiring contribution disclosure and limiting total campaign expenditures will surely increase these entry costs. Given present conditions, however, the potential entry of a third party is more important. The primary role of a third party is to discipline the governing party. This role is served by a credible threat to split the vote of the governing party. This strategy is risky, however, because a split of the majority can lead to the victory of a minority candidate and policies. The election of 1912 is an example. At present, the interests of those considering a third party on the right are probably best served by a visible effort to organize another party and select a credible candidate, followed by an offer to the Republican party to withdraw the third-party candidate in exchange for a public concession on several major substantive issues.[8] An actual third-party candidacy would probably be counterproductive to the interests of its suporters.

A president has a large vote advantage over any other candidate of the governing party. Some recent evidence, based on the popular vote for president from 1936 to 1972, suggests that this advantage is about 5 percent of the total major-party vote.[9] Moreover, this advantage would be offset only by a 10 percent decline in real per capita income between election years, a one-third increase in real per capita taxes, or a war. The effect of this advantage is that a president has a very large range of discretion on major policies that is consistent with his reelection. One or more substantial disasters is necessary to defeat a president who runs for reelection. In this century only Taft and Hoover were defeated in such a race, the first because of a split in the Republican party and the second because of a major depression, and no incumbent president has been defeated since 1932.

The source of this advantage is less clear. Since there was no apparent advantage to the incumbent president before 1936, however, it is plausible to attribute this advantage to the president's use of the new media, radio and television. The president's sustained unpaid access to these media contrasts with the high cost of access by any other candidate. If this explanation is correct, the president's advantage could be reduced by restricting his unpaid access to national television to, say, four hours each year, making his party pay for any incremental coverage. Or maybe an incumbent president would be required to win two-thirds of the electoral college votes for reelection. These suggestions may sound rather extreme, but some change appears necessary to induce better performance during the president's first term.

What motivates a president during his second term? More importantly, what would motivate a president to maximize the votes for the successor candidate of his party? Presidents retire to a life of ease, and their reputation seems largely independent of the success of their party. Presidents "use" their party to secure election and then depreciate the political capital of the party during their term in office. There is no political analog of the stock option that would motivate presidents to be concerned about their party beyond their tenure in office. This end-

[8] Naming the vice-presidential candidate should be considered a symbolic, not a substantive, issue.

[9] Niskanen, "Economic and Fiscal Effects on the Popular Vote."

period effect increases the president's discretion in his second term; governmental outcomes become entirely dependent on his personal motivations and the constraints on his power. One might hope that a president's concern for his reputation would be sufficient to motivate responsive behavior, but this concern is a weak reed. Even Hoover's reputation was revived during his years as an elder statesman.

What might be done to reduce the president's discretion in his second term? The Twenty-second Amendment could be repealed, but that action would merely maintain the normal advantage of the incumbent and indefinitely defer the end-period effect. My preferences are to maintain a finite tenure but to use some other instrument to motivate a president to be concerned about the future interests of his party. My own suggestions—to make the president's pension, any public spending for a retirement staff or a library, and the like a function of the percentage of the popular vote for the successor candidates of his party—should not be regarded as entirely fanciful. My ultimate concern, of course, is not the interest of any specific party but the motivation of the president to maximize the votes for himself or a successor candidate of his party. Vote-maximizing behavior (or profit-maximizing behavior, for that matter) does not always serve the public interest, but there does not seem to be any feasible attractive alternative.

Congress. Congress is an assembly of special interests. Could it be otherwise? Probably not, as long as congressmen are elected from single-member geographic districts. The primary problem of Congress is that individual congressmen have very little incentive, inherent in their position, to promote good law. This problem is the result of a massive and pervasive free-rider phenomenon within Congress.

Consider the following example. A congressman faces three actions that would use the same amount of his time, staff resources, and political capital. One action would generate $2 million of net benefits in his district and net costs of $10,000 in the other 434 districts. The second action would generate $1 million of net benefits in every district. The third action, opposition to the first type of special-interest program in another district, would save $10,000 in his district and 433 other districts and reduce the net benefits in one district by $2 million. The first action thus would generate aggregate net costs of $2.34 million, the second would generate aggregate net benefits of $435 million, and the third would generate aggregate net benefits of $2.34 million. In this case, an individual congressman would choose only the first action. Moreover, he would continue to pursue such special-interest programs for his own district until the ratio of marginal benefits to his district over the marginal input of his own time and other resources is less than that for the second type of action.

From his perspective, the least productive use of his time would be to identify and to organize opposition to special-interest programs that benefit another district. A recent statement by Senator Muskie reflects a perception of this problem: "Everyone recognizes the need for oversight, but other things come along, and it gets pushed further and further down the ladder until it disappears."[10] An average congressional district bears about 1/435 of total federal taxes. Even if there is a strong relation between district benefits and the perceived rewards of its congressmen, there is probably no other role in American society for which the decision maker bears a smaller proportion of the total benefits and costs of his actions. Congressmen are quick to take credit, not surprisingly, for special-interest programs for their district, for defense contracts awarded to firms in their district, and the like. No congressman, to my knowledge, has ever held a press conference to announce that by great effort on his own part he has saved ten cents for every family in the United States.

What can be done about this massive free-rider problem? One change would be to elect congressmen by a national proportional-representation system, but this solution would be a larger change in our political system than we would be prepared to consider and would create other significant problems of its own. A more important change consistent with our political traditions would be to enforce a constitutional prohibition on special-interest programs. One part of the free-rider problem is the result of the *combination* of geographic districts and special-interest programs. A restriction of federal activities to those that promote "the common Defense and the general Welfare of the United States," a radical eighteenth-century idea that is the only statement of objectives in our formal Constitution, would reduce much of this problem. Even if federal activities are limited to general-interest programs and policies, there is still a problem of inducing efficient monitoring of federal activities. One suggestion is to create a special prize fund, administered by an independent body, that would provide campaign funds to those congressmen who are recognized as especially effective monitors. Another suggestion is to create incentives for private monitoring of

[10] Allan Otten, "Oversight," *Wall Street Journal*, Mar. 6, 1975.

federal activities by permitting class action suits against the government for demonstrably inefficient performance.[11] As H. L. Hunt is reported to have said, "If this country is worth saving, it's worth saving at a profit."[12] Some such changes are necessary to induce congressmen and private individuals to make a living and a reputation by promoting good law and good public performance.

Members of Congress have a great advantage over any other potential candidate. In 1970, for example, 95.2 percent of incumbent candidates for the House of Representatives and 76.7 percent of incumbent candidates for the Senate were reelected.[13] Most elections are not even close: only 13 percent of the elections for both houses were decided by a vote margin of less than 5 percent. For the House, the proportion of close races has declined from 22 percent in 1958.[14] A recent study estimates the incumbent's advantage to be about 12 percent of the major-party vote in House races and about 6.5 percent in Senate races.[15] The same study estimates the advantage of an incumbent representative to be equivalent to about $200,000 of campaign spending and the advantage of an incumbent senator to be equivalent to about $80,000 per congressional district in his state. Moreover, the incumbent's advantage will surely be increased by the recent campaign finance laws, which establish limits on total campaign spending that are less than the average equivalent value of the incumbent's advantage and are less than was spent by *any* successful nonincumbent running against an incumbent in recent elections. Once elected, members of Congress have a longer potential tenure and as little discipline on their behavior as, say, university professors.

This great advantage of incumbents has mixed effects. On the one hand it makes them less dependent on serving their district, so it increases their opportunity to serve the general interest. On the other hand, this advantage reduces their incentive to be responsive to anyone.

[11] This prospect excites me. I would be among the first to organize a profit-seeking firm to monitor government performance if some such device for capturing part of the rewards of monitoring were authorized.

[12] Quoted in David Friedman, *The Machinery of Freedom* (New York: Harper & Row, 1973), p. 222.

[13] U.S. Census Bureau, *Statistical Abstract of the United States* (Washington, D.C.: Government Printing Office, 1974), Table 694.

[14] Edward Tufte, "The Relationship between Seats and Votes in Two-Party Systems," *American Political Science Review*, June, 1973, p. 550.

[15] William Welch, "The Economics of Campaign Funds," *Public Choice*, Winter, 1975, p. 95.

We seem to have created an institution in which we are almost entirely dependent on the personal motivations of its members. This advantage makes a positive model of congressional behavior more dependent on information about individual congressmen and the sociology of the Washington environment. As I observed in an earlier work, "this condition provides an opportunity for both statesmanship and skullduggery but puts the voter in the unfortunate position of being absolutely dependent on the politician's motivations and the constraints on his power. And one man's statesmanship may be another man's skullduggery."[16] I cannot believe that representative government with life tenure for our representatives serves the interests of the American population.

Incumbents pass the laws. For this reason it is not clear how or whether the incumbent's advantage can be reduced, and I have no clever solutions for this problem. The first types of actions that should be considered are to strip away those recent contributions to the incumbent's advantage: the campaign spending limits, the increase in the personal staffs, unpaid access to the mails and media, and so on. Public financing of campaigns, if authorized, should be restricted only to opposition candidates. Maybe a change in the election laws should be considered so that incumbents would be required to win, say, 60 percent of the popular vote. In the absence of a national initiative process or a constitutional convention, however, I do not know how these changes can be effected.

Most of the work of Congress is performed in a set of permanent functional committees. Each of these committees has an effective monopoly of the right to formulate and review legislation and to monitor government performance in a specific area. In other words, no member of Congress, except under special circumstances, may submit a bill for a floor vote or undertake a major policy or program review without approval of the relevant committee. Members serve on a committee for extended periods, and the composition of most committees does not change much faster than the composition of Congress. Moreover, several recent studies have confirmed that committee members generally have stronger preferences for government action in the area of the committee's responsibility than do other members of Congress.[17] Senator Proxmire has observed that "The net result of all of this . . . is that the Committee

---

[16] William A. Niskanen, *Bureaucracy and Representative Government* (Chicago: Aldine Publishing Co., 1971), p. 137.

[17] David Rohde and Kenneth Shepsle, "Democratic Committee Assignments in

structure develops a built-in bias toward higher budgets. Because the people who serve on each committee have an interest in seeing the budget for which they are responsible increase, they often fail to encourage careful evaluation and analysis of expenditures."[18]

The structure of committees in Congress, as it developed historically, was not anticipated by the constitutional founders, who feared the institutionalization of factions. Some system of committees, however, was made necessary by the growth in the size of Congress and the scale of government. The present system of monopoly committees, however, strengthens the committees relative to the body of Congress, effectively prohibits a fundamental review of existing legislation, reinforces the expansionary interests of the bureaus and regulatory commissions, and confirms the worst fears of the constitutional founders.

Several types of changes in the committee system should be considered. One type of change would maintain the structure of committees; members of Congress, however, would be randomly assigned and periodically reassigned. As an alternative, new bills would be randomly assigned among committees. This type of change would sacrifice the advantages of specialization and expertise to assure that committee decisions would be more representative of the interests of the whole Congress. A more fundamental change would be to allow competitive committees: any group, say 5 percent, of the members could form an *ad hoc* committee to review a bill or the performance of a specific program. This committee could then report a recommended bill for a floor vote, possibly in parallel with a bill reported out of the relevant permanent committee. The whole of Congress, then, could choose among two or more competing and considered proposals on a given issue. This proposal is more consistent with the type of *ad hoc* committee of the supporters of a bill that was envisioned by the constitutional founders. Changes in the rules of the House and Senate are sufficient to implement this plan. And most members of a Congress that is concerned about its efficacy may be willing to trade a reduction of their power in one area of federal activities for an increase in their power in all other areas. A

---

the House of Representatives," *American Political Science Review*, Sept., 1973; and others.

[18] U.S. Congress, Joint Economic Committee, Subcommittee on Economy in Government, *The Analysis and Evaluation of Public Expenditure: The PPB System*, 91st Cong., 1st sess., 1969.

fundamental reform of Congress is both feasible and necessary to preserve representative government.

The Bureaucracy. The federal bureaucracy has become the fourth branch of government. Since I have written extensively about the problems of bureaucratic supply of government services,[19] this paper summarizes only the main features of my analysis. The primary problems of the bureaucratic supply of government services are due to the structure of the bureaucracy and the incentives of bureaucrats.

Most bureaus are monopoly suppliers of the services they provide. Competition among bureaus is discouraged and is periodically reduced by organizational reforms that place competing bureaus in a common department. Any form of monopoly creates problems, but monopoly bureaus create distinctively different problems, primarily because bureau managers are not allowed to appropriate any part of the difference between available revenues and costs as personal income. In other words, there is no way to make a buck by maximizing the "profits" of a bureau; this leads bureau managers to use up the potential monopoly profits in various forms of wasteful activity.

The combination of these two conditions leads to the following major types of effects: (1) a bureau's budget will be larger than that desired by a majority of Congress; (2) some part of the excess budget will be used up in production inefficiency; that is, a given level of output will be produced at a higher-than-necessary cost; and (3) some part of the excess budget will be used up in oversupply of the service. Each of these effects, unfortunately, is reinforced by the review of a bureau's proposals and performance by a monopoly committee of Congress. Some empirical evidence is developing about the magnitude of each of these effects, and more needs to be done, but the direction of the effects is clear.

Every president in recent decades has been frustrated by the unresponsiveness and inefficiency of the bureaucracy; it is easy to understand why our chief executives have retreated to golf, images of a new frontier or great society, or foreign adventures. But they have been badly advised. We need more competition among bureaus, not less. We need a system of financial rewards for efficient management, not

---

[19] Niskanen, *Bureaucracy and Representative Government*; and William A. Niskanen, "Bureaucracy and the Interests of Bureaucrats," Working Paper No. 24 (Berkeley: University of California Graduate School of Public Policy, Apr., 1975).

formula increases in civil service salaries. We need more contracting with private firms for the supply of government services, not the extension of government into private markets. We need more use of vouchers so that recipients can buy services where their interests are best served, not the proliferation of new monopoly bureaus.

STATE AND LOCAL GOVERNMENT

State and local governments manifest most of the types of imperfections shown by the federal political processes. The magnitude of the resulting problems, however, is much less than that of the federal government's problems for three reasons: the absolute level of state and local budgets is lower, the range of authorized functions is smaller, and people have an opportunity to "vote with their feet," that is, to choose their government by commuting or moving. In general, the more restricted the range of governmental functions and the lower the cost of moving to another jurisdiction, the less important are the characteristics of political institutions and processes. For this reason, for example, consumers are essentially indifferent to the governance of private firms if they have an opportunity to buy other goods and services from a number of local suppliers. The imperfections in the "market" for state and local government services are intermediate between those of the federal government and those of the commercial market. Most of these imperfections are similar to those of the federal government, they are important, and they deserve special study that is beyond the scope of this paper. There are two specific and increasing flaws in the market for state and local government service, however, that deserve attention.

State and local governments are increasingly dependent on subventions from the federal government. From fiscal year 1947 through fiscal year 1976, federal grants increased from $1.7 billion to $50.8 billion, an increase from 11 percent to about 22 percent of total state and local revenues.[20] Another form of subvention that is not widely recognized as such is the deduction of most state and local taxes from income subject to federal taxes. For fiscal year 1976, personal deductions for state and local taxes on income, sales, property, and gasoline are

[20] U.S. Office of the President, *Economic Report of the President, Transmitted to Congress Feb. 1975* (Washington, D.C.: Government Printing Office, 1975).

expected to reduce federal tax revenues by $16.1 billion.[21] Total federal subventions to state and local government are thus expected to be $66.9 billion, an amount that is nearly equal to the expected federal deficit.

The primary effect of these subventions is to reduce the perceived tax price of state and local government services. On the average, tax-payers pay state and local governments only seventy to seventy-five cents for each dollar of state and local spending. Thus, the quantity of state and local services they demand through the political process is increased and their concern about inefficiency in the supply of these services is reduced. It is not surprising why state and local officials are so enthusiastic about these subventions.

These subventions have several other corrosive effects. They have created the new fiscal distinction between "hard" money and "soft" money; "hard" money, in this case, is money that is hard to raise from local taxpayers. The federal subventions have provided the leverage for increased federal intervention in state and local decisions and, to the same extent, have reduced the range of freedom of action by state and local officials. Some federal grants have had an equalizing effect on spending for specific services among state and local governments; this effect has reduced the incentive to vote by moving and the disciplinary effect of potential moves.

There is a conceptual case for federal grants whereby a substantial part of the benefits of services provided in one state or local government accrue to residents of other states. It is not generally recognized, however, that state and local governments also export a substantial part of their taxes to residents in other states. In the absence of any federal subventions, it is not at all clear that state and local governments would provide a lower-than-optimal level of services in terms of the interests of all affected people. The "new federalism" has probably contributed to an erosion of a responsive and efficient federal system. Federal officials have an opportunity to improve both federal fiscal conditions and the efficiency of state and local governments by first eliminating both general revenue sharing and the deduction of state and local taxes; as these formula subventions have little appeal in Congress, this seems to be the obvious place to start to restore responsible fiscal federalism.

[21] U.S. Department of the Budget, *Budget of the United States Government: Special Analysis* (Washington, D.C.: Government Printing Office, 1976).

Counties, cities, school districts, and so on, are, in effect, state-chartered local government monopolies. In the last several decades, state governments have increased the monopoly power of local governments by a massive consolidation of school districts, restrictions of the opportunity to create new cities in unincorporated areas, effective prohibition of the opportunity to secede from an existing local government, and, more recently, encouragement of regional governments in major metropolitan areas. The increasing monopoly power of local government would be appropriate if there were strong economies of scale in the provision of local services and if the political process passed these economies through to residents in the form of superior services or lower taxes. The rhetoric of municipal reform usually emphasizes these potential economies of scale, but the accumulating evidence suggests the contrary: for all major municipal services, all of the potential economies of scale appear to be achieved by cities and school districts with ten thousand to one hundred thousand residents.[22] The monopoly power of larger local governments appears to be used up in the form of higher municipal salaries, wasteful activities, and an erosion of service quality. Our major cities and school districts are too large for responsive and efficient government.

Municipal reformers often recommend that the state develop a "blueprint" for the optimal structure of local government. This plan would surely make matters worse, however intelligent, informed, conscientious, and benevolent the planners and legislators might be. The appropriate approach would be to let the structure of local government evolve in response to the preferences of each self-defined community. The first step would be to eliminate those provisions of the state municipal and education codes that effectively prohibit secession from existing units of government. The state should draw up some general guidelines for the process of local government formation and stand out of the way. The state guidelines should specify a voting rule to assure that there is a perceived community of interests and the rules for the disposition of existing assets and debt. The primary effect of this approach would be to permit people, with their neighbors, to have a local government of their own choosing without moving, and the pri-

---

22 For a summary of this evidence, see William A. Niskanen and Mickey Levy, "Cities and Schools: A Case for Community Government in California," Working Paper No. 14 (Berkeley: University of California Graduate School of Public Policy, June, 1974).

mary beneficiaries would be spatially concentrated political minorities who have strong preferences to live in a given area. Mistakes will be made, but people are less likely to make mistakes in terms of their own interests than any elected or appointed body would be. Moreover, the right to make one's own mistakes is the essence of a society of free people. The experimentation and diversity that would result are the basis for the vitality of a federal system. State governments that face increasing demands to bail out our major cities may soon recognize this approach as a preferable alternative.

PROSPECT AND PROMISE

Two hundred years ago, Americans started a revolution to provide for a government of their own choosing. At that time they were more sure of the form of government they opposed than of the form of government they would put in its place. After eight weary years of war and several years of floundering, a constitutional convention, meeting independently from the Congress, worked out a form of government that has lasted to this day. That was no mean accomplishment. Our government is the oldest surviving republic in the world.

As of 1976, after eight weary years of war and several years of floundering, it is time to reconsider our form of government. Again there seems to be more consensus about the problems of our existing government than about the form of government that would serve us better, but this is the essential basis for an effective dialogue on constitutional change. Our bicentennial celebration could serve no greater purpose than to stimulate a broad national dialogue on the constitution for a society of free people. Although the world has changed a great deal in the last two centuries, it is not clear that our understanding about constitutional government has improved. May I suggest that we start a dialogue on constitutional change by reconsidering those major departures we have made from the formal Constitution developed in Philadelphia in that hot summer of 1787.

Chapter 4

Social Security in the 1970's

COLIN D. CAMPBELL

ONE of the interesting developments in economics in the 1970's is the spurt of interest in the study of the social security system. Until recently, social security as a subject of inquiry has been neglected. Except within the Social Security Administration (SSA) itself, very little research has been done on the subject. The number of economists doing research on social security has increased significantly in recent years, and one can expect much more discussion of problems related to the system. This chapter first gives the background for the growing interest in social security and then surveys the major topics that economists are working on.

The current research interest in social security concerns primarily the program of old-age and survivors insurance (OASI), the largest of the various insurance programs in the system. There has been much less interest in the other types of public insurance—unemployment insurance, disability insurance, and medicare—or in the various types of welfare activities included in the system. Under OASI, a person is entitled to a pension at age sixty-five. Or, if he wishes to retire early, he may receive an actuarially reduced pension at age sixty-two. Widows may receive reduced pension at age sixty. Dependents—children and spouses of insured workers—may receive pensions in case of the death of the insured.

THE LARGE DIMENSIONS OF OASI

There are several reasons why economists have become interested in social security. One of them is that the program has become extremely large. Expenditures and revenues for social security are now a major item in the federal government's budget. In fiscal year 1975 total payroll tax collections for old-age, survivors, disability, and health insurance (OASDHI), excluding collections for the state programs of unemployment insurance, amounted to $76.5 billion, 27 percent of total federal tax revenues. In the same year, the total amount of benefits for OASDHI accounted for approximately 22 percent of total federal government outlays.

Another indication of the growing significance of social security is that the tax rate necessary to finance it has become very large. The social security system is financed by payroll taxes levied on an employer's taxable payroll and earmarked for the purpose of covering the cost of the program; half of the tax comes out of the wage contracted with the employee, and half does not. In 1976 the taxable payroll of employers consists of the amount paid to each employee up to $15,300 a year, and the tax rate is 11.7 percent, making the maximum tax payment per person $1,790 a year. Social security taxes have not always been this large, and until recently these taxes were relatively small. Table 4–1 shows the rise in the tax rates for social security from 1937 to 1976. From 1937 to 1949 the tax rate was only 2 percent, and the maximum wage base was only $3,000.

For most persons today, payroll taxes amount to a significant portion of their income. The present maximum wage base for the payroll tax is close to the average family income. For families with below-average income, social security taxes amount to 11.7 percent of their income (assuming that the portion of the tax on the employer is shifted to the employee in lower wages). In families with more than one taxpayer, the social security tax is especially high. For example, if a husband and wife each earned $15,300, the family payroll tax would be $3,580 a year. An increasing number of families now pay these relatively high payroll taxes as a result of the significant movement of married women into the labor force since World War II. Currently, more than 22 million married women workers, half of the total number of married women, are in the labor force. The self-employed, on the other hand, pay relatively low payroll taxes—at present 68 percent of the taxes paid by the employer-employee combined.[1] There are over 6 million self-employed persons paying social security taxes.

Another measure of the size of the social security system is that 90

[1] Until 1963 the payroll tax rate for the self-employed was 75 percent of that of employed persons. Between 1963 and 1972 it gradually fell to about 72 percent. From 1972 to 1973 it was reduced from 72 percent to 68 percent. The report of the 1974 Advisory Council on Social Security has recommended that the payroll tax rate on the self-employed be returned to 75 percent of that of employed persons.

TABLE 4–1
Social Security Tax Rates for OASDI and Medicare*

Year	Tax Rate (excluding Medicare) (percent)	Maximum Wage Base (dollars)	Maximum Tax Payment per Year (excluding Medicare) (dollars)	Tax Rate (including Medicare) (percent)	Maximum Tax Payment per Year (including Medicare) (dollars)
1937–1949	2	3,000	60	—	—
1950	3	3,000	90	—	—
1951–1953	3	3,600	108	—	—
1954	4	3,600	144	—	—
1955–1956	4	4,200	168	—	—
1957–1958	4.5	4,200	189	—	—
1959	5	4,800	240	—	—
1960–1961	6	4,800	288	—	—
1962	6.25	4,800	300	—	—
1963–1965	7.25	4,800	348	—	—
1966	7.7	6,600	508	8.4	554
1967	7.8	6,600	515	8.8	581
1968	7.6	7,800	593	8.8	686
1969–1970	8.4	7,800	655	9.6	749
1971	9.2	7,800	718	10.4	811
1972	9.2	9,000	828	10.4	936
1973	9.7	10,800	1,048	11.7	1,264
1974	9.9	13,200	1,307	11.7	1,544
1975	9.9	14,100	1,396	11.7	1,650
1976	9.9	15,300	1,515	11.7	1,790

SOURCE: *Social Security Bulletin, Annual Statistical Supplement, 1973*, p. 29.

* The tax rate excluding medicare is scheduled to increase to 11.9 percent in 2011. The tax rate including medicare is scheduled to increase to 12.1 percent in 1978, 12.6 percent in 1981, and 12.9 percent in 1986. Starting in 1975, the maximum wage base is scheduled to be increased annually with the percentage rise in the average of taxable wages.

million persons—94 percent of the labor force—are currently paying taxes for social security. Because the coverage of social security is compulsory and has been expanded to include almost every type of labor income, payroll taxes must be paid by almost everyone. The principal groups excluded are about 2.6 million federal government employees, 2 million state and local government employees who have chosen not to belong to the program, and several hundred thousand railroad workers, who have their own federal government retirement system. Congress may expand the coverage of social security to include these groups during the next few years. The 1974 Advisory Council on Social Security recommended to Congress that the coverage be made universal.[2]

The number of OASDI beneficiaries has also become very large and has risen to over 30 million persons. Approximately 20 million beneficiaries are sixty-five years of age and older, about 3 million are between ages sixty-two and sixty-four, and the remaining 7 million are persons under sixty-two years of age who are receiving disability benefits or are dependents of insured workers who are deceased. Retirement before age sixty-five has been very popular. In 1956, women were allowed to retire at age sixty-two with actuarially reduced benefits. In 1961, this same privilege was extended to men, and legislation in 1967 permitted widows to retire at age sixty.

About 90 percent of the persons sixty-five and over receive old-age benefits. Some persons do not qualify because of the eligibility requirements. Men who reach sixty-five in 1975 must have worked in covered employment for twenty-four quarters and earned at least $50 per quarter; women must have worked for twenty-one quarters in order to be qualified. Also, in order to receive old-age benefits, partial retirement is compulsory. In 1976 a person could earn only $230 a month, or $2,760 a year, without a reduction in benefits. In any month in which earnings exceed $230, one dollar of benefits is deducted for each $2 earned up until one's benefit is eliminated altogether.

Social security benefits have now become a substantial part of the average American's provision for old age. In the early years of the program when retired persons had not been able to accumulate earnings credits over a long period of time, the amount of their benefits was often very small. In July, 1975, the minimum pension was raised to $1,215 a year for a single person and $1,823 for an aged couple. The maximum pension was raised to $4,100 for a single person and $6,150 for an aged couple. In between the lower and upper limits, the size of the pension depends primarily on a worker's earnings prior to retirement—the larger his earnings, the larger his pension.

Social security replacement ratios—the ratio of the pension received to pre-retirement earnings—have become higher than most persons realize.[3] For an aged couple with a relatively low pre-retirement income of

[2] U.S. Congress, House, *Reports of the Quadrennial Advisory Council on Social Security*, 94th Cong., 1st sess., Mar. 10, 1975, House Doc. No. 75, p. 2.
[3] Peter Henle, "Recent Trends in Retirement Benefits Related to Earnings,"

$4,400 (close to the minimum wage) the replacement ratio is over 70 percent because the benefit formula is favorably weighted for persons with lower earnings. A construction worker with a pre-retirement income close to the maximum wage base of the payroll tax who also has an aged wife would have a replacement ratio of about 45 percent. For an aged couple with an income as high as $24,000, the replacement ratio would be approximately 22 percent. Replacement ratios are relatively low for persons with high earnings because there is an upper limit to taxable earnings and thus the amount of benefit paid.

SOCIAL SECURITY AS A TAX TRANSFER PROGRAM

A second reason for the growing interest of economists in the study of social security is that a new conception of the system has been developed. Many persons now look upon the social security system as a tax-transfer or intergenerational transfer program rather than as an insurance program. Only gradually have persons realized the significance of the new approach. When social security was set up in 1937, the benefits were frequently referred to as annuities. The tax payments were called premiums and are even today called contributions. The SSA intended to accumulate a large trust fund. Basic features of the program still give the impression that persons are purchasing insurance for themselves. Retired persons may receive benefits regardless of need if they have paid social security taxes. A worker must pay in for a certain length of time in order to be eligible for benefits. The amount of the benefit one is entitled to is related somewhat to the amount of taxes paid in. If a person wishes to retire at age 62, he may do so if he is willing to take a smaller pension. The reliance on record keeping and actuaries also gives workers the impression that they are paying for their old-age pensions. The insurance concept of OASI is popular even today. However, most students of social security use the new tax transfer model, even though they sometimes view the insurance concept as a myth that is socially desirable.

In the tax transfer approach, the taxpayer is conceived of as paying taxes not for his *own* benefits when he retires, but to provide benefits for those who are already retired. The benefits of present workers are to be financed by the taxes paid by the working population as of some fu-

Monthly Labor Review 95 (June, 1972): 12–20 (republished as The Brookings Institution Reprint 241, Washington, D.C., 1972).

ture date. This intergenerational transfer, once started, is expected to continue indefinitely in the future. The individual is still viewed as having a right to benefits when he retires, not because he has paid for them, but because he gave up part of his earnings during his working life to support the aged during their retirement.

Another difference is that the financing of social security as a tax transfer program is on a pay-as-you-go basis. The funds to pay benefits come from the taxes currently collected, and the amount of the taxes collected each year depends approximately on the total amount of the benefits to be paid out. A small reserve fund is required only for unexpected needs.

If OASI were a true insurance system, it would have accumulated a reserve fund sufficiently large to meet its financial obligations at any time. As with private insurance, the payments to individuals would come partly from the interest received from the investments in the fund and partly from the repayment of principal. Even though the present system originally expected to accumulate a large reserve fund, OASI is now explicitly on a pay-as-you-go basis, and the new tax transfer concept of social security has the advantage of being more realistic than the old approach. If viewed as insurance, the reserve fund that has been accumulated is much too small. The federal old-age insurance program in 1975 had unfunded liabilities amounting to approximately $2.7 trillion.

A third difference between a funded insurance system and a tax transfer system is in the rate of return assumed to be received by individuals. As insurance, this return would be determined primarily by the rate of interest earned on securities suitable for an insurance company. The Federal Old Age and Survivors Trust Fund is required by law to invest its small reserve fund solely in U.S. government securities. In the tax transfer approach, the individual worker is conceived of as receiving an *implicit* rate of return dependent on the rate of growth of total earnings. As stated by those who developed this point of view, the individual "shares in the growth of the economy." This implicit return is illustrated by the formula

$$tY_2 = tY_1(1+r)^n,$$

where Y_1 = taxable earnings of generation one,
   Y_2 = taxable earnings of generation two,
   t = payroll tax rate,
   r = percent increase in taxable earnings per year, and
   n = number of years.

When generation one is part of the working population, it pays a portion of its earnings, tY_1, to support the retired. If it is assumed that generation two also pays t percent of its earnings to finance social security benefits, the sum of money paid by generation two to finance the pensions of generation one, tY_2, will be much larger than tY_1. How much larger will depend on the percentage increase in earnings per year and the number of years covered, as shown in the formula by $(1 + r)^n$.

A fourth difference is that in the tax transfer approach, the relationship between taxes paid in by the individual worker and the benefits he receives may be less rigid than in the insurance approach. As insurance, one would expect a fairly precise relationship—the larger a worker's tax payments, the larger the benefit he would be entitled to. As a tax transfer program, however, persons are not viewed as purchasing their own insurance, and benefits may be distributed according to need rather than on the basis of the amount of taxes the individual has paid in. OASI benefits are actually based in part on considerations of need, even though they are also "wage related." For example, the policy of setting lower benefits for single persons than for married couples, even though both have paid in the same amount of taxes, is based on the belief that married couples have greater need than single persons. Other OASI policies based on need are the setting of a minimum benefit regardless of a worker's earnings record, the retirement test which limits old-age benefits to persons over sixty-five who have stopped working, and the regulation limiting the pensions of married women workers either to the pension they have earned or the benefit they are entitled to as a wife.

A fifth difference is that in the tax transfer approach, the earmarking of certain taxes to finance retirement benefits may be much less important than in the insurance approach. In the tax transfer approach, earmarking is not necessary because the taxes for social security are not conceived of as a payment for the taxpayer's old-age insurance. To some proponents of the tax transfer approach, this lack of earmarking is a major advantage because they would like to replace the use of regressive payroll taxes to finance OASI by general revenues.

THE OBJECTIVES OF SOCIAL SECURITY

An additional reason for the renewed interest of economists in social security is the realization that the fundamental objectives of such a program are more varied than they were formerly thought to be. The most common view is that social security is a welfare program to provide all persons with an assured source of income when they can no longer earn an income because of old age or other reasons. One of its main features is that it accomplishes this goal without a needs test, which is considered to be humiliating. When viewed in this way, social security is a public program to redistribute income—transferring purchasing power from wage earners to the elderly retired. The system is considered to be one of the federal government's major humanitarian programs and an important achievement of the liberal political movement that started with the New Deal.

The recent development of the theory of public goods has led to a new explanation of the objective of social security. It is said that its objective is to compel all persons to provide for their old age so as not to become a burden to others. This objective sounds selfish rather than humanitarian. However, as the modern theory of public goods has spread, the importance of this objective has become more widely recognized. Providing for one's old age is considered to be a type of public good because without such provision a person may become a burden to others. Therefore, through government, persons agree to belong to a system in which everyone is compelled to provide for his old age. According to this objective, the persons who are benefited are not primarily the elderly, but those who might have had to support them. These would be the families of the indigent and those who might have contributed to private charities or paid taxes for public welfare programs for the elderly.

A third objective that has become important because of the rising rate of inflation since 1965 is the claim that a pension financed by intergenerational transfers is a better hedge against inflation than funded pension systems. The formula showing how the tax transfer system operates illustrates the way in which the rate of return received by OASI beneficiaries depends primarily on the growth of total earnings, including inflationary growth. Historically, the per capita real rate of growth in earnings in the United States has been from 2 to 3 percent a year. This rate is approximately the same as the historical real rate of interest on U.S. government bonds—a rate of return that might be earned by a funded annuity. If there were no inflation, the choice between a tax transfer program and a funded program would be a toss-up. However, with inflation, a tax transfer system appears to be better than a funded system. Recent experience indicates that private annuities may not be able to offer customers full protection against inflation because nominal rates of return on stocks and bonds do not quickly adjust to discount the rate of inflation.

So far in this chapter I have reviewed the reasons for the current interest among economists in the social security system. The next part of the chapter reviews five major questions on which economists are presently doing research: (1) the financing of OASI, (2) the effect of OASI on the labor force participation of older persons, (3) the effect of OASI on personal saving, (4) the inequities in the system, and (5) the effect of social security on the distribution of income.

THE FINANCING OF OASI

The financing of social security became a major topic of concern in 1974. It is now widely believed that the current payroll tax rates projected in the Social Security Act and its amendments are below those that are going to be necessary to cover the cost of the present benefit program. The social security law requires projections of the payroll tax rate necessary to cover the cost of OASDI benefits for the next seventy-five years. As shown in Table 4-2, the current tax rates for OASDI (excluding medicare) are 9.9 percent through the year 2010 and 11.9 percent starting in 2011. Estimates of the higher payroll tax rates that are now believed to be required because of the unexpected decline in the birth rate during the past decade are also shown in Table 4-2. These estimates are from the report on the 1974 Advisory Council on Social Security. Including the tax for medicare, total payroll tax rates would be several percent-

TABLE 4–2

Tax Rate for OASDI (Excluding Medicare) as a
Percentage of Covered Wages

| Currently Scheduled | | Adjusted for Declining Birth Rate | |
Years	Rate (percent)	Years	Rate (percent)
1974–2010	9.9	1976–1979	10.9
		1980–1984	11.1
2011–2048	11.9	1985–2004	11.8
		2005–2014	12.3
		2015–2024	14.2
		2025–2050	16.1

SOURCE: *Social Security Bulletin: Annual Statistical Supplement, 1973*, p. 29; and U.S. Congress, House, *Reports of the Quadrennial Advisory Council on Social Security*, 94th Cong., 1st sess., House Doc. 94–75, March 10, 1975, p. 114.

age points above those given in this table and would rise to nearly 20 percent by the year 2025.

There is a technical flaw referred to as "double-indexing" in the 1972 amendment to the Social Security Act providing for escalated benefits. This flaw could cause payroll tax rates to rise even more rapidly than the adjusted rates shown in Table 4-2. The payroll tax rates shown in that table assume that the Social Security Act will be amended to eliminate this flaw. As the law now stands, not only are old-age *benefits* at each level of average monthly earnings raised as the consumer price index rises, but average monthly *earnings* (on which benefits are based) are also automatically raised. As a result, inflation causes social security replacement ratios to rise, and the more rapid the rate of inflation, the higher the replacement ratios. In order to finance the resulting higher replacement ratios, larger payroll tax rates would be necessary.

The basic reason for the current financial difficulties of OASI is the very large rise in social security benefits that has occurred during the past decade. It is not widely realized that from 1965 to 1974 the average monthly benefit for retired workers (excluding dependents) increased 123 percent (from $84 to $187). Only a portion of this increase can be accounted for by inflation. During this period the consumer price index increased 56 percent, and the increase in average gross weekly earnings in manufacturing was 64 percent.

In order to pay for this substantial increase in benefits, Congress raised payroll tax rates sharply. In 1965 the combined employer-employee tax rate was only 7.25 percent on wages up to $4,800 compared to the 1976 rate of 11.7 percent on wages up to $15,300. The maximum tax payment per year in 1965 was only $348 ($174 taken from the employee's wage and $174 paid by the employer) compared to the present $1,790. Unfortunately, despite these sharp increases, tax rates were not raised enough.

A little-understood factor that contributed to these very large increases in social security benefits is the recent change in the actuarial methodology used by the SSA.[4] Before this change, benefit increases were very moderate, and without this change Congress would probably not have raised benefits nearly as much. A curious feature of the social security system is that before 1972 the actuarial estimates of payroll tax

[4] Michael K. Taussig, "Recent Changes in Social Security Financing," *Proceedings of the 25th Anniversary Meeting, Industrial Relations Research Association*, Dec., 1972, pp. 241–247.

revenues and social security benefits were based on the unrealistic assumption that each worker's earnings for the next seventy-five years would be constant.[5] In 1972 this assumption was changed to one of rising levels of wages.[6] Under the old assumption of constant earnings, payroll tax collections were typically larger than had been estimated and resulted in periodic surpluses in the OASDI trust funds.[7] Congress would then adjust benefits upward, and such benefit increases would be possible without any increase in payroll tax rates. One thing that can be said for the old actuarial methodology is that it resulted in a social security program that was seldom faced by financial problems like those the present program has. The level earnings assumption was not as unreasonable as it appears if it were understood that Congress would periodically raise benefits when increased earnings levels created budget surpluses. It was a more conservative procedure than present policy because social security benefits were raised some time after economic growth had actually occurred.[8]

The new methodology unfortunately led Congress to raise benefits sharply. Under the old methodology, projected *future* payroll tax rates would have had to be much higher and probably would have been unacceptable to Congress. With the new assumption of rising earnings, the projected future payroll tax rates necessary to cover benefits were much lower than they would formerly have been and were politically acceptable. Without the change to the assumption of rising wages, the social security actuaries would not have been able to project the need for a tax rate for OASDI of no more than 9.9 percent up to 2011 and 11.9 percent up to 2048. Although the new tax rates were high, Congress thought they would be sufficient for the foreseeable future.

It is now realized that the 1972 projected payroll tax rates of 9.9

[5] Charles Killingsworth and Gertrude Schroeder, "Long-Range Cost Estimates for Old-Age Insurance," *Quarterly Journal of Economics* 65 (May, 1951): 199–213.

[6] This change was recommended by a panel of actuaries and economists to the 1971 Advisory Council on Social Security and was accepted by the OASDI Board of Trustees and by Congress; see U.S. Congress, House, *Reports of the 1971 Advisory Council on Social Security*, 92d Cong., 1st sess., Apr. 5, 1971, House Doc. No. 80.

[7] Because benefits are based on earnings, estimates of benefits were also too low, but not as much lower than predicted as revenues were. Also, the weighted benefit formula providing relatively high replacement ratios for workers with low earnings records assured an excess of revenues over costs since, as earnings grew, more covered workers moved into the low-replacement-ratio earnings ranges.

[8] Robert J. Myers, "Social Security's Hidden Hazards," *Wall Street Journal*, July 28, 1972, p. 8.

percent and 11.9 percent were too low primarily because the social security actuaries were using old projections of birth rates that were too high.[9] The social security actuaries were slow to adjust their projections of fertility to the downward trend that started about fifteen years ago. As a result of overestimating the rate of increase in population, payroll tax receipts were overstated. In a pay-as-you-go system, a decline in population growth reduces the size of the working population relative to the retired population. In order to keep old-age benefits increasing as fast as earnings, tax rates on the working population must be raised.[10]

THE EFFECT ON LABOR-FORCE PARTICIPATION

Another issue that has become of interest to economists is the claim that old-age and survivors insurance has significantly reduced the participation of the elderly in the labor force. One reason why OASI encourages retirement is that persons are not entitled to their full old-age pension if they earn more than $230 a month. In 1976, for any earnings over $230 a month ($2,760 a year), a person's pension is reduced $1 for every additional $2 earned, up until the pension is completely exhausted. This is equivalent to a marginal tax rate of 50 percent on additional earnings.[11]

---

[9] Robert S. Kaplan and Roman L. Weil, *An Actuarial Audit of the Social Security System* (Washington, D.C.: Department of the Treasury, 1974).

[10] The following formulas illustrate the direct relationship between the tax rate on earnings in a pay-as-you-go system and the ratio of retired beneficiaries to workers:

$$t N_w W = N_b B,$$

and
$$t = N_b / N_w \times B/W,$$

where: t = average tax rate on earnings,

N_w = number of workers,

W = average earnings of workers covered by old-age insurance,

N_b = number of retired beneficiaries, and

B = average old-age benefits.

See Michael K. Taussig, "The Social Security Retirement Program and Welfare Reform," in U.S. Congress, Joint Economic Committee, Subcommittee on Fiscal Policy, *Issues in the Coordination of Public Welfare Programs*, Studies in Public Welfare Paper No. 7, 93d Cong., 1st sess., July 2, 1973, p. 21.

[11] The amount forfeited may be quite small if earnings are kept below $230 a month during part of the year. In such months, a person receives his full pension regardless of the amount of his annual earnings. If a single person entitled to the maximum annual pension of $4,100, for example, could earn a substantial amount in one month or less than $230 in the other eleven months, he would suffer a loss of only $340 in his annual pension.

A second way in which OASI may reduce labor-force participation is by providing older persons with income in the form of old-age benefits. The social security system would have this effect even if retirement were not compulsory. Public opinion surveys indicate that a large percentage of older workers will decide to retire as soon as they can count on a dollar amount of income that they consider sufficient to cover their needs.[12]

An interesting aspect of studies of the relationship between OASI and labor-force participation is that the conclusions of the studies by the staff of the SSA have usually been the opposite of those by economists outside the system. Ever since the start of the social security system, the research staff of the SSA has periodically investigated the reasons why beneficiaries retire.[13] Researchers within the SSA have usually concluded that OASI has had very little effect on labor-force participation among elderly persons. The principal method used in these studies is to interview retired persons. The studies have concluded that almost all persons retire involuntarily because of bad health, difficulties finding a job, or reaching compulsory retirement age. When asked, retired persons seldom say that they were influenced by the availability of social security benefits or that they were deterred from working by the work-income test. Looked at realistically, persons within the SSA would not be expected to conduct studies which blame the organization in which they are employed for a decline in the participation of elderly persons in the labor force.[14]

Despite these studies by the SSA, examination of the statistical series on labor-force participation among the elderly, even without any

[12] See Richard E. Barfield and James N. Morgan, *Early Retirement, The Decision and the Experience: A Second Look* (Ann Arbor; Survey Research Center, Institute for Social Research, University of Michigan, 1974), pp. 1–7.

[13] Edna C. Wentworth, "Why Beneficiaries Retire," *Social Security Bulletin* 8 (Jan., 1945): 16–20; Margaret L. Stecker, "Beneficiaries Prefer to Work," *Social Security Bulletin* 14 (Jan., 1951): 15–17; Margaret L. Stecker, "Why Do Beneficiaries Retire? Who Among Them Return to Work?" *Social Security Bulletin* 18 (May, 1955): 3–12; Erdman Palmore, "Retirement Patterns among Aged Men: Findings of the 1963 Survey of the Aged," *Social Security Bulletin* 27 (Aug., 1964): 3–10; and Virginia Reno, "Why Men Stop Working at or before Age 65: Findings from the Survey of New Beneficiaries," *Social Security Bulletin* 34 (June, 1971): 3–17.

[14] This type of motivation for government employees is suggested in William A. Niskanan, Jr., *Bureaucracy and Representative Government* (Chicago: University of Chicago Press, 1971), pp. 36–41.

attempt at correlation analysis, strongly suggests that OASI has induced older persons to retire. For example, in the last four censuses (1940–1970), data on labor-force participation *by age* show a striking drop in the participation rate at age sixty-five, the age when persons become eligible for full social security benefits. Also, after the 1950's, when the coverage of the system was significantly expanded, the drop in labor-force participation at age sixty-five became much larger.

Data on the historical trend of labor-force participation of older persons also indicate that OASI has induced older persons to retire. Labor-force participation of men sixty-five years of age and over dropped from 48 percent in 1947 to 25 percent in 1972. During this period, persons insured by OASI (not including their dependents) rose from 15 percent to 66 percent of the total number of persons sixty-five and over. The decline in labor-force participation of older men has been much more rapid since 1950 than in earlier decades before the establishment of the social security system—except for the 1930's. The labor-force participation rate of men sixty-five and over declined 28 percent from 1950 to 1960 and 19 percent from 1960 to 1970 compared to less than 8 percent from 1890 to 1900, 12 percent over the twenty-year period from 1900 to 1920, and 3 percent from 1920 to 1930. The relatively large decline of 22 percent from 1930 to 1940 was probably caused by the extraordinary conditions resulting from the Great Depression and the welfare programs of the federal government that were introduced at that time. The decline during the 1930's was partly reversed during the 1940's when older men took advantage of the improved job opportunities during World War II. The labor-force participation rate for older men was approximately the same in 1950 as in 1940.

The importance of OASI as a cause of retirement is also indicated by the large response to the amendments to the Social Security Act permitting retirement before age sixty-five. About two-thirds of the women and more than half of the men now retire before age sixty-five. After the early retirement option for women was introduced in 1956, the census data show a larger drop in labor-force participation of women at age sixty-two than in earlier censuses. Also, when the early retirement option for men was introduced in 1961, the following census showed a larger drop in labor-force participation of men at age sixty-two than in previous censuses. The actuarial reduction in benefits when a person retires at age sixty-two has not had the expected effect of discouraging withdrawal from the labor force.[15] Benefits are reduced 5/9 of 1 percent for each month before age sixty-five that a person elects as his starting date; this adds up to a 20 percent reduction for retirement at age sixty-two. The principal regression analysis of early retirement by an economist outside the SSA has been made by Joseph F. Quinn.[16] He included in his analysis a large number of variables and concluded that the three most important factors causing early retirement were poor health, eligibility for social security benefits, and eligibility for a private or other public pension. He used data from the SSA's Longitudinal Retirement History Survey for 1969.

The negative impact of the work-income test on labor-force participation is indicated by the shift that has occurred from full-time to part-time employment among older men. The percentage of employed males sixty-five and over working less than thirty-five hours per week has increased from 20 percent in 1957 to 38 percent in 1972. The current policy of permitting persons to earn only $230 a month without loss of benefits would be expected to induce persons to limit the amount of work they do. In addition, persons may adjust to the work-income test by shifting to full-time, part-year employment.

The differences in OASI replacement ratios for different income levels also appear to have had an impact on the pattern of labor-force participation. Several statistical studies have found that retirement is more common among persons in low-income occupations than those in high-income occupations. One should expect retirement to be more common among lower-income groups because their OASI replacement ratios are higher than those of persons with high incomes. Also, persons with low earnings can increase the total income by taking their social security benefits as soon as they become eligible and working part-time. Consider the example of a married couple with a pre-retirement income of $4,000. Their pension of $2,880 in 1973 combined with the maximum earnings allowed at that time of $2,100 would amount to $4,980. The fact that retirement is less common among higher-paid occupations has been considered surprising by some students of social security because higher-paid persons have more resources for retirement. The later retirement of

[15] Patience Lauriat and William Rabin, "Men Who Claim Benefits before Age 65: Findings from the Survey of New Beneficiaries, 1960," *Social Security Bulletin* 33 (Nov., 1970): 22.

[16] Joseph F. Quinn, "Some Determinants of the Early Retirement Decision: A Cross-Sectional View," manuscript (Boston College, May 19, 1975).

persons with high incomes is usually attributed to such factors as work that is less demanding physically, more interesting jobs, or better health.

In addition to OASI, other factors such as the compulsory retirement policies of employers, the deterioration of the health of persons as they get older, rising standards of living, and the shift from agricultural to urban jobs undoubtedly have affected labor-force participation among elderly persons. Several studies using multiple regression analysis have been made to determine the relative importance of these various factors. William G. Bowen and T. Aldrich Finegan included in their comprehensive study of labor-force participation an analysis of the decline in labor-force participation of men between ages sixty-four and sixty-seven using a multiple regression analysis they had set up for men of ages fifty-five to sixty-four.[17] They estimated that about one-third of the drop between ages sixty-four and sixty-seven was the result of the increase in *other income* (primarily social security benefits). Only a small portion was the result of three years of aging (health)—a factor the SSA has considered important. About half of the decline could not be attributed to the factors for which data were available. The large unexplained portion could include the effect of such factors as OASI's work-income test, the compulsory retirement policies of employers, and the increased acceptance of retirement at age sixty-five.

Bowen and Finegan also used a multiple regression to determine the factors contributing to the secular decline in labor-force participation of older men from 1948 to 1965.[18] They estimated that, after adjusting for demographic factors, roughly three-fifths of the secular decline in labor-force participation of older men during this period was the result of the increase in income other than earnings.

Factors affecting the long-run decline in labor-force participation rates have also been studied through the use of multiple regression analysis by W. Kip Viscusi and Richard Zeckhauser.[19] They examined both annual data (1952–1971) and monthly data (1966–1972) on participation rates of persons sixty-five and over, stratified by both race and sex. They found that except for Negro females, increases in average social security benefits resulted in sizable reductions in labor-force par-

[17] William G. Bowen and T. Aldrich Finegan, *The Economics of Labor Force Participation* (Princeton: Princeton University Press, 1969), pp. 281–285.

[18] Ibid., pp. 355–358.

[19] W. Kip Viscusi and Richard Zeckhauser, "Welfare of the Elderly," manuscript (Harvard University, 1975), chap. 9.

ticipation rates. Also except for Negro females, increases in the amount of earnings allowed before one begins to lose benefits increased labor-force participation. The authors concluded that the lack of any effect of social security on the employment of Negro females was the result of the relatively large proportion of Negro females who were not social security beneficiaries because they had not worked in covered employment.

Michael J. Boskin has made a study of the effect of social security on labor-force participation using statistical techniques that are more re-fined than those that have been used in other studies.[20] He used data from the Survey Research Center's Panel Study of Income Dynamics in which the same households were interviewed annually for the five years 1968 through 1972. The households in the sample were headed by per-sons initially aged sixty-one through sixty-five. Using a Markov model of retirement behavior, he found that increases in social security bene-fits reduced labor-force participation and that increases in the amount of income forfeited because of the earnings test also increased the probabil-ity of retirement.

If OASI has a negative effect on labor-force participation, this is significant. It could cause OASI to fail to achieve its humanitarian ob-jective of shifting income from the young to the elderly. If older persons have been induced by OASI to work less, the increased transfer pay-ments received by them could be offset by a reduction in their earnings. Although the value of increased leisure to elderly persons may offset the loss of earnings, as a tax transfer program OASI is usually viewed as a program to raise the money income of elderly persons. In recent decades, the relative money income position of older families has, in fact, declined relative to all except the age group of fourteen to twenty-four. Between 1947 and 1972 the median income of families with the head age sixty-five and over increased only 3.2 times compared to between 3.7 and 4.1 times for most other age groups. This overall decline in the relative in-come position of older families occurred despite the increase in federal old-age benefits and old-age assistance from $1.5 billion in 1947 to $40.2 billion in 1972.

If OASI has induced older persons to retire, there would also be a cost in terms of real output. Martin Feldstein has estimated that if the labor-force participation rate of the elderly were the same now as in the 1930's, the increase in the total labor force would be less than 3 per-

<hr />

[20] Michael J. Boskin, "Social Security and Retirement," manuscript (Stanford University, Mar., 1975).

cent.[21] Also, in one of the earlier studies of the effect of OASI on retirement, Lowell Gallaway calculated that for the twelve-year period from 1949 to 1961, the reduction in GNP caused by induced retirement was 2.4 percent—a 0.2 percentage point decline in the annual growth rate.[22] This loss of output may be offset somewhat by the increased efficiency of business firms resulting from the earlier retirement of workers. Compulsory retirement programs and OASI undoubtedly assist many employers in solving personnel problems associated with aging, and employers support these programs for this reason. It is not easy for employers to decide which older employees should be kept and which should not be, and it may be less costly for management simply to compel all older employees to retire. Also, it may be difficult to hold able young workers on the job if promotion is blocked by older workers.

OASI AND SAVING

The third aspect of the social security system that has become of interest to economists—the effect of OASI on personal saving—has become an important topic of discussion since the publication of the startling findings of Feldstein on this topic.[23] With the exception of two empirical studies in the mid-1960's by Phillip Cagan and George Katona, economists both within the SSA and outside have generally ignored this topic. According to the studies by Cagan and Katona, a pension plan, if anything, raises the rate of saving.[24] From a theoretical point of view, this conclusion is surprising. If it is assumed that people save during their working years to provide for consumption during retirement—the life-cycle hypothesis of saving—a pension would tend to reduce the need for private saving.

The empirical analysis made by Feldstein concluded that the reduc-

[21] Martin Feldstein, "Social Security, Induced Retirement, and Aggregate Capital Accumulation," *Journal of Political Economy*, Sept.–Oct., 1974, p. 924.

[22] Lowell E. Gallaway, *The Retirement Decision: An Exploratory Essay*, Social Security Administration, Division of Research and Statistics, Research Report No. 9 (Washington, D.C.: Government Printing Office, 1965), pp. 41–48.

[23] Feldstein, "Social Security, Induced Retirement, and Aggregate Capital Accumulation," pp. 905–926.

[24] Phillip Cagan, *The Effect of Pension Plans on Aggregate Savings* (New York: National Bureau of Economic Research, 1965), and George Katona, *Private Pensions and Individual Savings* (Ann Arbor: Survey Research Center, Institute for Social Research, University of Michigan, 1964).

tion in personal saving because of OASI has been very large, even though this effect is not necessarily implied by his theoretical analysis. He believes that theoretically the effect on saving of belonging to the social security system is mixed. A social security pension tends to *reduce* saving if it is a substitute for other types of assets, but it may also tend to *increase* saving if it induces persons to retire earlier and thus to hold more assets in order to provide for a longer period of retirement. Whether a pension actually increases or decreases saving depends on the net effect of these two tendencies.

Feldstein estimated that in 1971 the effect of OASI was to cut private saving in half. Part of this effect was the result of the reduction in disposable income as a result of payroll taxation. In 1971 social security taxes reduced disposable income by $51 billion. Given a marginal propensity to save of 35 percent, the decline in disposable income would reduce saving by $18 billion.

In addition, and more important, Feldstein estimated the reduction in private saving because of the wealth effect of OASI. He calculated that in 1971 the sum of the present value of OASI benefits for everyone covered by the social security system amounted to $2 trillion—an amount equal to over one-third of total household assets including the value of social security benefits. Using a multiple regression equation which included as independent variables social security wealth, permanent income, the stock of household wealth excluding social security wealth, and retained earnings of business firms, he found with data from 1929 through 1971 (excluding the years 1941 through 1946) a good correlation between total social security wealth and consumption. On the basis of this finding he calculated that the reduction of private saving because of the wealth effect of OASI amounted to $43 billion. The wealth effect plus the income effect of OASI reduced personal saving in 1971 by a total of $61 billion. A significant conclusion of Feldstein's study is that in the long run OASI will reduce the private capital stock by 38 percent, and this will reduce the GNP 11 percent below what it would be without the reduction in saving caused by OASI.

To lessen the effect of OASI on private saving, Feldstein recommends that a much larger portion of OASI be funded. This would require raising payroll tax rates even higher than those in Table 4-2 and having budget surpluses in the OASI trust fund. By de-emphasizing pay-as-you-go financing, this suggestion runs counter to the established policy of the social security system. Building up the trust funds would reduce the volume of publicly held U.S. government securities and release funds to finance private capital expansion.

Feldstein's study of the effect of OASI on private saving has resulted in a lot of discussion. It will undoubtedly stimulate further research on this topic. Whatever the outcome of this debate, in the future students of social security may no longer uncritically assume that social security does not affect personal saving.

INEQUITIES IN OASI

The fourth aspect of OASI that economists are interested in is that some beneficiaries get a much better deal financially than others. If OASI were perfectly equitable, the amount of benefits a person received would depend solely on the amount of taxes he and his employer paid in and on the length of the period over which tax payments were made. Throughout the history of the social security system, OASI benefits have never been based solely on considerations of equity. Although partly guided by equity objectives, OASI policies have also taken into consideration the "adequacy" of the benefits provided.[25]

The attitude of students of social security toward the problem of inequities varies. While some believe that individual benefits ought to be more closely related to the taxes paid in by the individual and his employer, others reject the view that such financial considerations ought to be the basis for granting benefits. According to the point of view of those who reject equity as a goal, the tax selected to finance the social security program ought not to be considered as a payment for social security benefits, but ought to be the kind of tax that will reduce inequality of income and promote economic growth and efficiency.[26] They also believe that although the present labeling of the payroll tax as a contribution may have gained public acceptance of the program, the same effect could be achieved by other devices than the use of earmarked payroll taxes. In addition, they believe that benefit policy for the aged ought to be based on such factors as a person's living standard before retirement, current earnings, age, number of dependents, and whether that person

[25] Robert J. Myers, *Social Insurance and Allied Government Programs* (Homewood, Ill.: Richard D. Irwin, Inc., 1965), p. 6.

[26] Joseph A. Pechman, Henry J. Aaron, and Michael K. Taussig, *Social Security: Perspectives for Reform* (Washington, D.C.: The Brookings Institution, 1968), pp. 74–78.

is a retired worker or a survivor rather than on the amount of taxes paid in by the worker and his employer. Despite the lack of agreement on the importance of the inequities in the social security system, there is considerable interest in them.

The minimum social security benefit—one of the major sources of inequity in the system—is now $1,215 a year for a single person and $1,823 for an aged couple. During the early years of the program, the minimum benefit was said to be necessary because many persons reaching retirement age had so little coverage that the pension they would have received would have been extremely low. As the system has grown older, this reason for a minimum benefit no longer exists. Currently, a man retiring at age sixty-five who worked from 1937 to 1974 at the prevailing federal minimum wage would be entitled to a benefit almost double the minimum amount.

Despite the ending of the original justification for minimum benefits, Congress over the years has increased the minimum benefit more than twice as much as other OASI benefits. The principal consequence of this policy now is that persons not covered by OASI in their regular jobs are able to get a remarkable financial deal out of the social security system. Persons whose primary occupation has been in the federal government, state and local government, or the railroads can qualify for the minimum pension if they moonlight just long enough in covered employment, and they only have to earn fifty dollars each quarter. The value of the minimum OASI pension received by such persons far exceeds the value of the taxes they have paid in. To reduce somewhat this inequity, the 1974 Advisory Council on Social Security recommended (1) that when benefits are automatically raised in the future in order to keep up with prices, the minimum benefit should be held constant, and (2) that in the future, pensions based on a person's work in employment not covered by social security should be subtracted from their social security dependent's benefit.

Three groups that get a relatively bad deal financially from social security are (1) those who are single at retirement, whether a bachelor, a widower, or in some cases a divorced person; (2) those with relatively high earnings; and (3) married women workers. Even though a single person may have paid in the same amount of taxes as a person who has a wife, his pension is only two-thirds that of the married man because he does not receive a secondary benefit for a wife. The reason why persons who have relatively high earnings receive a low rate of return on the taxes paid in is that the benefit formula for OASI is progressive and benefits are not increased in proportion to the earnings base. As a result, persons with high incomes pay relatively more in taxes for their OASI benefits than persons with low incomes. Married women workers, the third group discriminated against, are treated badly because they and their husbands will typically receive pensions that are no larger than those of families in which the wife did not work and paid no taxes. A wife cannot get both the pension she is entitled to as a wife and the pension she has earned. In most cases, a married woman worker will not have worked long enough or at high enough wages to earn more than the pension she would have been entitled to as a wife. All three of these inequities are intentional and the result of efforts by Congress to base OASI benefits, in part, on criteria of need. Single persons are not supposed to need as large a pension as married couples. Lower-income groups are considered to be in greater need than higher-income groups. A working wife is not supposed to need both the wife's pension and the pension she has earned.[27]

A principal issue raised by policies that weaken the relationship between tax payments and social security benefits is their possible undesirable work-incentive effects.[28] Earmarking payroll taxes makes the disincentive effects of these taxes smaller than those of other taxes because paying a higher social security tax eventually results in higher retirement benefits. The requirement that wives pay social security taxes despite the limited advantages to them of belonging to the social security system may have induced some wives not to seek employment. Also, for a worker who did not plan to retire at age sixty-five and therefore would not be entitled to benefits, the payroll tax becomes a disincentive to work. In addition, for single persons who have relatively high tax-benefit ratios, the disincentive to work as a result of high payroll taxes will be greater than for married persons.

Self-employed persons, another distinct group under the social security program, have a relatively good deal because their tax rate is less than that paid by employees and their employers. Currently, their tax

[27] A serious inequity in the present system is that two-worker couples, who together happen to pay the same total taxes as a worker whose wife does not work, get slightly smaller total benefits than the one-worker couple. See *Reports of the Quadrennial Advisory Council on Social Security*, pp. 93–101.

[28] Martin Feldstein, "Toward a Reform of Social Security," *Public Interest*, Summer, 1974, p. 81.

rate is 68 percent, although formerly it was 75 percent of the combined employer-employee tax rate. Even though the self-employed pay lower taxes, they receive benefits that are just as large as those received by employees with similar earnings records. The reason given for the lower tax rate is that it offsets the different treatment of the self-employed under the federal income tax. Because they pay the entire payroll tax themselves, they pay income taxes on the total amount of the payroll tax. In contrast, employees pay income taxes on only one-half the combined employer-employee payroll tax because half the payroll tax is paid by their employers. Although there is some justification for the lower payroll tax paid by the self-employed, the present reduction in this tax may be excessive. The 1974 Advisory Council on Social Security recommended that the tax rate on the self-employed be raised back to 75 percent of the combined employer-employee tax rate.

A final source of inequity is the work-income test. Persons over sixty-five who receive substantial earnings are not entitled to an OASI pension. Not only do such persons lose their OASI pensions, but when they retire they get pensions only slightly larger than those received by persons who retired at age sixty-five. There are two ways of lessening this inequity: (1) the work-income test could be eliminated and persons could be given pensions at age sixty-five whether or not they have any earnings, and (2) the work-income test could be retained and persons retiring after sixty-five could receive a full actuarial increase in their benefits. A step was made in this direction in the 1972 amendment to the Social Security Act, which provides a 1 percent increase in benefits for each year employed beyond age sixty-five, although actuarially 1 percent is nowhere near as large as it ought to be.

The principal general program to create a more equitable system of old-age insurance has been proposed by James Buchanan.[29] He would repeal the payroll tax and replace it with a requirement that all persons purchase a new type of United States Treasury issue known as Social Insurance Bonds. The amount purchased by each person would be a given percentage of his earned income as determined through the political process. The bonds would yield a rate of return equal to the rate of growth in earnings over the period between their purchase and their

[29] James M. Buchanan, "Social Insurance in a Growing Economy: A Proposal for Radical Reform," *National Tax Journal*, Dec., 1968, pp. 386–395. See also Taussig, "The Social Security Retirement Program and Welfare Reform," pp. 14–39.

maturity date.[30] At retirement, a person would convert the bonds he had accumulated into an annuity based on life expectancy at his age of retirement. As was shown by the formula for the intergenerational transfer model, persons making payments for social security may receive a rate of return on these payments because of the growth of earnings—assuming that the percentage of earnings taxed remains the same. Financing social security by purchases of bonds would have several advantages over payroll taxes. The bonds owned by persons would be an identifiable claim on the government, and persons would have a more accurate account of the expected value of their old-age annuity and a safeguard against errors in record keeping.

In Buchanan's proposal, the proceeds from the sale of the bonds would be used to finance current benefits. However, the system would not be on a pay-as-you-go basis because the amount of bonds purchased would depend on the amount of benefits persons wish to receive when they retire rather than on the current cost of the program. If the total amount of bonds sold during a year exceeded the total amount of benefit payments, the excess tax receipts would be used to cover other federal government expenditures; if bond sales were less than benefit payments, general revenues would be used to pay for part of the cost of OASI benefits.

Buchanan has shown that it would be possible to create a social security system based on intergenerational transfers that would be equitable. In addition, his proposal ought to help solve the serious current problem of how to keep the expansion of the social security program within reasonable limits. Under Buchanan's proposal, if people wished larger benefits, they would have to purchase more Social Insurance Bonds. This ought to keep the expansion of benefits under control. Also, a fundamental weakness of the current method of financing social security is that payroll tax rates are very sensitive to demographic changes. Because of the decline in the birth rate, the financing of OASI has become a major problem, and the tax rates necessary to finance the present program appear forbidding. In Buchanan's proposal, tax rates would de-

---

[30] Although the original proposal by Buchanan provided that Social Insurance Bonds might earn the higher of either the rate of interest on U.S. Treasury Bonds or the rate of growth of GNP, Edgar Browning has shown that this would not be possible. See "Social Insurance and Intergenerational Transfers," *Journal of Law and Economics*, Oct., 1973, pp. 215–237.

pend solely on the amount of the pensions desired rather than on demographic changes.

The program of reform proposed in the Brookings Institution study by Joseph Pechman, Henry Aaron, and Michael Taussig, entitled *Social Security, Perspectives for Reform*, is very different from Buchanan's reform program. They would de-emphasize considerations of equity and instead would use the system to distribute old-age benefits largely on the basis of need. A principal difficulty in their approach is that having benefits related to earnings has been very popular. Persons wishing to expand the social security system almost always propagate the insurance myth in which persons are viewed as purchasing an annuity for their old age. In addition, there is a fundamental difference between a social security program in which individuals are viewed as purchasing their own old-age pensions and one in which governmental officials allocate benefits in accordance with criteria of need. The reform program proposed by Pechman, Aaron, and Taussig and the program of reform proposed by Buchanan represent the opposing directions in which the social security system may develop.

EFFECT ON THE DISTRIBUTION OF INCOME

A final important aspect of OASI is its effect on the distribution of income. To many of its early supporters, the use of regressive payroll taxes was not considered to be a defect because social security was viewed as an insurance program. Both rich and poor were said to be paying for an annuity to be received during their old age. Financing OASI with earmarked payroll taxes was thought to be in accordance with the benefit principle of taxation. Also, to early supporters of the social security system the objective was to provide a minimum income only for those persons who were subject to "the personal hazards of life," such as old age.[31] The present objective of the federal government's antipoverty programs—providing a minimum income for *all* persons—was not generally accepted.

At first glance, if the social security system is viewed as a tax transfer program, the effect of OASI on the distribution of income appears to be highly progressive. On the average, the incomes of those who are employed are higher than the incomes of the retired. Transferring in-

[31] Robert J. Lampman, ed., *Social Security Perspectives: Essays by Edwin E. Witte* (Madison: University of Wisconsin, 1962), pp. 101–107.

come from those who are employed to those who are retired would result in less inequality. Unfortunately, these effects that appear progressive are the result of the usual changes in income over a person's lifetime—with income dropping during retirement years. To determine the progressivity of the social security system, it is necessary to examine its effect on lifetime incomes.

OASI reduces a person's income during his earning years and increases his income during retirement. For each person, the accumulated value of the taxes paid in may be compared with the discounted value of the benefit he can expect to receive, assuming average life expectancy. Over their lifetimes, persons who have relatively low tax benefit ratios would gain from the social security system, and those with high tax benefit ratios would lose out. OASI would tend to equalize the lifetime distribution of income if the tax benefit ratios were typically lower for the low-income groups than for the higher-income groups.

A study recently made by Henry Aaron of the effect of OASI on the lifetime distribution of income has concluded that OASI has a regressive effect.[32] A principal reason for this effect is that persons with high incomes typically start work at a later age. Because the lower-income groups pay taxes over a longer period of time than the upper-income groups, their tax/benefit ratios tend to be relatively high. A second important reason for the regressivity of OASI is that persons in high-income occupations have a longer life expectancy. Because persons with higher incomes tend to receive old-age benefits over a longer period of time, their tax/benefit ratios are relatively low.

Aaron was not able to include in his study all of the aspects of OASI that might affect lifetime incomes. A factor omitted that might have a contrary tendency is the fact that lower-income groups tend to retire earlier than persons in higher-income groups. This would have a progressive impact on lifetime incomes because persons who retire at sixty-five or earlier would tend to have lower tax/benefit ratios than those who work full-time beyond age sixty-five. Several other factors omitted from Aaron's analysis would probably reinforce his conclusion that the system is regressive. The lower tax rate paid by the self-employed would have a regressive effect on lifetime income distribution if a disproportional number of self-employed persons were in high-income groups.

[32] Henry Aaron, "Demographic Effects on the Equity of Social Security Benefits" (Paper presented to the International Economic Association, Conference on the Economics of Public Services, Turin, Italy, Apr. 1–6, 1974).

Because of the lower tax rate paid by the self-employed, their tax/benefit ratios are relatively low. Also, working couples have relatively high tax/benefit ratios because both husband and wife pay taxes. If the number of working couples among lower-income groups were disproportionately large, this also would have a regressive effect.

To evaluate completely the impact of OASI on lifetime incomes, the interrelationship between payroll taxes and individual income taxes would have to be accounted for. For example, social security benefits are not subject to the personal income tax, an important advantage to retired persons with high incomes. In addition, the portion of the payroll tax paid by the employer is excluded from an individual's income tax base. This tends to make the individual income tax less progressive. If the amount of tax paid by the employer had been included, it would be taxed at a person's marginal tax rate—which would be higher the larger a person's income.

Most efforts to reform the social security system have been concerned with its possible undesirable effects on income distribution.[33] A program that taxes the earnings of all workers at a tax rate of 11.7 percent no matter how low their incomes is a major impediment to the federal government's antipoverty program. To eliminate the undesirable effects of the payroll tax on persons with relatively low incomes, it has been proposed that the payroll tax be integrated with the individual income tax so that payroll taxes would be refunded to workers whose incomes are so low that they pay no individual income taxes. Opponents of payroll taxes also advocate replacing the payroll tax as the exclusive method of financing the social security system and relying partly on general revenues. The purpose of the use of general revenues would be to reduce the taxes on the poor.

SUMMARY

An important characteristic of the recent research on the social security system is that it has been concerned primarily with the way in which this program affects the operation of the overall economic system rather than with the internal operation of the social security system itself. The questions being studied are broader than the typical concerns

[33] Pechman, Aaron, and Taussig, *Social Security*; and John A. Brittain, *The Payroll Tax for Social Security* (Washington, D.C.: The Brookings Institution, 1972).

of students of social security in the past. The principal conclusion to be drawn from this review is that there is no basis at all for the traditional point of view that the system is working well. Because of the decline in the birth rate, it appears that payroll tax rates are going to have to be raised sharply without any improvement in benefits. In addition, the disincentive effects of social security on saving and labor-force participation may be eroding the resource base of the economy and thus of the social security system itself. The lack of a close relationship between the amount of payroll taxes paid by an individual and his employer and the OASI benefits one can expect to receive not only is inequitable, but probably aggravates the disincentive effects that the social security system appears to have on labor-force participation and saving. Also, recent research indicates that these harmful effects are not compensated for by beneficial effects on the distribution of income.

About all one can claim for the system is that it has been a help to those who might have had to care for the indigent aged if there were no social security system. The economists doing this new research are questioning pay-as-you-go financing, the loose relationship between payroll taxes and OASI benefits, and OASI's policies of encouraging retirement. If the social security system is having harmful effects on the rate of saving, capital formation, increases in productivity, and economic growth, policy proposals to alter and revise the program will undoubtedly be forthcoming.

Chapter 5

Government Transfer Spending

JAMES BUCHANAN

> If the society were annually to employ all the labour which it can annually purchase, as the quantity of labour would increase greatly every year, so the produce of every succeeding year would be of vastly greater value than that of the foregoing. But there is no country in which the whole annual produce is employed in maintaining the industrious. The idle everywhere consume a great part of it; and according to the different proportions in which it is annually divided between those two different orders of people, its ordinary or average value must either annually increase, or diminish, or continue the same from one year to another.
>
> ADAM SMITH, *Wealth of Nations*

HORROR stories about public spending and its growth emerge directly from almost any cursory look at the subject. No great amount of thought is required on anyone's part to describe plausibly predictable scenarios that almost no one could desire, regardless of his ideological position. I shall not spend much time here on such constructions.[1] But a minimum initial dosage of data may establish a frame of mind that is necessary for a hard-headed analysis of our situation. As Samuel Johnson is alleged to have remarked, men constantly need reminding about things they already know.

In 1975 total government spending in the United States economy amounted to more than one-third of the gross national product. More than one dollar out of every three dollars of value produced was spent

---

I am indebted to my colleague Gordon Tullock for his helpful comments on an earlier draft of this essay.

[1] For a series of papers that present and analyze the data in some detail, see Thomas Borcherding, ed., *Budgets and Bureaucrats: Sources of Government Growth* (Durham, N.C.: Duke University Press, 1976).

through public or governmental channels and was directed in patterns of outlay determined by some collective decision process rather than by the choices of individuals in their private capacities. (And this statistic does not include the effects of government regulations in modifying private behavior.) The formally computed share of total public expenditure in United States GNP increased from 27 percent in 1960, roughly a 25 percent change over the decade and one-half between 1960 and 1975. Extrapolation alone suggests that by the year 2000 public spending will approach one-half of the GNP. And we must, of course, keep in mind that governmental activities are included, valued simply at cost. But of course simple extrapolation becomes highly misleading, since the productive bases upon which any growth in real output depends may become so eroded that the very increase in the formal public-sector share of the nominal GNP will be accelerated long before 1990 or even 1984.

Perhaps even more disturbing than the increasing and absolutely large public-sector share in the GNP is the relatively sudden change that has occurred in the effective composition of this share since the 1960's and that shows no signs of tailing off. I refer here to the shift within public spending itself away from use of resources or so-called productive outlays, in proportional terms, and toward transfer or nonproductive governmental outlays. For the so-called productive public expenditures, the outlays on the purchase of real goods and services that are provided through government, an argument can be made, within limits, to the effect that these goods and services are themselves indirect inputs for the generation of national product.[2] The movement of goods is facilitated by publicly provided highways; public education supposedly increases the supply of productive human capital; policemen protect private property and make the economy more efficient thereby. The list could be extended. No such argument can be adduced with

[2] This seemingly straightforward statement requires specific assumptions in order for it to hold. In a world where real goods and services are provided publicly through pure Niskanen bureaus, each one of which successfully extracts all of the potential fiscal surplus through oversupply, there is no net addition to value generated by the public sector. On the other hand, if the goods and services so provided are genuinely nonexcludable, and hence impossible to provide through markets, and, further, if public supply necessarily implies pure Niskanen bureaucracy, there is no net inefficiency generated because of the existence of the public sector. At the limit, the community secures neither net gains nor net losses from supplying public goods and services to itself. For description of the Niskanen bureau, see William A. Niskanen, *Bureaucracy and Representative Government* (Chicago: Aldine-Atherton, Inc., 1971).

respect to transfer spending. Resources are not, of course, "used up" directly in the pure transfer process, but purchasing power must be drawn from payments made to productive resource owners and shifted to individuals and groups in ways unrelated to productivity. The effects on overall economic productivity in the economy must be unidirectional; the increase in transfers can only have the net effect of sapping the sources of economic growth. Another way of putting this point is to say that within limits an argument can be made for the efficiency of productive outlays of governments, but no comparable efficiency basis justifies transfer outlays.[3] For the most part, the transfer outlays must be justified on grounds of nonefficiency, and the conflict between the objectives for transfers and efficiency must be squarely acknowledged.

Let us look briefly at the data on the increase in the transfer share of federal spending. In 1960 this part of the budget amounted only to 5.6 percent of the GNP, having changed relatively little over the 1950's, up only from 5.3 percent in 1950. By 1974, however, total transfer spending by government exceeded 10 percent of the GNP. In absolute totals, transfer spending doubled between 1970 and 1975 alone, moving up from under $80 billion to almost $160 billion. No one would dare predict a leveling off, or even a deceleration, of the rate of increase. It seems well within the realm of plausibility that by 1984 we shall be devoting one-fourth of our GNP to transfer payments alone.

In this chapter I want to concentrate attention on the effects of these increases in transfer payments on the national economy. I shall simply leave out of the account the growth in nontransfer spending which exerts different and perhaps equally important effects.

BASIC SOCIAL SECURITY

We may look first at the basic component of the social security system in the United States, the OASI program of retirement, survivors', and disability benefits. For fiscal year 1976, these payments alone will approximate $75 billion, or roughly 5 percent of the GNP. This figure

---

[3] A limited amount of transfer activity can be rationalized on grounds of efficiency if utility interdependence exists. This aspect of transfer policy has recently been widely discussed under the rubric of Pareto-optimal redistribution. For the basic paper, see Harold Hochman and James Rodgers, "Pareto Optimal Redistribution," *American Economic Review* 59 (Sept., 1969): 542–557. Even if this argument is accepted, however, it does not seem wholly comparable to that which may be adduced to support nontransfer activity.

represents an increase from a mere $1 billion in 1950 and from a low $11 billion in 1960, and it is a near doubling of the $38 billion of 1970. What has been the economic effect of this explosive growth in these transfer payments, and what will be the effect of the predicted continued acceleration of this growth?[4]

In order to analyze these questions systematically, it is useful to construct a model that isolates specific features of the program. Consider the following model. Suppose that there are only two age groups (generations) living at any particular time: a retired group and a working group. All members of one generation are productive workers, and we may, for purposes of simplification, assume them to be equal. No members of the other generation work; they live off past earnings, gifts from the working generation, or receipt of public transfers. We suppose here that a political decision is made, in period T_0, to implement a public retirement program only after a time lag, only in, say, T_{30}, when all members of Generation 2 will have become retired and the work force will be made up of the succeeding Generation 3. This assumption means that members of Generation 1, the retired persons at the time of the initial legislation, are totally unaffected; they secure no retirement benefits. We may, through this device, concentrate on the behavior of members of Generation 2, who remain working in the periods before the transfers commence but who will all be retired when these payments start. How will the members of Generation 2 react? I shall present two differing hypotheses which yield contrasting results, and I shall then attempt to determine which of the two seems more in keeping with observed empirical reality.

Ricardo-Barro Model. We may label the first scenario after its classical originator and its most modern expositor.[5] A central assumption in this scenario is the existence of strong family ties between succeeding generations; that is, between 1 and 2, between 2 and 3, between 3 and 4, and so on. When the public or governmental retirement program is announced to be effective in the future, members of Generation 2, those who are currently working and who will themselves be the first recipients

[4] For a general discussion, see Colin Campbell, "Social Insurance in the United States: A Program in Search of an Explanation," *Journal of Law and Economics* 12 (Oct., 1969): 249–266.

[5] David Ricardo, *Works and Correspondence*, vol. 1, *Principles of Political Economy and Taxation* (Cambridge: Cambridge University Press, 1951), pp. 244–249; Robert J. Barro, "Are Government Bonds Net Wealth?" *Journal of Political Economy* 82 (Nov.–Dec., 1974): 1095–1118.

of the publicly provided retirement benefits, will act as if they hold legitimate claims against the community. These claims will come due on retirement, and it is assumed that they will be fully honored by the community. The present value of these claims will be included as a part of the net wealth of Generation 2 during their working years. Holding these claims against the government, members of Generation 2 will act to reduce their own private saving aimed directly at supporting their own income needs during retirement years. In the limit, the latter can be reduced dollar-for-dollar with the present value of the public claim.

But who is to pay off the claims when they come due? Who is to pay off the implicit public debt that is created by the announcement of the governmental retirement program? The only productive group in existence during the time when Generation 2 retires will be Generation 3. In the Ricardo-Barro model, members of Generation 2 will fully recognize the future obligations that the retirement program places on members of Generation 3, and members of Generation 2 will adjust their planned bequests, positive or negative, to just offset those obligations. In this scenario, therefore, Generation 2 will simply replace the accumulation of assets for their own retirement support with accumulation of assets for enhanced transfers to members of Generation 3. The net saving of Generation 2 is not affected by the introduction of the public pension scheme. As a result of Generation 2's behavior, members of Generation 3 will have direct ownership of a larger capital stock and hence a larger income than they would have in the absence of the public transfer obligation. Thus, members of Generation 3 can meet the commitment for financing the pension payments to members of Generation 2 as the latter retire and shift out of the productive labor force. The aggregate stock of private capital is essentially unchanged by the introduction and operation of the public or governmental retirement scheme, and upon the full implementation of the program, the set of public transfers simply replaces the drawing-down of privately accumulated claims by recipients.

Feldstein Model. The contrasting model may be associated with Martin Feldstein, its most articulate modern proponent.[6] In this scenario, the members of Generation 2, the productive group at the time that the future benefit program is announced, will treat the newly created claims to future payments as net wealth. They will reduce the private

[6] Martin Feldstein, "Social Security, Induced Retirement, and Aggregate Capital Accumulation," *Journal of Political Economy* 82 (Sept.–Oct., 1974): 905–926.

accumulation of assets designed to finance their own retirement income support. To this point the two analytical models are equivalent, but in the Feldstein construction, members of Generation 2 will not, as a result of the introduction of the public pension scheme, modify their planned bequests to members of Generation 3. Essentially, persons behave in accordance with a life-cycle model for rational choice, and family ties with Generation 3 are such that planned bequests are not affected.

In the Feldstein scenario, therefore, the important announcement effect of the public pension scheme is to reduce aggregate private saving. When the retirement claims come due, when prior commitments must be honored by the government, members of Generation 3 find themselves with a capital stock no larger than they would have had in the absence of the transfer system. As a result, the transfers to members of Generation 2 represent a dead-weight burden, so to speak, against the income receipts of the productive members of the community, in this case Generation 3.

Evaluation. The two models produce dramatically differing results, even in the extremely simplified setting that is postulated, one that is designed to eliminate many of the familiar effects. Any assessment of the present social security structure depends critically on which of the two scenarios is accepted in broad and general terms. At base, the choice between the two must be made on empirical grounds. Feldstein attempts to support his analysis with empirical estimates based on time series data from the United States. He estimates that the social security system has reduced total private saving by roughly 38 percent. This reduction will, over the long term, exert roughly similar effects on the level of private capital stock. Barro makes no attempt to support his contrasting analysis with empirical estimates.

I am not competent to examine critically Feldstein's empirical tests of his analysis. But without resort to complex data or to the intricacies of econometrics, straightforward empirical observation seems strongly to support the Feldstein rather than the Ricardo-Barro scenario. To establish this conclusion it is necessary to look at the historical record in a public-choice framework.

By 1975 the United States social security system had gone through forty years of history. Careful examination of the political decisions made over this long period should shed some light on the economic incidence of the institutions. I should note that the United States system, as it was introduced and as it has operated, is not equivalent to that analyzed in the simplified model above. Benefit payments were commenced immediately and not after a generation's lag, as in the simplified setting used above. But we may still get some general results by staying with the simplified model while extending it with care to the actual institutions in existence.

Under the setting postulated, suppose that at the time that the public or governmental pension system is enacted members of Generation 2, those who are scheduled to be the first benefit recipients, are taxed at sufficiently high levels to offset fully the present values of the benefit claims which they secure. In other words, assume that strict actuarial funding is followed from the outset of the system; genuine insurance principles are followed. The tax revenues during the periods before Generation 2 retires would then be accumulated in a special pension fund or reserve which would be invested in public or private debt instruments or capital assets. Under this scheme, the fund balances would just be sufficient to finance the pension transfers to members of Generation 2 as they retire and present their claims. In recognition of this fund accumulation, members of Generation 2, at the time of enactment, will have no motive to modify the rate of private bequests to Generation 3, regardless of family ties, since there will be no net burden imposed on Generation 3 by the whole scheme.

The important conclusion, for purposes of differentiating between the two scenarios sketched out above, is that the fully funded and actuarially sound system of public or governmental pension transfers is not different, in effect, from the nonfunded system described in the Ricardo-Barro scenario. Members of Generation 2 put aside, in both sequences, funds that are just sufficient to finance their own retirement, in the one case (Ricardo-Barro) via the enhanced bequests to Generation 3 and in the other case (full-funding) via the system's fund balances. Members of Generation 3 secure no net increment to private assets under the funded pension scheme, but they incur no offsetting obligations to pay direct transfers to Generation 2.

This basic equivalence may be acknowledged, but what does this tell us about the explanatory power of the two scenarios? It suggests that *if* the Ricardo-Barro model is descriptive of the behavior of persons of Generation 2, those persons should be roughly *indifferent* to a fully funded scheme for public pensions or the unfunded scheme outlined above. Evidence for such indifference would consist in roughly equal political support for the alternative structures.

But the political record offers the contrary. Despite much initial discussion about the social security system being based on "sound insurance principles," and despite the continued misuse of the word "insurance," the observed political decisions about the system have never reflected a willingness on the part of decision makers to adopt full funding. Over an initial period, almost by necessity, a fund was accumulated, but it was never sufficiently large to offset the present values of future benefit claims. By the 1950's the absence of fund accumulation appropriate for general insurance principles came to be widely acknowledged, and the system was transformed into a straightforward transfer mechanism, with taxes being maintained roughly in balance with the benefit payout required. The net indebtedness of the social security system, treated actuarially, has been estimated at roughly $2.4 trillion, although the specific estimates here are difficult to compute. The main point is, however, clear. Political decision makers, who have presumably been responsive to the desires of constituents, at least indirectly, have definitely preferred the unfunded to the funded system. In the context of our simple two-generation construction, therefore, this suggests that members of Generation 2, the working group, elect politicians who refrain from imposing taxes for the purpose of accumulating fund reserves. The historical record indicates that politicians impose taxes only as required to meet current benefit obligations that the system has incurred. The evidence could scarcely be stronger in support of the essential Feldstein hypothesis. Over the forty-year period of its existence, the social security system has embodied the creation of claims against incomes of later periods, claims that have been treated as net wealth by potential beneficiaries and which have not been offset by the accumulation of either private or public assets.

One component of the so-called crisis in the system is the fact that these claims are coming due in ever-increasing magnitude, as the figures noted earlier suggest. Those who produce incomes currently are being called upon to transfer increasing shares of those incomes to those who have what they consider to be legitimate claims. Private saving in the economy is lower than it would be without the public transfers for three reasons. First, current taxpayers are led to expect that they, too, will be qualified to receive social security benefits on retirement. These future claims substitute for private saving that might be designed to provide retirement income support. Second, because private saving has been lower over the period of the system's existence, the capital stock is lower than it might have been. Thus, income before transfers, income from which private saving might be made, is lower. Finally, private saving that might be forthcoming for other purposes, over and beyond basic retirement income support, is reduced because disposable income is curtailed by the necessity to meet the increasing transfer burden.

Demographic Shifts. These results emerge even if we project that the population will maintain a constant age profile, with the ratio between the working population and the retired population remaining unchanged. If major changes in this ratio occur, the analysis must be modified. Consider our model of separated generations again. Suppose that Generation 2 arrives at retirement and that its claims for support are financed by taxes on Generation 3. The latter, in its turn, anticipates support from Generation 4, which will be the productive group upon Generation 3's retirement. But let us now assume that Generation 4 is substantially smaller than Generation 3; the birth rate falls between Generation 2 and Generation 3. In that case, Generation 4 will find its transfer burden increased for yet another reason. And with this increased burden there will be still further reductions in disposable income, from which private saving and, ultimately, private capital formation must be made. These demographic shifts are of major importance in assessing the viability of the United States social security system beyond the 1980's. Because of the sharp curtailment in crude birth rates that occurred after the late 1950's, fear is now increasingly expressed about the ability of those who will be economically productive in the years after the turn of the century to finance the transfers that will be required to meet the claims of those who are members of the "baby-boom" generation and who will reach retirement in that period. If the Ricardo-Barro behavioral hypothesis should be correct, it should be possible to observe a major shift in the savings habits of the baby-boom generation as it moves into the income-producing stages of its life cycle. Accompanying the decline in the crude birth rate there should be observed an increase in private savings motivated by the recognition of the transfer burden that this generation will place on the next via the social security system. Has such a change been noted?

Early Retirement. The analysis to this point has assumed that individuals have no choice about which generation or which group they belong to. If we modify the basic model slightly to allow for some degree of individual choice between working and receiving pension support, we can add yet another dimension to the transfer problem. If a person may, on his own option, choose to retire early and to qualify for income support, even if at some reduced level, such behavior exerts a double effect. By shifting out of the work force, a person reduces the overall income base from which transfers are made, even if he does not qualify for a retirement pension. But, if he does so qualify, he will add to the transfer burden from the reduced income base. The inducement for such behavior will, of course, increase as the level of transfer taxes increases.[7]

NONGENERALITY IN THE SOCIAL SECURITY SYSTEM

In its idealized form, the most important feature of a basic social security system is its generality. Potential beneficiaries include a very large proportion of the total population, and actual beneficiaries qualify for the receipt of transfers largely on the basis of age. That is, each person becomes old, and the aging process is something that cannot be individually controlled.

This feature of generality is important for both the financing and the political support of the system. To the extent that almost every member of the productive working population can anticipate the receipt of transfers on his own future retirement, taxes to finance payment to those currently retired may be rationalized on some basis of "intergenerational transfer" instead of on the more questionable criteria of equity or efficiency applicable for more general levies. In this context, individuals who pay taxes can plausibly accept the total tax/benefit structure as an "exchange" of sorts. Comparisons can be made between present values of tax obligations over a period of a person's working years and present values of future benefits over a period of anticipated retirement years. In the framework of our earlier example, members of Generation 3 may finance the retirement benefits for members of Generation 2, when they come due, on the expectation that they are indirectly "purchasing" claims against members of Generation 4, who will, in subsequent years, be called upon to finance Generation 3's retirement. In an idealized and fully mature system, there would be a present-value equivalence between a person's payments into the system

---

[7] For an analytical and empirical study which indicates that retirement is strongly influenced by the current social security system, see Michael J. Boskin, "Social Security and Early Retirement," mimeographed (Stanford University and National Bureau of Economic Research, Mar., 1975).

and the transfers he secures from the system, computed or estimated on genuine actuarial principles. To the extent that a system approximates this ideal, it can be treated as an intergenerational exchange of sorts, and there is no need to raise issues of equity about the financing.[8]

As it has developed, and as noted above, however, the United States system has not approximated this ideal. Persons who have qualified for retirement income transfers, and persons who anticipate retiring before the mid-1980's, have secured extremely favorable "bargains" from the system. The value of the benefits secured from the system far exceeds the value of payments made to the system, appropriately computed. This bargain will not, however, continue for those who commence retirement in the late 1980's and beyond unless benefit levels are increased above those now anticipated. And such real increases in benefits seem increasingly unlikely, given the observed demographic shift already mentioned. For young workers in the 1970's and beyond, the "exchange" of present taxes for future benefits that the system promises is a bad bargain, and possibly a very bad one, indeed.

To the extent that large numbers of workers recognize this fact, the political support for the whole social security structure may be threatened. Young workers in the 1970's may properly ask: Why should I pay taxes to support old people who have got a fine bargain while I am almost certain to get a bad deal? The young workers in the 1980's can ask this question much more emphatically. If the implicit intergenerational exchange comes to be treated as not offering "mutual gains," the system of payroll taxes becomes vulnerable. And the generality features of the structure will seem to be increasingly replaced by overtly discriminatory features. If those retiring before the mid-1980's secure such a better deal than all those who come after them, what is the "justification" for the observed differential treatment?

---

[8] This was the model upon which my proposal for the issuance of Social Security Bonds was based. Compulsory purchase of such bonds, in lieu of the payroll tax, would cause purchasers (potential benefit recipients) to treat future claims more clearly as net wealth in their personal portfolios and, at the same time, create more definitive obligations on the part of the system to meet such claims. My proposal involved the usage of funds from bond "sales" to finance current pension claims; no creation of assets was implied. Thus, the effects on real capital formation, under my scheme, might even be more severe than those under the present scheme, because of the enhanced security of future claims. The Feldstein concern about real capital formation would be increased. For my proposal, see my "Social Insurance in a Growing Economy: A Proposal for Radical Reform," *National Tax Journal* 21 (Dec., 1968): 386–395.

These issues would be present even if there were no additional discriminatory features embodied in the United States system. But there are many other departures from an idealized general system of retirement benefits than the failure of Congress to adjust tax rates in past years. Even with a single-age cohort group, the structure of taxes and benefits tends differentially to favor the low-wage earner, the self-employed, and the worker with dependents who do not work. The structure tends to penalize the high-wage earner, the single worker, and the working wife or husband of a working marriage partner.

These discriminatory features, of both sorts, prevent the developing opposition from being contained and controlled by the introduction of a private pension option. If a system meets the idealized pattern of generality, persons could be allowed to opt out, to select private pension schemes, insuring thereby that the overall objective of social security for the aged would be met. But because of the departures from generality, the United States system must remain a compulsory one, with opting out disallowed. If such an option were opened up, there would be an immediate exodus of young workers, single workers, and working married couples—precisely those groups who anticipate the unfavorable intergenerational exchanges. This exodus would, of course, leave the older workers, the self-employed, and the low-wage earners in the system, tending thereby to accelerate the necessity of reducing project benefit levels or of increasing tax rates, steps which would, in turn, accelerate the exodus from the system.

If provisions for opting out are not possible, how is the political response to the mounting criticism of the social security transfer system to take shape? What plausible predictions can be made for policy change in the 1980's? Support has continued to increase for general treasury financing of at least some part of the system's obligations. In early 1975 the official advisory council on the system recommended that those transfer payments not strictly retirement-related, such as medicare payments, should be funded from general revenue sources and not from payroll taxes.

Steps in this direction will probably be taken as the system's transfer budget balance comes to be increasingly threatened in the late 1970's and early 1980's. But resort to the financing of social security transfer from general tax monies, even if it is only partial, must necessarily exert major policy consequences. The pretense of an independent financial entity incorporating an intergenerational exchange through a "trust fund" would be destroyed, and the distribution of transfer benefits would have to be evaluated against orthodox criteria of "need" instead of automatic or general eligibility. The general tax financing of benefit payments would lead directly to demands for means tests for recipients. Potential beneficiaries could no longer anticipate transfer payments as "rights" in the trust-fund context. General-fund financing would probably guarantee that persons who own assets valued above some cutoff level would be denied benefits, regardless of their record of payroll tax payments through their productive earning period. The cutoff level here will tend to be somewhat above the asset holdings of the median beneficiary, at least in some anticipatory setting. To set the cutoff level to insure that only those persons at the lower extremes qualify for transfers would lead to political abandonment of the whole system.

The introduction of any means test for receiving benefits will, however, tend to accentuate the effect on private saving and private capital formation emphasized by Feldstein. If a person anticipates that he will qualify for retirement income support only if the value of accumulated assets falls below defined limits, rational behavior will, of course, dictate that asset accumulation be held within these limits. It is difficult to conceive of a more direct discouragement to private saving for the middle-income earners. And this impact on the behavior of middle-income earners would more than offset the opposing effects on the very-high-income earners, who may be led to increase rates of private saving because they can no longer place positive discounted values on social security claims.

As the social security system shifts away from its independent financial status and toward incorporation into the general budget account of the federal government, there will also arise tax-side pressures for change. Allegations about the regressivity of payroll taxes remain wholly irrelevant as long as the fiction or mystique of intergenerational exchange is maintained and as long as the system is treated as a benefit-tax package on the individual level of consideration. Once this nexus is dropped and means tests are introduced on the receipts side of the ledger, there must arise intense demands for modifying the structure of taxes, for removing the limits on earnings subject to the tax, and for dropping the proportional rate structure itself. Political experience has demonstrated the willingness of the Congress to increase the income bases for the tax, and quite independently of the relationship to potential pension receipts. As the benefits side is further modified by means tests, attempts will be made to introduce progressive elements into the payroll tax structure.

The most plausible prediction suggests that the United States social security system will come increasingly to resemble a "welfare" or "discriminatory transfer" system and decreasingly to resemble an idealized general system of retirement-income support. But there is one vital difference between them that might be projected for the social security system and the standard program of discriminatory transfers, to be discussed briefly below. Because the existing institutions were developed from, and the acceptance of the institutions was based on, the conception of a general system of retirement-income support, massive quantitative significance seems insured. Attempts to maintain a large part of the widespread political support that the program secured over the first forty years of its existence will guarantee that at least a majority of workers can anticipate the receipt of transfer benefits on retirement. But, with the effective divorce of the level of these benefits from the payment of taxes, both individually and for the system as a whole, there will be little, if any, pressure for containment. The system can, therefore, become the institutional means for massive income and/or wealth transfers from the upper-income receipts to those who expect to qualify for benefits. The social security system can well become the institutional vehicle through which a majority, acting in its own self-interest, "legitimizes" its direct exploitation of the high-income minority, something that it cannot do either with respect to the progressive-tax financing of genuinely public goods and services or with the provisions of welfare benefits to differentially favored minorities.[9]

The particular scenario might be sketched in somewhat more detail. Congress will face continuing pressures from the current and future claimants under the social security system for an increase in the level and range of benefits. At the same time, Congress will face pressures from current taxpayers, as taxpayers, against rising real tax burdens. To the extent that the set of effective taxpayers can be reduced to a minority by introducing progressivity in the rate structure and by increasing the wage-salary base, the political weights are shifted toward expansions. As the Goldwater episode, which politicians will not quickly

___

[9] In this context, the social security system may approximate the institutional embodiment of the limiting set of transfers discussed in my paper "The Political Economy of Franchise in the Welfare State," in *Essays on Capitalism and Freedom*, ed R. Seldon (Charlottesville: University Press of Virginia, 1975).

forget, demonstrated in 1964, social security is a sacred cow in the United States. Recognition of political reality suggests that it is not the "bankruptcy" of the system that threatens future benefit recipients, but instead the "political transfer potential" of the system which threatens to sap the productive strength of the national economy.

WELFARE TRANSFERS

Any analysis and discussion of the explosive growth in federal transfer payments over the 1965–1975 decade must give primary attention to the basic social security system. But account must also be taken of other transfer payments which, in total, are of roughly equal quantitative significance. The set of transfers which might be discussed under the single "welfare" rubric amounted to somewhat more than $17 billion in fiscal year 1975.

These transfers include those made under the Supplemental Security Income Program, covering direct assistance to the aged (not covered under OASI), the blind and the disabled—roughly $5 billion for fiscal year 1975. The second major componnt of the welfare transfers is the aid to states for maintenance payments to families with dependent children (AFDC). This program was roughly $5 billion in size in fiscal year 1975. Housing subsidies amounted to another $2 billion, and food stamp outlays to more than $3.5 billion. Child nutrition programs added a final $2 billion to the welfare payments total.

In contrast with the transfers made under the social security program, certain components of the welfare system arouse significant political and public opposition. Survey data suggest that welfare spending is among the least desired of budget outlays on behalf of the voting public. Nevertheless, we observe a continued increase in the levels of welfare spending in almost all categories and regardless of the rate of growth or the prosperity of the national economy. How is this growth to be explained?

Welfare transfers may, for this purpose, be classified into two distinct groups: those made to persons who qualify on the basis of criteria that are not behaviorally induced, and those made on eligibility criteria that are within the control of the recipient. The first set includes payments made to the aged poor not covered by OASI payments, to the blind, and to the disabled and could be extended beyond the strict set of welfare transfers to include at least some of the payments to veterans. The welfare payments which arouse the main public clamour are those for which persons can become eligible by modifying their own behavior. These include AFDC transfers to women who qualify for welfare payments when their male cohorts "desert" them, payments which also increase as they increase the number of children. The income criteria determining eligibility for food stamps are so loosely drawn that both students and strikers can qualify. Transfer programs of these types are essentially open-ended, with the outlays coming to be largely uncontrollable. And at this juncture in the discussion the role of the federal bureaucracy cannot be overlooked. Evidence is accumulating to indicate that the bureaucracy plays a major role in the rate of growth in federal spending of all sorts, and this bureaucratic influence seems notably true with respect to welfare spending. Bureaucrats in the welfare agencies are rewarded in terms of the case loads that their agencies carry; it is to their own advantage to see eligibility lists increased, not reduced.

Nonetheless, and despite the extremely rapid rates of increase that have been observed in the whole set of welfare transfers, this sector of the federal transfer program seems ultimately more manageable than the social security sector. This conclusion is based on the political or public-choice reasons already noted above. By the nature of the case, welfare transfers will tend to benefit differentially favored minorities of the population. And although these minorities may, through such agencies as the welfare rights organizations, exert considerable direct political pressures, the budget increases must still secure the implicit sanction of the political spokesmen and representatives of the majority of the population. Explicit espousal of vastly expanded programs for welfare transfers is the path to political suicide, as George McGovern found out in 1972, and proposals for replacing the piecemeal separate program with a general program of income maintenance, the so-called negative income tax, meet relatively stiff opposition, as Richard Nixon found out in 1970.

TRANSFER PAYMENTS AND NATIONAL ECONOMIC GROWTH

Space does not permit a discussion of remaining major elements in the set of federal transfer programs, among the most notable of which are payments to veterans and payments to the unemployed. It will, however, be useful to examine, in very general terms, the impact of increasing transfer payments, both in relative and absolute terms, on the national economy. As we have noted, the rate of private saving and private capital formation has been substantially reduced because of the social security system's failure to accumulate a reserve fund. More directly, any transfer payment must reduce the income left for the free disposition of the primary income earner. To the extent that the income earner retains options which allow him to shift to nonpecuniary sources of utility, some reduction in work effort must accompany every increase in transfer spending. Incentives to work and to save out of income earned from work are necessarily related directly to the differential between retained or disposable incomes and the level of transfers made.

Insofar as a larger and larger share of the taxes required to finance transfers comes to be placed on capital, there will be differential effects on the rate of capital accumulation. Those who are competent in the manipulation of growth models can probably offer useful insights on alternative scenarios. I can make only some general suggestions here. Suppose that the rate of capital accumulation depends on disposable income left in the command of productive income earners. Suppose, further, that the national economy is in some long-run dynamic equilibrium; it is on a steady growth path. There will exist a specific relationship between the size of the aggregate capital stock and the level of income generated. Onto this steadily growing economy let us impose a reduction in disposable incomes of the productive income earners because of the transfer of funds to specific groups in the economy, groups which do not make current economic contributions. This reduction in disposable income will, of course, reduce the rate of private saving. But note that there will also be produced a disequilibrium between the size of the capital stock and the level of current income that is disposable. Owners of capital will have an incentive to draw down stocks in order to maintain incomes above the levels which would be possible in the absence of capital withdrawal. For a transition period, it seems quite possible that there would take place a net reduction in the aggregate stock of capital. At the end of this transition, the capital stock would be reduced to a level commensurate with the lowered level of income that is sustainable, given the continuation of the transfer policy.

I have discussed with my colleagues a parable that was intended to illustrate this situation, at least in part. Suppose that somewhere in a remote mountain valley there lives a farmer who produces apples for sale on the market. His only capital is standing apple trees, which he can also market for firewood if he chooses. He has gone along for years replacing his trees as they die out and adding a few new seedlings each year, thus expanding his orchard and, ultimately, his apple crop. Now, lo and behold, one year a thief appears who steals x percent of the apples from the trees. The farmer may react by reducing the rate at which he expands his orchard, but he also may sell off his standing trees for firewood. For the thief there is a genuine maximization problem: What is the optimal percentage of the crop to steal, given his predictions about the responses of the farmer?

This is about where we are with transfer policy. Concern has been expressed about the response of saving, investment, and labor supply to the increasing taxes required to finance transfers to the nonproductive members of society. Implicitly, economists have examined the maximization problem for the transferees, based on the fear that they might overshoot the proper target as defined by the transferees' own interest. But this position overlooks the possible secondary or strategic reactions of the apple farmer. When will he begin to behave strategically? When will he take one of the other options open to him? He can, of course, quit farming and become a thief. And he can (or can he?) decide that the way to protect his apples is by catching and punishing the thief. As applied to transfer policy, when and how will those who earn incomes from productive activity react explicitly against the increasing drainage coercively imposed on them by government? But what if there are more thieves than farmers? How near have we come to Plato's definition of "democracy"?

This is nothing more than a rough-and-ready sketch of the sort of analysis that could be carried out, starting from an empirically relevant basis, on the observed dramatic increases in the levels of transfer spending by government. It is time that economists commenced to apply their learned expertise to such issues as these. Whether or not such applications would result in a change in the direction of budgetary emphasis, including a possible reduction in the rate at which government spending, overall, is increasing, may be questioned. Honest assessment must yield pessimistic predictions about the maintenance of the private sector in the national economy. Government cannot continue to grow at the rate it did over the decade between 1965 and 1975. But the way in which Leviathan is contained becomes all-important for the preservation of the ideals of liberty and freedom that the United States has historically represented.[10]

[10] For a general discussion of the problems of controlling Leviathan, see my book *The Limits of Liberty: Between Anarchy and Leviathan* (Chicago: University of Chicago Press, 1975).

Chapter 6

Regulating the Regulators

GORDON TULLOCK

IN the United States there are a considerable number of regulatory commissions dealing with various aspects of the economy. The point of this chapter is, first, to discuss the various explanations for their behavior which have been offered by economists and then briefly to discuss what can be done about the problem.

Until quite recently almost all economics books discussed the regulation of various industries in terms of a natural monopoly model. It is by no means obvious that the people who set up the regulatory commissions had this model in mind. As a particularly clear-cut case, the airline industry at the time the Civil Aeronautics Board (CAB) was established was vigorously competitive and showed no signs of even potential monopolization. Nevertheless, the economic discussion of that industry in the texts was largely in terms of a natural monopoly and the difficulties of dealing with it. Why this was so I do not know, but it has to be conceded that the natural monopoly, a concept which normally goes hand-in-hand with decreasing marginal costs, presents very difficult problems both for economic theory and for choice of policy. These problems were discussed at length in the traditional literature.

In the early 1940's it was frequently pointed out that in a natural monopoly the regulatory commission, by forcing the price down to the price that would have prevailed under competitive conditions, could deprive the owners of the monopoly profits while at the same time insuring that output would be the same as one would anticipate under competition. The demonstration is, of course, a matter of simple diagrammatics. Unfortunately, although this proposition is true on its assumption, it is not true in the real world for a variety of reasons which were fairly well known to substantially all economists. In the first place, the regulators would not know what the price would be in a competitive market and would have to calculate it in some way. The method theoretically in use was to choose that price which gave the utility a "fair" return on capital.

The theoretical problems with using this specification are obvious. First, the utility or regulated industry is no longer under any great pressure to be efficient, since the return on its capital will be the same whether it is efficient or inefficient, provided only that it is not so inefficient that it has to stop operating altogether. Second, the public utility regulators must have a superhuman ability to guess what the appropriate rate of interest is. If they select an interest rate that is too low, the industry will be driven out of business eventually; if they select one that is even marginally higher than the cost of capital to the utility, then the utility is motivated to overinvest. The latter phenomenon was known long before Averich and Johnson formalized it.

The use of a target rate of return was not adopted on the basis of any economic advice but as a result of some court decisions. The courts had argued that the exercise of police power could not be used to confiscate people's property and hence that the regulated industries must be guaranteed a rate of return equivalent to that which their money could earn elsewhere. It should be noted that this particular rule, strictly speaking, cannot be implemented. The problem is that any industry faces the possibility of falling upon hard times which will lead to its eventual elimination. If demand falls enough, then it is impossible with *any* rate schedule to provide the rate of return required.

The doctrine of fair return, together with the belief that the bulk of the industries were natural monopolies—that is, had declining marginal costs—could provide a justification for the differentiated prices uniformly charged in the regulated industries. If there are declining marginal costs, then a two-part or perhaps two-thousand-part tariff can be Pareto optimal if it is properly computed. Further, if one is required to obtain a fixed return on capital, then a differentiated fee schedule may make it possible to provide that minimum profit, even if the industry would be driven out of business in a competitive situation in which it is compelled to charge its marginal cost for all units sold.

I do not, of course, charge the early students in this area with naïveté; they were fully aware of the fact that there were other reasons for wanting to have a differentiated fee schedule and generally were quite critical of the specific schedules which were adopted in the regulated industries. However, even though they believed they faced a natural monopoly situation, they thought that no optimal solution was likely and that the case was a choice of evils.

One of the things which immediately occurs to modern students of that period is that those economists who opposed the whole concept of regulation deserve much more credit from their fellow professionals than they have in fact received. They may have been simple conservatives who objected to any new ideas, but the arguments they offered against the new regulation technique on the whole seem sounder than the arguments offered by those in favor of it from the perspective of almost one hundred years of regulation.

In practice, of course, although the courts mouthed the formula of a fair rate of return, they did not in fact enforce it particularly vigorously. For one thing, they did not know what the fair rate of return was, and for another there were various political pressures upon them as well as upon the regulatory commissions. At the time I was studying my one course in economics, I was also occasionally using the Chicago El, a privately owned company which was being driven into bankruptcy and beyond by a rate that did not cover the cost of service.[1] In practice, then, the rates of return were not very clearly specified or held to any particular goal by the regulatory commissions, although as a general rule they were not permitted to become conspicuously high or, except in certain times of depression, conspicuously low.

All of these facts were known to the economists in the thirties, forties, and early fifties, and there was a good deal of criticism of the regulatory process. This criticism, however, normally was put in the context of the problems of operating a natural monopoly, and the difficulty of suggesting alternatives which would work better was usually emphasized.

The realization that the whole natural-monopoly/declining-cost industry framework might be erroneous appeared upon the economic scene relatively recently, which is astonishing in light of the fact that careful historical investigation of the establishment of regulatory commissions normally indicates that one of the first things done was to reduce the

[1] That the rate restriction, rather than anything else, was the problem is obvious from the fact that after the city of Chicago took over the El, at a price which discounted the continuing loss the El was likely to incur, it promptly and very sharply raised the rate. The city did not run the El very efficiently, but it did demonstrate that the rates charged before the El was municipalized were massively under the revenue-maximizing level.

amount of competition then in existence. Indeed, as a general rule, although not in every single case, the regulated industries were prominent among those who urged the establishment of the commission. Electric power, for example, was provided by several companies in many cities of the United States at the time regulation was adopted. I can still remember that in my high school civics text the principal argument offered for regulating the utilities was that the existence of the separate poles and wires of a great many different electric light companies was unsightly.[2]

The realization that many of the regulatory commissions had restricted competition broke almost like a new dawn on the discussion of this subject. George Stigler's remark that those who object to a regulatory commission encouraging monopoly are rather like those who object to a dentist pulling teeth was perhaps typical. A great many things that had been hard to explain under the previous theory suddenly fell into place.

Of course, if the regulated industries were natural monopolies, then we are back to the initial problem, because although the regulatory commissions might be creating monopolies where monopolies did not have to exist, they might also simply have speeded up the movement to monopoly status. The question of whether the various regulated industries had the characteristics of a natural monopoly was discussed a good deal in the early days of regulation. In particular, the question of whether there was declining marginal cost or the usual rising marginal cost was subject to a good deal of technical discussion in the fields of railroads and electric power, although no very firm conclusions were reached.

Let me digress. I am rather of the opinion that most of the regulated industries are not in any sense natural monopolies. The only exception I make is for the telephone company, and I am not really convinced in that case. Electricity, as I mentioned before, was provided competitively before regulation in many places. That competition may have been unsightly, but there is no evidence that it was inefficient.

---

[2] If one goes back and looks at the actual literature at the time regulation was adopted for the electric utility industry, it will be found that although the appearance of the streets was an important argument, there was at least some reference to the natural monopoly thesis. As a general rule, the argument against the natural monopoly thesis was put in the form of a prediction that if nothing were done, cutthroat competition would lead to the reduction of the number of companies to one, which would then be an exploitative monopoly.

Further, the unsightliness of electric power distribution could have been taken care of without establishing monopolies. In any event, there is a competitive wholesale market in electricity, and the retailing of electricity does not seem to be subject to very much in the way of economies of scale, so very small retailing institutions which had monopolies over small areas, but which bought their electricity in the competitive market, would seem to have been the optimal arrangement *if* there is an element of natural monopoly.

In England, water was provided by pipes in a highly competitive manner up to about 1850, and the switch to a monopoly water system was made allegedly for health reasons. It is no doubt true that the particular set of competitive companies in England in the 1840's provided water of rather poor quality, but it is also highly probable that the centralized water system did, too. The problem was that the germ theory of disease had not yet been discovered. In any event, the technology of water delivery is not necessarily tied to pipes. For example, a very posh suburb of Athens uses truck-delivered water with a highly competitive market and different qualities of water available at varying prices.

Up to about 1900 many American cities used a somewhat similar technology, that is, wagons, for the removal of human waste. Anyone who has been in the Orient knows that in many Oriental cities a lot of night soil is removed privately by coolies with buckets or small carts. Whether this method is feasible for present-day Western use, I do not know.

One thing I take it we can all agree on is that the transportation industries do not have anything much in the way of a natural monopoly, and their present cartelized state is entirely a gift from the government. It does not follow that there were not elements of monopoly in railroad transportation in the 1880's. It should be noted, however, that the regulations actually adopted in the 1880's, among other things, reduced the competitive nature of railroads and increased their average profits almost immediately on the organization of the Interstate Commerce Commission.

But this is a digression. Those scholars who suddenly realized that the regulatory commissions were in part running monopolies mostly felt that there would be no monopoly without the regulatory commissions. However, as far as I know, they never argued that in *all* cases there would not be a natural monopoly.

The view of regulatory commissions as essentially administering cartels that were hard to organize privately is, I think, presently orthodox among what I might call the "advanced quarter" of the economics profession. It has not yet penetrated into the elementary texts except some of the new left wing texts, which use it as another argument against what they perceive as a capitalist order. But if this view is currently orthodox, three waves of the future in explaining the regulatory process are now clearly visible.

The first modification of the cartel management view of government regulation is the theory of unbudgeted income transfer. Even a superficial examination of any existing regulatory authority will find a great many practices which do not maximize profits. The CAB, for example, has adopted a rate schedule for airlines which does not take into account the cost savings on long flights. It also requires airlines to offer services to certain places they would rather not serve and provides rates for tourist passengers which implicitly subsidize first-class passengers.

These phenomena can be accounted for if one assumes that among the beneficiaries of the cartel operation are certain specific categories of customers as well as the owners. Thus, in order to organize the cartel it is necessary to obtain some external support, and this support is obtained from various customer groups.[3] Unfortunately, as far as we can tell, most of the particular customer groups benefited would be benefited even more if the industry were competitive. But still, the existence of regulatory apparatus does make it possible to transfer funds from some groups of people to other groups of people without its appearance in the government budget and thus may have political advantage. Certainly all regulated industries are compelled by their regulators to do a good deal of this kind of thing.

So much for the first of my new waves; the second, a completely nihilistic new wave, implies that the regulatory commissions really are not doing anything at all except behaving randomly. James Q. Wilson suggested that what actually happens when a new regulatory commission is set up is that the commission simply "begins regulating."[4] In other words, it establishes a set of regulations without giving them very much thought and then, as time goes by, gradually elaborates on and applies

3 R. A. Posner, "Taxation by Regulation," *Bell Journal of Economics and Management Science* 2 (Spring, 1971): 22–50.

4 James Q. Wilson, "The Dead Hand of Regulation," *The Public Interest* 33 (Fall, 1971): 39–58.

these regulations. According to this theory, the firms in the industry either adapt to these regulations or die out. After a while, the existing members of the industry which have adapted have an obvious interest in the continuance of the regulations in substantially their existing form. The principal beneficiaries of the regulation, if this theory is correct, are the technical specialists in the regulation themselves who gain a rent on their specialized knowledge and abilities. Thus, the professional civil servants and that part of the bar which practices before each regulatory commission are the primary beneficiaries of the regulation.

There is clearly some element of truth in this allegation, as there is in all of the others we have discussed so far. It is notable that regulated industries do not appear to be particularly profitable, which argues against the pure cartel theory,[5] and the particular groups who "receive income transfers" as a result of regulation frequently end up paying higher prices than they would pay in a competitive market. The special discount fares on airlines, for example, are commonly higher than the fares charged in that part of the industry which has escaped government cartelization.

The third new wave is not quite as nihilistic as the second but is perhaps more deadly as a criticism of regulation. John Chant and Keith Acheson,[6] looking into the functioning of the Bank of Canada, have suggested that its behavior can best be explained not on grounds that it is attempting to operate the Canadian financial system in a way that is to the benefit of Canada and doing it ineptly, but on the grounds that it is attempting to maximize the personal well-being of members of the board and, in particular, the president of the Bank of Canada and doing this fairly well, granted the restraints to which it has been subjected.

Paul L. Jaskow argues more or less the same with respect to the various state regulatory commissions which control electric power rates.[7] He suggests that their behavior is best understood not as an effort to maximize the well-being of the citizens of their state or to provide the electric utilities with a fair rate of return (or even a monopoly rate of

[5] See Gordon Tullock, "The Transitional Gains Trap," *Bell Journal of Economics and Management Science* 6 (Fall, 1975): 671–678.

[6] They have presented their point of view in several articles, but for present purposes see John F. Chant and Keith Acheson, "The Choice of Monetary Instruments and the Theory of Bureaucracy," *Public Choice* 12 (Spring, 1972): 13–33.

[7] Paul L. Jaskow, "Inflation and Environmental Concern: Structural Change in the Process of Public Utility Price Regulation," *Journal of Law and Economics* 17 (Oct., 1974): 291–327.

return), but simply as maximizing their own utility. In both of these cases, the regulatory commission is assumed to maximize its utility not by selling decisions at auction, which is what would occur to most economists (but which may carry with it too high a possibility of very sharp reductions in utility by way of prison sentences), but by what we might call flak minimization. In more traditional economic parlance, the commission seeks a quiet life.

Public utility regulating commissions, for example, normally find themselves confronted with a very large number of requests for changes from the public utility which are not opposed by anyone. Their usual routine is simply to grant those requests, this being the least troublesome route. When there is opposition, as there sometimes is, the commissions feel unhappy, tend to delay any decision, and aim at that decision which will cause the least difficulty.

According to Chant and Acheson, the Canadian National Bank is more active in its role.[8] One of the objectives of the Canadian National is to make it hard for people to assess its performance, both by making statements about its policy which are unintelligible in themselves and which are intended to make monetary theory unintelligible, and by the use of indirect control instruments, the effects of which are hard to measure. It also tends to give in readily to pressures from people who are in a position to seriously injure it—for example, the Treasury Department—even if this involves the necessity of inconveniencing other, less influential people. Recently, Russell and Shelton have produced and partially tested a model of regulatory agency behavior in which a good many of these variables are present.[9] The model is, in its present form, rather crude, but it is an important first step.

It seems to me that there is at least some element of truth in each of these explanations of the regulatory process I have surveyed. It should not surprise my readers, however, that I rather prefer the last one. The reason, of course, is that it is the only explanation which looks with any attention at all at the personal advantages and disadvantages of the members of the regulatory board. All of the others assume that the regulatory board is attempting to carry out some theoretical policy or other regardless of whether that policy is sensible, nonsensical, or even random (as in the case of the nihilist proposal). Only the final explanation deals

---

[8] Chant and Acheson, "Choice of Monetary Instruments."

[9] Milton Russell and Robert B. Shelton, "A Model of Regulatory Agency Behavior," *Public Choice* 20 (Winter, 1974): 47–62.

with the factors that directly affect the utility of the commission members in their capacity as persons, not in their capacity as members (or perhaps patrons) of some much larger group.

The initial monopolistic price control model assumes that the commissioners act to maximize the well-being of the society as a whole; the cartel model assumes that they act to maximize the well-being of the firms in the industry; the income transfer model assumes that they act to benefit a whole set of various groups, although they themselves are members of few or any of them. The nihilist random behavior model assumes that they are interested in any event in carrying out existing regulations, insofar as they can be carried out, and in making required changes in those regulations. There is no obvious reason why the members of the board should gain in any of these models.

The final suggestion, which is that the boards are acting to advance their own self-interest, seems more realistic. However, it should be kept clearly in mind that the fact that a man is working in his own self-interest does not mean that he may not also be benefiting other people. Adam Smith's baker was a selfish man, but he produced good bread at a reasonable price. It is the usual routine for people establishing organizations, and who actually want them to work, to try to set them up in such a way that the personal interests of the participants in the organization support the goal at which they aim. A company, for example, hiring an attorney to appear before the Interstate Commerce Commission is concerned to prevent the attorney from maximizing his own personal interest, which surely is to collect his fee and do very little about the matter. It controls him by threatening to fire him, and thus reduce his future income, if he does not win in a fair number of cases. The government at least to some extent purports to use the same method. Promotions are supposed to depend on performance in the previous job. Similarly, reappointments to administrative boards would, I suppose, be affected by the level of performance in the first term.

Therefore, there is nothing in any sense critical in saying that members of commissions are essentially motivated by their own personal concerns. That is, after all, the way most people are motivated, and what we aim at is a set of institutions such that the personal maximization on the part of an individual leads him to take that action which also maximizes the social good.[10] This goal is hard to attain under most cir-

[10] See Gordon Tullock, *The Politics of Bureaucracy* (Washington, D.C.: Public Affairs Press, 1965).

cumstances, and I doubt that there are any cases where we actually achieve total maximization in an absolutely perfect way, but the competitive market does a reasonable job.

This latest theory of the behavior of regulatory commissions, then, is simply a statement of the obvious, together with a strong implication that for regulatory commissions the rewards available to members are such that they are led into socially perverse behavior. Is there anything we can do to change this situation?

Let us begin by considering the motives of members of regulatory commissions. Presumably they are like most of us, by which I mean they are not completely and unswervingly interested in their own material well-being. They have at least some interest in maximizing the public welfare as they see it, but, as is the case with most of us, the amount they will sacrifice to this end is distinctly limited. Further, they may well have personal preferences with respect to the regulated industry which they are now in a position to control, as long as the costs are not too great. For example, it seems likely that in the 1930's Southern regulated electric utilities would have been well advised to keep Negroes off their boards of directors. Now, in most of the country, in any event, a regulated utility would be well advised to have a Negro and a woman on its board.

Presumably the racial composition of the board of directors is more or less irrelevant to the functioning efficiency of the utility, but there are other areas in which the personal preferences of the regulatory commission may have more effect. They may have various aesthetic ideas about the operation of the industry. It has been suggested, for example, that the electric power regulatory boards have required a much higher degree of investment in the avoidance of potential brownouts than is economically rational. The ability to recover quickly from a storm also may be imposed upon the utility companies beyond its actual economic value. It is also possible that splendid, large, modern plants are favored on aesthetic grounds by members of the boards (particularly if they are given a conducted tour in fairly luxurious conditions), and thus there may be overinvestment in such equipment.

It would seem likely, however, that all of these are relatively modest inefficiencies. The desire of the board to reduce pressures to which it is subjected and, in a more general sense, to improve its position of power could have greater effects, particularly since, as a general rule, the members of regulatory boards are not on the boards for very long periods of time and therefore presumably do not take long-range views in these matters. Avoiding trouble right now by giving in to certain environmental groups may cause severe power shortages five years in the future, but by then it will be a different commission. The present members will have pleasanter lives, their wives will be snubbed less frequently at garden clubs, and they may even be the subject of laudatory editorials if they prevent the construction of new electric plants and let the future take care of itself.

So far we have hardly discussed what to an economist would appear to be the largest single conflict of interest facing the regulatory commission, that is, the prospect of direct corruption of one sort or another. As a general rule, the members of the regulatory commission have favors to give out which are worth many, many millions of dollars. If they decide to sell those favors instead of giving them away, no economist could be terribly surprised. As far as I know, there is little evidence that the members of the boards and commissions regulating various utilities do this kind of thing on any significant scale. Even the Texas Railroad Commission has seldom been accused of corruption, and the members do not seem to live in the kind of luxury which the receipt of even 0.01 percent of the economic value of their decisions would insure. We may presume that the reason for this comparative honesty has to do with the prospects of getting caught.

As a sort of fallout from Watergate, the bribery accounts of various large companies, including Gulf Oil, have become to some extent a matter of public knowledge. The extraordinary feature of them is their extremely small size, considering the value of the economic interests of these corporations. Gulf appears to have been handing out something like $500,000 a year, and surely there are many individual regulations for which a modest change would be worth vastly more than that to Gulf.

Leaving aside this mystery, it is likely that the most important single case in which individual preferences of commission members clash with the well-being of society has to do with the individual commission members' desire for leisure. If an individual member of the commission works hard and thoroughly understands a given policy or case, he generates a public good for the whole of society by his action, but the cost is borne entirely by him, since he is not paid by the hour of actual work. Under the circumstances, one would anticipate that he would underinvest in becoming informed about his job.[11] There is no empirical evidence directly measuring commission activity in this area, but certainly a casual reading of commissions' decisions would seem to imply that they are enjoying a good deal of leisure when they could be burning the midnight oil studying the subject matter of their board.

Another group in our society which faces exactly the same conflict is, of course, the judges. Here there is some empirical evidence, and this empirical evidence does seem to support the proposition that they are extremely lazy.[12] The same can be said about college professors once they have achieved tenure. A certain number of them (as is also true with a certain number of judges and a certain number of commissioners on utility boards) do, indeed, work very hard. We may presume that they put out this effort because they are interested in the subject matter of their studies as a sort of hobby and they invest energy in it. Still, it seems likely that the largest conflict between the interests of the members of commissions and boards and the principles they are supposed to implement does lie in this area of leisure.

What to do, then? In the private market, as we have mentioned, straightforward material motives are frequently arranged so that an individual ends up pursuing the public good although that pursuit is no part of his intention. That is not *always* true, of course, in the private market, but we find it occurs quite commonly. Is there anything we can learn from the public market to make use of the same kind of carrot and stick to improve the activity of regulatory groups?

If we could somehow have the salaries of the members of a regulatory board vary according to the efficiency with which they carry out their duties, they would have a strong material motive to carry them out efficiently. The problem is that determining output measurement for government activities is very difficult and, in the case of a regulatory board, perhaps impossible, even in principle. The problem that makes rating the efficiency of regulatory boards so hard is that they are usually attempting to operate on several parameters simultaneously. The Federal Reserve Board is interested in both the rate of inflation and the rate of

[11] Gordon Tullock, "Public Decisions as Public Goods," *Journal of Political Economy* 79 (July–Aug., 1971): 913–918.

[12] Gordon Tullock, "On the Efficient Organization of Trials," *Kyklos* 28, fasc. 4 (1975): 745–762.

unemployment (to say nothing of the rate of interest). Similarly, electric utility commissions should be interested in both prices and the rate of investment in new equipment for the future. Any reward system would necessarily involve an implicit tradeoff between at least two factors, and if this tradeoff were different in the reward system from that given by nature, then the commission would be led to aim at a systematically erroneous target.

Our general lack of any very good ideas about the parameters involved creates a very undesirable operating condition for systems aiming at rewarding commission members in proportion to their performance. However, I am not certain that we could not do something along these lines. I am inclined to the view that even with a good deal of research we would end up unable to adjust commission members' salaries to their performance of the desired social goal, but I could be wrong. In any event, the rewards which we could obtain if we *did* succeed in developing such a payment scheme would be so great that research on this subject would seem desirable even if the odds are against success.

In this respect, government commissions are not radically different from other government activities. It is clear that we could greatly improve governmental efficiency if we had good measures of government output and used those measures to punish or reward government officials. Unfortunately, the measures do not now exist, but we can hope that there will be progress along these lines in time.

If, for the time being, we cannot make the rewards to the commissioners depend upon their performance, are there other techniques we can use? One that is very widely used in our government, and indeed has been widely used in governments since as far back as we have any historic record, is the effort to avoid conflicts of interest. This technique does not make the reward to the member of government positively dependent upon his performance, but it attempts to eliminate from his reward system certain perverse effects. The judge who is directly concerned with the issue brought before him is subject to a penalty and reward system which is likely to lead to an undesirable outcome. Similarly, the electric power commissioner who happened to be the largest shareholder in the local electric utility might be thought to have other interests than those of the public in his mind when he made his decisions. In a way, the rules against bribery and corruption are merely a special example of this desire to avoid the particular type of perverse incentive system we call conflict of interest. The man who accepts a bribe in return for his decision has a conflict of interest with respect to that decision.

I do not wish to argue that this immemorially ancient policy is unwise, but it clearly does not get us very far. Every government official has a clear-cut conflict of interest between his own personal desire for leisure and his desire to carry out his own preference function on the one hand and the public interest, which he is supposed to serve, on the other. There is no way of avoiding this particular conflict of interest except to provide material incentives for carrying out the public interest, and that raises the issues we have discussed before. As I mentioned above, the empirical evidence about judges does indicate that they are comparatively lazy people, and anyone who has paid much attention to his faculty environment realizes that the same can be said of a great number of professors.

The assumption that the members of the commission are not interested in doing too much work or undergoing too much pain to carry out the duties of the commission and, insofar as they do make decisions, to maximize their own utility unfortunately does not get us very far, either. In the first place, it is clear that on these assumptions we could justify all of the descriptions of commission behavior which have been presented before. Presumably, those commissioners would be flak-minimizers in the sense that they would not like to be subject to public criticism and pressure. That being so, we would anticipate that they would have some tendency to push the general price level down if there were monopoly profits that could be squeezed;[13] they would tend to create monopolies because that would please members of the industry; they would tend to transfer funds to politically organized groups; they would tend to behave more or less randomly on many decisions and, in fact, would have strong tendency to follow the advice (not with concentrated attention, of course) of their professional civil servants and the most persuasive attorney they had heard recently; and, last but not least, they would attempt to increase their power and reduce direct pressure in various ways.

The problem with this hypothesis, however, is that although it can

[13] See Louis DeAlessi, "An Economic Analysis of Government Ownership and Regulation: Theory and the Evidence from the Electric Power Industry," *Public Choice* 19 (Fall, 1974): 1–42.

explain all of these things fairly easily, it can also explain all sorts of other patterns of behavior. Strictly speaking, economic theory assumes that everyone maximizes utility, and the use of measurable material gains as a goal, that is, profit maximization, is normally thought of as an approximation of the real world rather than a perfect measure. Nevertheless, the areas where economic analysis has been most helpful are those areas where this approximation is very good, for example, in the private sector. Once we move into areas where that approximation is poor, it becomes much harder to make predictions. The prediction that a corporation will maximize profits is seldom absolutely true, but it is usually very close to the truth. When we drop out the profit motive, there are many possible arguments in individuals' utility functions. Further, psychologists have given us very little guidance in these matters, and we have little knowledge except that different people seem to get utility from different things. Under the circumstances, making specific predictions is very hard to do.

What we can fairly certainly say, with respect to utility maximizers, is that they are unlikely to give overwhelming weight to their preference of any particular social goal. The effort to avoid conflict of interest, which is a five-thousand-year-old technique, assumes that maximizing the public interest is one of the arguments in the utility of at least carefully selected individuals and, if any prospect of maximizing the other arguments can be eliminated, the individual will maximize public interest. The problem we have mentioned above is, of course, the conflict between the individual's desire for leisure and the necessary hard work involved in maximizing the public interest, but it is fairly obvious that there are apt to be many, many other arguments in the individual's utility function which conflict to at least some extent with maximizing the public interest and cannot be eliminated by at least existing provisions on reducing conflicts of interest.[14]

We can easily find various things we would anticipate most commissioners would attempt to maximize. Improving their power, having

[14] The oath of poverty, which used to be prominent in the organization of much of the Catholic Church, may have been a more effective way of eliminating conflicts of interest than is more modern, much more restricted legislation. Certainly a believer who anticipated facing divine judgment would be much more strongly motivated to carry out what he thought was the will of God than is the modern commissioner to carry out the public interest.

good personal relations with people around them, and not working too hard are obviously examples. Unfortunately, it would appear that all three of these, in the particular environment in which most commissions operate, would tend to lead to perverse results. Further, they are to some extent in conflict with each other, and we have no idea of the tradeoffs that might result. As a final complication, presumably there are many other factors in the commissioner's utility function, and we have no good information about them.

As I suppose no one will be surprised to hear, it seems to me that this final view of the functioning of a commission is, on the whole, a strong argument against depending upon such organizations. Of course, the fact that one particular type of organization works badly does not prove that another is better. The fact that we can assume that regulatory commissions will function with a very low level of efficiency and at least in part will behave in a perverse manner may not prove that they are worse than permitting the monopolies to go along unchecked. Nevertheless, it is clear that we should look for other institutional structures to deal with the problem.

The obvious other institutional structure is, of course, the competitive market. Since it is my opinion and, I take it, the opinion of the bulk of the economists who have dealt with the problem in recent years that most, if not all, of our "natural monopolies" are actually artificial monopolies created by law, it is obvious that simply permitting competition would be one way of dealing with the regulating boards and commissions. The CAB and the ICC clearly have no excuse for further existence. I presume that they will continue in existence, but the reason they will is simply that their beneficiaries have political power, not that there is any social interest in retaining them.

For those areas, if there are some, in which competition is impossible, we should seek out (if we can) nonregulatory solutions, a number of which have been suggested—for example, what I call the Tullock-Demsetz proposal for putting the utilities out on bids.[15] The fact that the

---

[15] See Gordon Tullock, "Entry Barriers in Politics," *American Economic Review* 55 (May, 1965): 458–466; and Harold Demsetz, "Why Regulation Utilities?" *Journal of Law and Economics* 11 (Apr., 1968): 55–66. Note that I call it the Tullock-Demsetz proposal; almost everyone else calls it the Demsetz proposal. It is undeniably true that I got into print first, but it is also true that my particular discussion of this issue was not really serious; I was using it as a stalking horse for a totally different subject, whereas Demsetz made a serious proposal in the area.

individual monopoly would have to be bid out for fairly long periods of time and, indeed, the fact that it is hard to change the monopolist once you have him because of the capital investment problem make this particular solution probably not generally applicable. It should be noted, however, that many of our utilities were originally built under institutional systems that look very much like the Demsetz proposal. The most recent example is, of course, the development of the natural gas industry in the last thirty years, but the introduction of electricity and water in many cities proceeded under much the same circumstances.[16]

Another nonregulatory solution might be the so-called cooperative. There are two variants of this proposal. My own, which is intended for electric utilities only, involves very local cooperatives (a few blocks), presumably run by the householders who purchase their electricity and their maintenance, probably by contract, from larger entities in a competitive market. The other variant, which involves large electricity companies, provides for a cooperative in which the members have votes proportional to their bills in the preceding year. I am dubious about the prospects of raising adequate capital under the latter technique, but it does seem to me to be very much worth further exploration.

All of these proposals have been ways of attempting to get the monopolistic industry to behave, at least to some extent, in a nonmonopolistic manner. I should like to close this chapter by suggesting that perhaps instead of doing that, we should attempt to simply take the monopoly profits for state uses while leaving the monopoly itself undisturbed. The argument against monopoly is, generally speaking, that it generates a welfare loss because there is always a welfare triangle created by the use of the monopoly price. If we assume that the utilities generally cannot perfectly discriminate, that argument would be true in their case. It is not often noted in discussion of monopoly, but the use of any tax raises exactly the same issue and, indeed, the diagrams used in texts on public finance to discuss the problem of excess burden are essentially identical to those used to show welfare loss in industrial organization texts.

Granted that the government must have revenue and that the taxes will generate an excess burden, the prospect of simply taking over the

[16] Of course, this development of electricity and water occurred in those areas where they were introduced without competition, generally *after* the laws banning competition had been enacted and, therefore, mainly confined to the smaller cities.

monopoly profit and having substantially the same kind of excess burden as other taxes create is attractive, if we can think of nothing that could be done about the monopoly otherwise. Of course, a simple tax on the output of the public utility would be taken as a cost, and the public utility would maximize its monopoly profit on top of that cost. A tax on profits sets up somewhat more complex reactions, but once again one would assume that the utility would respond to such a tax. Therefore, a tax which is an effort to get the monopoly profit and which is not to be based on a totally unlikely amount of knowledge about the production efficiency of the utility must be based on something else.

The ideal thing to tax, of course, would be the potential market of the utility. Obviously we cannot measure the potential market exactly, but it is not obvious that we could not find reasonably attractive proxies. The total income as shown on income tax returns generated in a given area might not be a bad measure of the size of the demand for electricity. No doubt that method could be improved upon, but let me use it as an example for the rest of this discussion.

Suppose, then, that the legislature enacts a tax on electric utilities which is some function of the total income in the area served by each utility. Note that this tax does not affect any of the marginal decisions of the utility but does affect its ability to acquire new capital. Assuming that the tax was approximately the right size, this effect would not be damaging. Further, it should be noted that the optimal tax, assuming that our proxy for potential demand is correct, would be that tax which maximized the long-run revenue of the taxing authority. Taxing authorities, for a variety of reasons, usually have fairly strong motives to want to get as much money as they can, and urging them to select that tax rate which maximizes their revenue would put the advising economist, for once, in the position of pressing the government along directions which it would like to follow anyway. Thus, it seems to me not unlikely that fairly accurate taxes might be assessed in this area.

This technique, of course, leaves the monopoly in place and leaves the welfare loss of monopoly in full existence. However, it should permit the reduction of taxes somewhere else in the economy, and hence a welfare gain elsewhere.[17] This is clearly not an ideal policy, but it may be the best we can do.

---

[17] Note that I say "permit"; I will not guarantee that the government actually will do it.

Doing the best we can do is all we can do anywhere. It is just that in some areas, and clearly the regulation of natural monopolies is such an area, the restraints seem to be less pleasant than they are elsewhere. It would be nice if the problem would simply go away, but it shows no signs of doing so. Under the circumstances, the best we can do probably will not be very good.

Chapter 7

The Modern Corporation as an Efficiency Instrument

OLIVER WILLIAMSON

ALTHOUGH others plainly disagree, I submit that the modern corporation should be assigned a relatively narrow social purpose. What commend the corporation most as a mode of economic organization are its efficiency attributes. As I hope the materials in this chapter make clear, the corporation has often served this purpose well in the distant and recent past; subject to appropriate constraints, it can continue to do so in the future.

This is not to suggest that the single-minded pursuit of profits should exempt the corporation from public policy scrutiny. Monopoly problems may be posed which plainly warrant concern and, where feasible, correction; the corporation may generate social costs (for example, pollution) for which it should be made responsible; and vigilance should be maintained lest corporate resources be used to corrupt political processes. But to divert the corporation from the pursuit of profits to assume a wider set of social responsibilities is of dubious merit. The corporation's attributes as an efficiency instrument would presumably be diluted in the process; its main contribution to social welfare would accordingly be compromised.

A transactions cost approach is used to study the corporation as an instrument of adaptive efficiency. Although this approach is "modern" in some ways, it was anticipated by the work of both John R. Commons and Ronald Coase in the 1930's.[1] Thus, Commons took the position that the transaction should be regarded as the ultimate unit of economic investigation, which is substantially the approach that is developed herein, and Coase's seminal paper on the nature of the firm was concerned, as I

---

[1] J. R. Commons, *Institutional Economics: Its Place in Political Economy* (Madison: University of Wisconsin Press, 1934), pp. 4, 5, 8; R. H. Coase, "The Nature of the Firm," *Economica*, n.s. 4 (1937): 386–405.

am, with the properties of markets and internal organization as these relate to economizing on transaction costs. More specifically, I develop the argument that the modern corporation is usefully regarded as an instrument for mitigating frictions that are associated with the operation of labor, intermediate product, and capital markets. The argument relies extensively on materials that I have developed elsewhere, most of which appear in *Markets and Hierarchies*.[2]

The transaction cost approach (alternatively referred to as the contracting approach or as the markets and hierarchies approach) may be contrasted with several other "modern" approaches to the study of the corporation. Probably the conventional view is that the corporation is analytically indistinguishable from the neoclassical firm, which is to say that it is a production function to which a profit maximization objective has been assigned. A quite different view is that the modern corporation is a bureaucratically organized planning instrument that manages or manipulates final product markets to its advantage.[3] A sympathetic variant of this second view is that the hierarchical mode of organization which characterizes the modern corporation has the purpose and/or effect of regimenting workers.[4]

Section one of this chapter sets out the rudiments of the markets and hierarchies approach. Aspects of labor-market organization are examined in section two, where the use of internal organization to harmonize antagonistic interests is described. The third section considers vertical integration as an alternative to market-mediated exchange for intermediate products. Issues of competition in the capital market and conglomerate organization are treated in section four. Comments on the alternative views mentioned above and some remarks regarding future research follow.

THE MARKETS AND HIERARCHIES APPROACH[5]

The markets and hierarchies approach may be stated compactly as follows: (1) markets and firms are alternative instruments for complet-

[2] O. E. Williamson, *Markets and Hierarchies: Analysis and Antitrust Implications* (New York: The Free Press, 1975).

[3] J. K. Galbraith, *The New Industrial State* (New York: Houghton Mifflin Co., 1967).

[4] D. M. Gordon, "Recession is Capitalism as Usual," *New York Times Magazine*, Apr. 27, 1975, pp. 18ff.

[5] The argument in this section closely follows my article, "The Economics of

ing a related set of transactions; (2) whether a set of transactions ought to be executed between firms (across markets) or within a firm depends on the relative efficiency of each mode; (3) the costs of writing and executing complex contracts across a market vary with the characteristics of the human decision makers who are involved with the transaction on the one hand and the objective properties of the firms and of the market on the other; (4) although the human and transactional factors which impede exchanges between firms (across a market) manifest themselves somewhat differently within the firm, the same set of factors applies to both. A symmetrical analysis of trading, therefore, requires that the transactional limits of internal organization as well as the transactional sources of market failure be acknowledged. Moreover, just as market structure matters in assessing the efficacy of trades in the marketplace, so internal structure matters in assessing internal organization.

The transaction cost approach is interdisciplinary, drawing extensively on contributions from both economics and organization theory. The literature on market failure, contingent claims contracting, and recent organizational design supplies the requisite economic background.[6] The literature on administrative man and strategic behavior provides the main contributions from organization theory.[7]

With this basis the markets and hierarchies approach attempts to identify a set of market or environmental factors which, together with a related set of human factors, explains the circumstances under which complex contracts involving contingent claims will be costly to write, execute, and enforce. Faced with such difficulties, and considering the risks that simple, and therefore incomplete, contingent claims contracts pose,[8] the firm may decide to bypass the market and resort to hierarchical

---

Antitrust: Transaction Cost Considerations," *University of Pennsylvania Law Review* 122 (June, 1974): 1442–1447.

[6] See, for example, respectively, K. J. Arrow, "The Organization of Economic Activity," in U.S. Congress, Joint Economic Committee, *The Analysis and Evaluation of Public Expenditure: The PPB System*, 91st Cong., 1st sess., 1969, pp. 59–73; J. E. Meade, *The Controlled Economy* (London: Allen and Unwin, Ltd., 1971), pp. 147–188; and L. Hurwicz, "On Informationally Decentralized Systems," in *Decision and Organization*, ed. C. B. McGuire and R. Radner (Amsterdam: North-Holland, 1972).

[7] See, for example, respectively, H. A. Simon, *Models of Man* (New York: Wiley, 1957); I. Goffman, *Strategic Interaction* (Philadelphia: University of Pennsylvania Press, 1969).

[8] This is merely a necessary but not sufficient condition for internal organization to supplant the market. Internal organization also experiences distortion. Shifting a transaction from the market to a firm requires that a net efficiency gain be shown.

modes of organization. Transactions that might otherwise be handled in the market would then be performed internally and governed by administrative processes.

Uncertainty and small-numbers exchange relations, in which one party's choice of trading partners is restricted, are the environmental factors to which market failure is ascribed. Unless joined by a related set of human factors, however, such environmental conditions need not impede market exchange. The pairing of uncertainty with bounded rationality and the joining of small numbers with what I will refer to as opportunism are especially important.

Consider first the pairing of bounded rationality with uncertainty. The principle of bounded rationality has been defined by Herbert Simon in this way: "The capacity of the human mind for formulating and solving complex problems is very small compared with the size of the problems whose solution is required for objectively rational behavior in the real world."[9] That definition refers both to neurophysiological limits on the capacity to receive, store, retrieve, and process information without error and to definitional limits inherent in language.[10] If these limits make it very costly or impossible to identify future contingencies and to specify, *ex ante*, appropriate adaptations thereto, long-term contracts may be supplanted by internal organization. Recourse to the internal organization of transactions permits adaptations to uncertainty to be accomplished by administrative processes as each problem arises. Thus, rather than attempting to anticipate all possible contingencies from the outset, we permit the future to unfold. Internal organization in this way

[9] Simon, *Models of Man*, p. 198.

[10] The implications for contractual purposes of joining bounded rationality with uncertainty are suggested by the following description of the decision process: "For even moderately complex problems . . . the entire decision tree cannot be generated. There are several reasons why this is so: one is the size of the tree. The number of alternative paths in complex decision problems is very large. . . . A second reason is that in most decision situations, unlike chess, neither the alternative paths nor a rule for generating them is available. . . . A third reason is the problem of estimating consequences. . . . For many problems, consequences of alternatives are difficult, if not impossible, to estimate. The comprehensive decision model is not feasible for most interesting decision problems" (J. Feldman and H. Kanter, "Organizational Decision Making," in *Handbook of Organizations*, ed. J. March [Chicago: Rand-McNally, 1965], p. 615). The infeasibility, or prohibitive cost, of describing the comprehensive decision tree and making *ex ante* optimal choices at every node means that collusive agreements must, except in implausibly simple circumstances, be highly incomplete documents.

economizes on the bounded rationality attributes of decision makers in circumstances where prices are not "sufficient statistics" and uncertainty is substantial.[11]

However, rather than resort to internal organization when long-term contingent claims contracts are thought to be defective (too costly or perhaps infeasible), why not employ short-term contracts instead? Appropriate adaptations to changing market circumstances can then be introduced at the contract renewal interval, thereby avoiding the prohibitive costs of *ex ante* specification. The pairing of opportunism with small-numbers exchange relations, however, creates other obstacles to market transactions.

Developing this set of issues is somewhat involved. Suffice it to observe here that (1) opportunism refers to a lack of candor or honesty in transactions, to include the seeking of self-interest with guile; (2) opportunistic inclinations pose little risk to trading partners as long as competitive (large-numbers) exchange relations obtain; (3) many transactions which at the outset involve a large number of qualified bidders are transformed in the process of contract execution—often because of economies of scale and accrued cost advantages attributable to successful bidders learning more about the job as they perform their work (learning by doing)—so that a small-numbers supply condition effectively obtains at the contract renewal interval; and (4) short-term contracting is costly and risky when opportunism and small-numbers relations are joined. The argument will be developed further in other sections of this chapter.

In consideration of the problems that both long- and short-term contracts are subject to—by reason of bounded rationality and uncertainty in the first instance and the pairing of opportunism with small-numbers relations in the second—internal organization may be used instead. With internal organization, issues are handled as they arise rather than in an exhaustive contingent planning fashion from the outset.[12] The resulting adaptive, sequential decision-making process is the internal or-

---

[11] In circumstances, however, where prices are sufficient statistics, reliance on the price system serves to economize on bounded rationality. See F. Hayek, "The Use of Knowledge in Society," *American Economic Review* 35 (Sept., 1945): 519–530.

[12] This is oversimplified. International organization also provides for contingencies by developing what are referred to as "performance programs," which are sometimes quite elaborate. Such programs are more easily adapted to unforeseen contingencies than are interfirm contracts, for the reasons given in the text. For a discussion

ganizational counterpart of short-term contracting and serves to economize on bounded rationality. Opportunism does not pose the same difficulties for such internal, sequential supply relations that it does when negotiations take place across a market because (1) internal divisions do not have preemptive claims on profit streams, but act under common ownership and supervision to more nearly maximize joint profits instead, and (2) the internal incentive and control machinery is much more extensive and refined than that which obtains in market exchanges.[13] The firm is thereby better able to take the long view for investment purposes (and hence is more prepared to put specialized plants and equipment in place) while simultaneously adjusting to changing market circumstances in an adaptive, sequential manner.

Having said this, I hasten to add that if internal organization serves frequently to attenuate bounded rationality and opportunism problems, it does not eliminate either condition. Of special relevance in this connection are two propositions: (1) the limitations of internal organization in both bounded rationality and opportunistic respects vary directly with firm size when organization form is held constant, but (2) organization form—that is, the way in which activities in the firm are hierarchically structured—matters. The import of this latter proposition is developed in the discussion of conglomerates below.

Moreover, the choice between firm and market ought not to be regarded as fixed. Both firms and markets change over time in ways which may render an initial assignment of transactions to the firm or market inappropriate. The degree of uncertainty associated with the transactions in question may diminish; market growth may support large numbers of suppliers in competition with one another, and information disparities between the parties often shrink. Also, changes in technology may occur, altering the degree to which limits of bounded rationality apply. Thus, the efficacy of completing transactions by hierarchies or markets should be reassessed periodically.

---

of performance programs, see J. March and H. A. Simon, *Organizations* (New York: Wiley, 1958).

[13] Internal organization affords two further benefits: it helps to overcome conditions where one party holds information not available to the other without some expense (information impactedness), because internal audits are more powerful than external ones, and it is sometimes able to reduce uncertainty by promoting convergent expectations. Both of these benefits are important but less basic to the present argument than the effects of internal organization on bounded rationality and opportunism.

LABOR MARKETS

IDIOSYNCRATIC TASKS[14]

Peter Doeringer and Michael Piore describe idiosyncratic tasks in the following way:

> Almost every job involves some specific skills. Even the simplest custodial tasks are facilitated by familiarity with the physical environment specific to the workplace in which they are being performed. The apparently routine operation of standard machines can be importantly aided by familiarity with the particular piece of operating equipment. . . . In some cases workers are able to anticipate trouble and diagnose its source by subtle changes in the sound or smell of the equipment. Moreover, performance in some production or managerial jobs involves a team element, and a critical skill is the ability to operate effectively with the given members of the team. This ability is dependent upon the interaction skills of the personalities of the members, and the individual's work "skills" are specific in the sense that skills necessary to work on one team are never quite the same as those required on another.[15]

Friedrich Hayek describes the consequences of idiosyncracy as follows:

> . . . practically every individual has some advantage over all others in that he possesses unique information of which beneficial use might be made, but of which use can be made only if the decisions depending on it are left to him or are made with his active cooperation. We need to remember only how much we have to learn in any occupation after we have completed our theoretical training, how big a part of our working life we spend learning particular jobs, and how valuable an asset in all walks of life is knowledge of people, of local conditions, and special circumstances.[16]

More generally, there are at least four task idiosyncracies that can arise: (1) equipment idiosyncracies, due to incompletely standardized,

---

[14] The argument in this section follows O. E. Williamson, M. L. Wachter, and J. E. Harris, "Understanding the Employment Relation: The Analysis of Idiosyncratic Exchange," *Bell Journal of Economics and Management Science* 6 (Spring, 1975): 256–257, 276. Copyright 1975, The American Telephone and Telegraph Co. Reprinted with permission from *The Bell Journal of Economics and Management Science.*

[15] P. Doeringer and M. Piore, *Internal Labor Markets and Manpower Analysis* (Lexington, Mass.: Lexington Books, 1971), p. 84.

[16] Hayek, "Use of Knowledge," pp. 521–522.

albeit common, equipment, the unique characteristics of which become known through experience; (2) process idiosyncracies, which are fashioned or "adopted" by the worker and his associates in specific operating contexts; (3) informal team accommodations, attributable to mutual adaptation among parties engaged in recurrent contact but which are upset, to the possible detriment of group performance, when membership is altered; and (4) communication idiosyncracies with respect to information channels and codes that are of value only within the firm. Given that "technology is [partly] unwritten and that part of the specificity derives from improvements which the work force itself introduces, workers are in a position to perfect their monopoly over the knowledge of the technology should there be an incentive to do so."[17]

Training for idiosyncratic jobs ordinarily takes place in an on-the-job context. Classroom training is unsuitable both because the attributes of uniqueness associated with particular operations, machines, work groups, and, more generally, atmospheres of the workplaces may be impossible to replicate in the classroom and because job incumbents, who are in possession of the requisite skills and knowledge with which the new recruit or candidate must become familiar, may be unable to describe, demonstrate, or otherwise impart this information except in an operational context.[18] Teaching by doing thus facilitates the process of learning by doing. Where such attributes of uniqueness and teaching are at all important, specific exposure in the workplace at some stage becomes essential. Outsiders who lack specific experience can thus achieve parity with insiders only by being hired and incurring the necessary start-up costs.

The success of on-the-job training is plainly conditional on the attitudes of incumbent employees toward disclosure of information. Both individually and as a group, incumbents are in possession of a valuable resource (knowledge) and can be expected to reveal it fully and candidly only in exchange for value. The way the employment relation is structured turns out to be important in this connection. The danger is that incumbent employees will hoard information to their personal advantage and engage in a series of bilateral monopolistic exchanges with the management to the detriment of both the firm and other employees as well.

---

[17] Doeringer and Piore, *Internal Labor Markets*, p. 84.
[18] Ibid., p. 20.

ORGANIZATIONAL IMPLICATIONS

The efficiency properties of what have come to be known as internal labor markets have been developed elsewhere.[19] The basic argument is that the bargaining and strategic posturing that infect individualistic markets contracting for idiosyncratic jobs have consequences of inefficiency that can be overcome by shifting to collective organization. The resulting internal labor markets serve to promote efficiency by attaching wages to jobs instead of to individuals, thereby foreclosing individual bargaining. The resulting wage structure reflects objective long-term job values instead of current bargaining exigencies. Internal promotion ladders encourage a positive worker attitude toward on-the-job training and enable the firm to reward cooperative behavior. A grievance procedure, with impartial arbitration as the usual final step, allows the firm and the workers to deal with continually changing conditions in a relatively nonlitigious manner. Contract revision and renewal take place in an atmosphere of mutual restraint in which the parties are committed to continuing accommodation. Unionization commonly facilitates the orderly achievement of these results, though it is not strictly necessary, especially in small organizations.

Reorganization of Steel. A specific example of such a transformation—albeit imperfect, since it represents the evolution of an internal labor market at its early stages—is afforded by an examination of task idiosyncracies in the steel industry at the turn of the century. The system that existed in 1890 is referred to by Katherine Stone as the "contract system."[20] The practices employed in steel making were evidently a continuation of those which had developed earlier in the iron industry. Skilled workers contracted both with the steel companies and with unskilled workers to perform the necessary heavy manual labor. The steel companies provided equipment and raw materials and marketed the product.

The companies sometimes negotiated specific piece rates for the performance of various activities,[21] but at other times an overall labor rate was negotiated with the union. An example of the latter, in which the union first negotiated an overall rate and subsequently divided it by function, is the following:

[19] Williamson, Wachter, and Harris, "Understanding the Employment Relation."

[20] K. Stone, "The Origins of Job Structures in the Steel Industry," *Review of Radical Political Economies*, Summer, 1974, pp. 61–97.

[21] Ibid., p. 63.

When the Columbus Rolling Mill Company contracted to reheat and roll some railroad tracks in January, 1874, . . . the union elected a committee of four to consult with the plant superintendent about the price the workmen were to receive for the work. They agreed on a scale of $1.13 per ton, which the committee brought back to the lodge for its approval.

There followed an intriguing process. The members soon accepted the company offer, then turned to the major task of dividing the $1.13 among themselves. Each member stated his own price. When they were added up, the total was 3¾ cents higher than the company offer. By a careful revision of the figures, each runback buggyman was cut 2 cents, and the gang buggyman given an extra ¼ of a cent to settle the bill. By the final reckoning, 19¼ cents went to the roller, 13 cents to the rougher up, 10 cents to the rougher down, 9 cents to the catcher, 8¼ cents to each of the four hookers, 5 cents each to the runout hooker and the two runback buggymen, and 13¾ cents to the gang buggyman, half of whose earnings were turned over to his non-union helper.[22]

The Amalgamated Association of Iron, Steel, and Tin Workers, which was the union to which the skilled workers belong, was reputed to be the strongest union of its day. It gave "the skilled workers authority over every aspect of steel production."[23] Like the "inside contractor system" in the arms industry, which it resembled and which is described below, the contracting system in steel was characterized by costly haggling and inflexibility. Operating inefficiency developed, and innovations were suppressed. Examples cited by Stone include the following:

1. The consent and approval of the executive committee within each department was needed to fill a vacant position.

2. The details of the work were subject to recurring dispute.

3. Output per worker was restricted.

4. Production procedures were proscribed: ". . . the proportion of scrap that might be used in running a furnace was fixed; the quality of pig-iron was stated; the puddlers' use of brick and fire clay was forbidden, with exceptions; the labor of assistants was defined."

5. Presumably to perfect and maintain their monopoly over jobs, skilled workers were prohibited from teaching other workers.

---

[22] Stone (ibid., p. 64) relies on David Montgomery for this example (undated ref., pp. 3–4).

[23] Stone, "Origins of Job Structures," p. 64.

6. Changes in the physical plant could not be made without the approval of the executive committee of the union, which prevented the company from realizing greater labor productivity by reorganizing or mechanizing labor tasks.

7. Innovations of a labor-saving kind were discouraged: "The many innovations introduced between 1860 and 1890, of which the most notable was the Bessemer converter, increased the size and capacity of the furnaces and mills, but they generally did not replace men with machines."[24]

The resulting inefficiencies were apparent to the companies. Andrew Carnegie and Henry Clay Frick resolved to challenge the union at Carnegie's Homestead mill, which was reputed to be the strongest lodge of the Amalgamated Association. A lockout was ordered in 1892, and Frick announced that the mill would thenceforth be operated non-union. Violence resulted, with members of the union pitted against scabs and Pinkerton agents. The support of state and federal governments helped Carnegie and Frick prevail. Whether emboldened by the success of Carnegie and Frick, or out of realization that their competitive viability rested on their being likewise able to disaffiliate with the Amalgamated Association, other steel companies challenged and beat the union as well. Association membership, which peaked at twenty-five thousand in 1892, was down to ten thousand in 1898. By 1910 the entire steel industry was non-union. The effects of the breaking of the power of the skilled workers are summarized by Stone as follows: "The decade that followed the Homestead defeat brought unprecedented developments in every stage of steel-making. The rate of innovation in steel has never been equaled. Electric trolleys, the pig casting machine, the Jones mixer, and mechanical ladle cars transformed the blast furnace. Electric traveling cranes in the Bessemer converter, and the Wellman charger in the open hearth did away with almost all the manual aspects of steel production proper. And electric cars and rising-and-falling tables made the rolling mills a continuous operation."[25]

Having broken the union's grip on procedures did not, however, assure the steel industry that its labor force would thereafter be organized efficiently. Such efficiency required that new institutional structures be devised. The objectives of the steps that were taken seem mainly to have been designed to (1) supply affirmative incentives for

[24] Ibid., pp. 64–65.
[25] Ibid., p. 66.

productivity, (2) tie the interests of the workers to the firm over the long term, (3) develop the requisite work skills among inexperienced workers, and (4) organize the work to preclude subsequent loss of control by the company. Although Stone interprets the various steps that were taken to realize these objectives as pernicious and evidence of a continuing class struggle between workers and employers,[26] I would like to emphasize a different aspect: the incentive to challenge the union in the first place and the efforts to organize labor subsequently were principally geared to achieving efficiency, the rewards for which, once the new methods were imitated by rivals and rates of return were driven down to competitive levels, were enjoyed by society.[27] Whether "a system of job rotation, one in which the workers themselves allocated work, would have been just as rational and effective a way of organizing production" is easy to assert but is surely unproven.[28] Indeed, my examination of the limitations of peer-group organizations elsewhere suggests that the self-organizing mode favored by Stone has severe disabilities.[29] By contrast, hierarchy has a number of features which, as compared with nonhierarchical modes of organization of the kind favored by Stone and others, give it a significant efficiency advantage. For example, hierarchy (1) extends the bounds on rationality by permitting the specialization of decision making and economizing on communication expense; (2) permits additional incentive and control techniques to be brought to bear in a more selective manner, thereby serving to curb small-numbers opportunism; (3) permits interdependent units to adapt to unforeseen contingencies in a coordinated way and furthermore serves to "absorb" uncertainty; (4) permits small-numbers bargaining indeterminacies to be resolved by fiat; and (5) extends the constitutional

[26] Ibid., p. 93.

[27] Carnegie and Frick were the early beneficiaries, while the skilled workers who lost their strategic position in the organization of steel making, together with rival firms that were as yet unadapted, were the early losers. But the reorganization accomplished by Carnegie and Frick could be easily imitated and, indeed, quickly was. The result is that costs of steel were considerably reduced and, as competition in the product market made its effects felt, prices were driven down to cost levels (which appears to have been the long-run outcome). The resulting economies thus redounded to the benefit of society at large. The upshot is that once systems considerations are taken into account, the social consequences of organizational innovations that have cost saving properties are commonly better than an examination of such phenomena in the short run or in isolation would reveal.

[28] Stone, "Origins of Job Structures," p. 166.

[29] Williamson, *Markets and Hierarchies*, chap. 3.

powers to perform an audit, thereby narrowing (prospectively at least) the information gap that obtains between autonomous agents.

These gains are not had without cost, however. Peer groups afford valued involvement relations that are upset, in some degree, by hierarchy. Not only is transparent inequality of rank objectionable to some individuals,[30] but auditing and experience rating may offend their sense of individual and collective well-being. Those individuals who value peer-group involvements highly will presumably be prepared to incur certain productivity losses—if indeed, for the reasons that I have set out elsewhere, such losses are commonly incurred when manufacturing (though perhaps not service) activities are organized as peer groups.

INTERMEDIATE PRODUCT MARKETS

Assume that the product in question is technically complex and that it needs to be supplied on a semicontinuous basis. Assume also that periodic redesign and/or volume changes, unless deterred by reason of contractual disabilities, are made in response to changing environmental conditions. Three alternative supply arrangements can be considered: a once-for-all contingent claims contract, an incomplete long-term contract, and a series of short-term contracts.

MARKET CONTRACTING

The operational limitations of complex contingent claims contracts are widely appreciated.[31] Bounded rationality makes it impossible, or prohibitively costly, to attempt to write the comprehensive contract in which contingent supply relations are exhaustively stipulated. Consider therefore an intermediate form of contracting—namely, incomplete long-term contracts which include a profit sharing arrangement—and sequential spot contracts.

That incomplete contracts, without more, pose trading risks is obvious: the natural posture for each party is to bargain opportunistically when contractual ambiguities develop. But might the hazards of contractual incompleteness be overcome by (1) introducing a general clause

[30] Note, however, that there was transparent inequality between the skilled workers and the unskilled workers, and the wage rates among skilled workers, both before and after the reorganization, varied. Stone, "Origins of Job Structures," p. 126.

[31] R. Radner, "Problems in the Theory of Markets under Uncertainty," *American Economic Review* 60 (May, 1970): 454–460; Meade, *Controlled Economy*.

into the contract to the effect that the parties agree to be guided during contract execution by joint profit maximization considerations and (2) inventing an appropriate sharing rule that would induce the parties to adhere to the agreement? The purpose of such an agreement is to encourage the parties to behave cooperatively, in a joint profit maximizing way, when unforeseen contingencies develop.

The issue is of interest not merely for our purposes here, but it also has a bearing on what Leonid Hurwicz refers to as "incentive compatibility."[32] The questions of concern to Hurwicz are (1) whether participants to a nonatomistic market exchange who do not openly defy the prescribed rules (the rule of principal interest is that they behave as price takers) can successfully cheat and (2) whether alternative rules of market exchange can be devised which lead to Pareto optimality. He shows that price-taking rules can be successfully evaded if parties employ false preference maps.[33] He also contends that autonomous bilateral trading with a sharing rule sometimes leads to joint profit maximization.[34]

This last result crucially depends, however, on an assumption that one of the parties behaves throughout as a fully truthful price taker. I submit that sharing rules will not reliably lead to joint profit maximization if both parties are treated *symmetrically* and are allowed to enter false statements or produce false signals. Consider the following sharing rule arrangements:

1. Faced with an unanticipated change in circumstances, the parties will (a) earn π_1 and π_2 respectively if no adaptation is made (that is, present period practices are unchanged from the previous period), and (b) earn $G > \pi_1 + \pi_2$ if they adapt in such a way as to maximize joint profits.

2. The rules for dividing G between the parties are as follows (where $0 < \alpha < 1$): (a) party 1 will receive αG if $\alpha G > \pi_1$ and $(1 - \alpha)G > \pi_2$, π_1 if $\alpha G < \pi_1$, or $G - \pi_2$ if $(1 - \alpha)G < \pi_2$ (in which case party 2 gets π_2 and $G - \pi_2 > \pi_1$), and (b) party 2 will receive $(1 - \alpha)G$ if $(1 - \alpha)G > \pi_2$ and $\alpha G > \pi_1$, π_2 if $(1 - \alpha)G < \pi_2$, or $G - \pi_1$ if $\alpha G < \pi_1$ (in which case party 1 gets π_1 and $G - \pi_1 > \pi_2$).

---

[32] Hurwicz, "On Informationally Decentralized Systems," pp. 320–334; L. Hurwicz, "The Design of Mechanisms for Resource Allocation," *American Economic Review* 63 (May, 1973): 23–27.

[33] Hurwicz, "On Informationally Decentralized Systems," pp. 324–332.

[34] Hurwicz, "Design of Mechanisms," pp. 25–26.

Since each party can do no worse and will usually do better by adapting and employing the sharing rule, the incomplete contract does not appear to impede efficiency or occasion costly haggling. Rather, the contrivance of a general clause and sharing rule seems to give the parties to an incomplete long-term contract the requisite incentives to adapt efficiently in joint profit maximizing.

But, as might be anticipated, there is a hitch. The foregoing assumes that π_1, π_2, and G are all known or can easily be estimated, while in fact they are unknown and, despite great effort and expense, can ordinarily be estimated only imperfectly. Uncertain revenue streams and, even more, uncertain cost streams must be estimated. To the extent that information sets incompletely overlap—which, given task idiosyncrasies and differential exposure to environmental circumstances, they clearly will—each party can be expected to supply incomplete and biased data to the estimators when it suits his purposes. Costly haggling predictably ensues. Hurwicz skirts these issues by assuming that one of the parties to the transaction is continuously truthful, which is plainly heroic.

Both complete and incomplete once-for-all contracts thus experience difficulties. The former are flawed by the great cost of anticipating contingencies and specifying efficient adaptations at the outset. Despite the contrivance of a general clause and sharing rule, the latter is beset by costly haggling. Might then short-term contracts be employed instead? These presumably would permit terms to be redrawn at the contract renewal interval; new information could be appropriately taken into account as events unwind, and only a short-term forecast of the immediate future would be required.

But while short-term contracts have advantages in these respects, they also pose distinctive problems of their own. Thus, if either (1) efficient supply requires investment in special-purpose, long-lived equipment or (2) the winner of the original contract acquires a cost advantage by reason of first-mover advantages (such as unique location or learning, including the acquisition of undisclosed or proprietary technical and managerial procedures and task-specific labor skills), then resort to short-term contracts as a means of filling a requirement for semicontinuous supply is unlikely to prove satisfactory. The difficulty with condition (1) is that optimal investment considerations favor the award of a long-term contract to permit the supplier to amortize his investment confidently. But, as just indicated, incomplete long-term contracts pose adaptive, sequential decision-making problems. Consequently, optimal investment and optimal sequential adaptation processes are in conflict in this instance.

Whether first-mover advantages, assuming that they exist, have any bearing on vertical integration might be disputed on the grounds that initial bidders will capitalize anticipated future gains. While this argument is surely correct, it is hardly dispositive. For one thing, unless the total supply requirements are stipulated, "buying-in" strategies are risky. Also, and in relation, the alternative supply price is not independent of the terms that the buyer may subsequently offer to rivals. Moreover, alternative supply price is merely an upper bound; an aggressive buyer may attempt to obtain a price at the level of current costs on each round. Haggling could be expected to ensue. Short-term contracts thus experience what may be serious limitations in circumstances where nontrivial first-mover advantages obtain.

It is relevant to note that the condition of technological interdependency involving flow-process economies between otherwise separable stages of production is really a special case of the argument of contractual incompleteness. The contractual dilemma is as follows: On the one hand, it may be prohibitively costly, if not infeasible, to specify contractually the full range of contingencies and stipulate appropriate responses between stages. On the other hand, if the contract is seriously incomplete in these respects but, once the original negotiations are settled, the contracting parties are locked into a bilateral exchange, the divergent interests between the parties will predictably lead to individually opportunistic behavior and joint losses. The advantages of integration thus are not that technological (flow-process) economies are unavailable to nonintegrated firms, but that integration harmonizes interests (or reconciles differences, often by fiat) and permits an efficient (adaptive, sequential) decision process to be used. More generally, arguments favorable to integration that turn on considerations of "supply reliability" commonly reduce to the issue of contractual incompleteness.

VERTICAL INTEGRATION

The Inside Contracting System. When the above-indicated limitations of autonomous contracting are considered, a shift from market to hierarchy warrants examination. However, rather than move immediately to common ownership combined with an employment relation, might the unified ownership of plant and equipment between the successive stages suffice? Consider in this connection what John Buttrick has described as the "inside contracting system": "Under the system of inside contracting, the management of a firm provided floor space and machinery, supplied raw material and working capital, and arranged for the sale of the final product. The gap between raw material and finished product, however, was filled not by paid employees arranged in (a) descending hierarchy . . . but by [inside] contractors, to whom the production job was delegated. They hired their own employees, supervised the work process, and received a [negotiated] piece rate from the company."[35] The system developed among New England manufacturing plants at the time of the Civil War and was continued in many of them until World War I. While not identical to the contracting arrangements in the steel industry before the Homestead strike, it bears an amazing resemblance to them.

The inside contracting system had the attractive attributes that it (1) provided for the aggregation at a single location of a series of primary work groups that were involved in successive manufacturing processes, thereby reducing transportation expense and assuring that a cheek-by-jowl association would develop, with corresponding economies of communication; (2) permitted the capitalist with relatively little technical knowledge to employ his capital productively while limiting his involvement to negotiating contracts with the inside department heads, inspecting and coordinating the output of the various departments, and taking responsibility for final sales; and (3) provided the inside contractors (first-level supervisors) with incentives for efficient labor performance in both supervisory and process innovation respects. In addition, although neither is mentioned by Buttrick, (4) the monopoly powers of the various inside contractors were, in relation to supply by an exclusive outside supplier, presumably limited by the capitalist's ownership of plant and equipment, and (5) problems of information impactedness, which might otherwise inhibit new investment, were avoided. The system nevertheless experienced numerous difficulties.[36] For example, (1) a bilateral monopoly position, albeit restrained, developed between the parties; (2) the periodic renegotiation of rates induced the contractor to hoard information and to delay process innovations; (3) the flow of components was difficult to regulate; (4) work-in-process inventories

35 J. Buttrick, "The Inside Contracting System," *Journal of Economic History* 12 (Summer, 1952): 201–202.

36 Ibid., pp. 210–215.

were excessive and, since each stage incurred only its own direct labor costs, later-stage processes were wasteful of components on which early-stage work was completed; and (5) contractor incomes were sometimes excessive in relation to those of the capitalist, endangering the status of company officials. The system moreover was beset by defective incentives in that (6) equipment was not used and maintained with appropriate care; (7) process innovations were biased in favor of labor-saving, as against materials-saving, innovations; and (8) incentives for product innovation were insufficient.

Buttrick attributes the supplanting of the inside contractor system by a hierarchical control apparatus in the Winchester Repeating Arms Company to the conjunction of internal personnel changes in the late 1800's with external "scientific management" developments in the early 1900's.[37] But whatever the immediate explanation for the abandonment of inside contracting at Winchester, or any other firm, it is evident that the inside contractor system possessed serious defects and that to the extent that a more comprehensive system of hierarchical controls served to mitigate these defects (and did not incur offsetting costs), an eventual change in organization form was to be expected.

Although defects 4 and 7 above might have been remedied by making simple changes in the internal pricing system, the other disabilities of inside contracting appear really to be immanent. Given uncertainty, from which arises the occasion to make coordinated adaptations between successive parts, and bounded rationality, from which the limitations on long-term contracts and the infeasibility of a flat (single-stage) hierarchy develop, the defects listed are manifestations of small-numbers bargaining relations in which conditions of opportunism and information impactedness obtain.

For example, suppose that all of the cost data and other related data bearing on the exchange were costlessly available to both capitalist and contractor (that is, there is no information impactedness). Long-term contracts containing a general clause and sharing rule (of the type described above) could then be written. Given that a large number of bidders are qualified to compete at the outset, the bilateral monopoly problem (defect 1) would vanish. Alternatively, if winners of original bids made self-enforcing promises not to exploit first-mover advantages at contract renewal intervals, short-term contracts could be written and the

[37] Ibid., pp. 213–220.

initial large-numbers condition would be sufficient to assure competitive supply relations throughout. Inasmuch, however, as both of these assumptions are a fiction (the necessary information is not costlessly available, and promises of the sort described are unreliable), the bilateral monopoly condition emerges.

The information hoarding and strategic delay of process innovations (defect 2) are manifestations of the gaming behavior which the absence of full information permits. Information relating to costs and technology was asymmetrically distributed to the advantage of the inside contractor. Without opportunism, this distribution would pose no problem. But the inside contractor evidently was opportunistic, whence defect 2 resulted.

The disruptions in component flows between the parts (defect 3) can be attributed in the first instance to contractual incompleteness (bounded rationality). In principle, this disruption could be overcome by relying on the capitalist to coordinate the parts flow in an adaptive, sequential manner. Given, however, that each inside contractor assesses the consequences of intervention by the capitalist in terms of the effect of his individual profit stream (again, promises to be guided by considerations of joint profit maximization are unenforceable), this corrective proves unacceptable. The defect, therefore, continues.

The status threat posed by defect 5 is somewhat special. I conjecture that it arises because the inside contractor was relatively secure against displacement (because of first-mover advantages) and because he was not fully candid in disclosing his true costs to the capitalist. The normal correspondence between hierarchical position and income was sometimes upset as a result, which the capitalist regarded as a status threat. Moreover, adverse efficiency consequences can result if the capitalist attempts to reassert his primacy by converting what could be instrumental contractual relationships into subordination relationships instead. Dysfunctional performance easily obtains when such power contests are waged.

The equipment utilization problems referred to in defect 6 are akin in their origins to the component flow problems discussed above, while the equipment maintenance problems are a reflection of free-riding behavior. The defective incentives for product innovation (defect 8) are due, probably, to appropriability problems. Although the capitalist has an interest in improving the product, he is able, given the first-mover advantages which inside contractors acquire, to introduce such changes only by securing the consent of these contractors. The prospect of having to bargain and the inability to appropriate the full value of product inno-vations reduces his incentive to undertake research and development efforts.[38]

The Employment Relation Extended. A chronic problem with which economic organization must contend is how to harness opportunism. For the reasons given above, individual workers sometimes acquire mo-nopoly power over jobs. Also, as the above discussion of the inside con-tracting system reveals, the same holds true for managers of functional departments. While individual interests are promoted by exercising these powers for private gain, the system as a whole incurs additional costs and may be rendered nonviable.

A systems solution that transforms the relation between the parties from one of qualified antagonism to more complete cooperation is clearly indicated. Extending the employment relation to include department managers serves to promote such an outcome. The firm offers man-agers job security and an internal equity system, in return for which managers agree to being evaluated in terms of their contribution to the system as a whole, as revealed in part by their attitude of cooperation.

What one wants to devise is a contractual relation that promises fair (competitive) returns, promotes adaptive efficiency, and is relatively sat-isfying in terms of the involvement experience. Inside contracting is de-ficient in the first two respects and may pose problems in the third. Shifting inside contractors from a quasi-autonomous bargaining status to an employment relation has advantages in the first two—and indeed pos-sibly all three—respects. Several things occur when the inside contractor becomes a manager. First, he no longer has claims on a semi-independent profit stream. Second, his operations become subject to an internal audit. His incentives to engage in opportunistic behavior are attenuated for the first of these reasons, and his advantage of information impactedness is reduced by the second. More generally, he becomes a member of a team and, as a member of the team, becomes subject to a different set of ex-pectations regarding his relation to the whole than is the case when quasi-autonomy is preserved and self-seeking is expected. Informal group influences are brought more systematically to bear when behavior con-trary to the interests of the firm occurs.

In addition to being audited and evaluated, managers are subject to

[38] See Buttrick's discussion of the Winchester Company's experience in this connection, ibid., p. 214.

a relatively refined internal reward and compliance machinery. The expectation that employment terms and prospects are subject to fine tuning adjustments serves to promote functional and check dysfunctional behavior.

CAPITAL MARKETS [39]

THE FRICTIONLESS FICTION

Received microtheory is loath to concede that capital markets may fail to operate frictionlessly. Partly for this reason, the fiction that managers operate firms in fully profit-maximizing ways is maintained. It is argued that any attempt by opportunistic managers to promote their own goals at the expense of corporate profitability would occasion intervention through the capital market. Effective control of the corporation would be transferred to those parties who perceived the lapse; profit-maximizing behavior would then be quickly restored.

Parties responsible for the detection and correction of deviant behavior in the firm would, of course, participate in the greater profits which the reconstituted management would realize. This participation would not, however, be large. One reason is that incumbent managements, by assumption, have little opportunity for inefficiency or malfeasance because any tendency toward waywardness would be quickly detected and costlessly extinguished. Accordingly, the incremental profit gain occasioned by takeover would be small. Moreover, the market for corporate control is presumably one in which large numbers of qualified takeover agents are noncollusively organized. Competitive offers assure that the takeover gains mainly redound to the stockholders.

Shorey Peterson's sanguine views on corporate behavior are roughly of this kind. He characterizes the latitude to disregard the profit goal as "small" and goes on to observe that "[f]ar from being an ordinary election, a proxy battle is a *catastrophic* event whose mere possibility is a threat, and not remote when affairs are in *conspicuous* disarray." Indeed, even "stockholder suits . . . may be provoked by evidence of *serious* self-dealing" (emphasis added). On the principle that the efficacy of legal prohibitions is to be judged "not by guilt discovered but by guilt dis-

[39] The argument here follows Williamson, "Economics of Antitrust," pp. 1480–1491.

couraged," he concludes that such suits, albeit rare, may have accomplished much in helping to police the corporate system.[40]

While I do not mean to suggest that such deterrence has not been important, Peterson's observations appear to me to be consistent with the proposition that traditional capital markets are beset by serious problems of information impactedness and incur nontrivial displacement costs if the incumbent management is disposed to resist the takeover effort. Why else the reference to catastrophic events, conspicuous disarray, and serious self-dealing? Systems that are described in these terms are not ones for which a delicately conceived control system can be said to be operating. As recent military history makes clear, controls that involve a large and discrete shock to the system are appropriate only when an offense reaches egregious proportions. The scope for opportunism, accordingly, is wider than Peterson seems prepared to concede.

The reasons why traditional control of management performance by the capital market is relatively crude are that internal conditions in the firm are not widely known or easy to discover (information impactedness) and that those seeking to gain control of the firm (takeover agents) might well take opportunistic advantage of the shareholders' bounded rationality. Information impactedness means that outsiders cannot make confident judgments that the firm has departed from profit maximizing standards, except with difficulty. The firm is a complex organization, and its performance is a joint consequence of exogenous economic events, rival behavior, and internal decisions. Causal inferences are correspondingly difficult to make, and, hence, opportunism is costly to detect. Moreover, once detected, convincing interested stockholders that a displacement effort ought to be supported encounters problems. Inasmuch as time and the analytical capacity of stockholders are not free goods (which is to say that the limits imposed by bounded rationality must be respected), the would-be takeover agent cannot simply display all of his evidence and expect stockholders to evaluate it and reach the "appropriate" conclusion. Rather, any appeal to the stockholders must be made in terms of highly digested interpretations of the facts. Although this helps to overcome the stockholder's bounded rationality problem, it poses another: How is the interested stockholder

---

[40] S. Peterson, "Corporate Control and Capitalism," *Quarterly Journal of Economics* 79 (Feb., 1965): 11, 21.

(or his agent) to distinguish between bona fide and opportunistic take-over agents?

The upshot of these remarks is that the transaction costs associated with *traditional* capital market processes for policing management, of the sort described by Peterson, are considerable. Correspondingly, the range of discretionary behavior open to incumbent managements is rather wider than Peterson and other supporters of the fiction of the frictionless capital market concede.[41]

One of the more attractive attributes of the conglomerate form of organization (of the appropriate kind) is that it serves to overcome certain of these limitations of traditional capital markets.[42] The argument, which I will develop below, essentially reduces to the proposition that conglomerate firms (of the appropriate kind) function as miniature capital markets with consequences for resource allocation which are, on balance, beneficial.

This argument poses, however, the following paradox: under conventional assumptions that more choices are always preferred to fewer, the banking system ought to have superior resource allocation properties to any miniature imitation thereof. Put differently, why should a miniature capital market ever be preferred to the real thing? As might be anticipated, transaction cost considerations supply the resolution. If decision makers could be easily apprised of an ever wider range of alternatives and choose intelligently among them, there would be no occasion to supplant the traditional market. But it is elementary that where complex events have to be evaluated, information processing capacities are quickly reached. As a result, expanding the range of choice may not only be without purpose but can have net detrimental effects. A trade-off between breadth of information, in which respect the banking system may be presumed to have the advantage, and depth of information,

---

[41] Smiley estimates that "per share transaction costs are approximately 14% of the market value of the shares after a successful [tender] offer" and suggests that such a cost level warrants "skepticism about the efficacy of the tender offer in constraining managers to act in the best interests of their shareholders" (R. Smiley, "The Economics of Tender Offers," [Ph.D. diss., Stanford University, July 1973], pp. 124–125).

[42] This assumes that the hierarchic structure and internal control processes of the conglomerate satisfy the requirements that I have stipulated elsewhere. Although there are certainly other types of conglomerates, those which lack an underlying efficiency rationale (as contrasted with a temporary financial rationale) will presumably be sorted out in the long run. Those which pose financial problems are best dealt with by the SEC. My discussion sidesteps these and focuses on antitrust issues.

which is the advantage of the specialized firm, is involved. The conglomerate can be regarded as an intermediate form that, ideally, optimizes with respect to the breadth-depth trade-off.[43] Although the number of alternatives considered by a conglomerate's management is limited, its knowledge (*ex post* and *ex ante*) with respect to each remains relatively deep. Operating as it does as an internal control agent, its auditing powers are more extensive and its control instruments are more selective than an external control agent can employ. Information impactedness is reduced as a result, and opportunism is attenuated in the process.

CONGLOMERATE ORGANIZATION

The failure on the part of received microtheory to regard the internal organization of the firm as interesting is, I believe, responsible for what Richard Posner has called "the puzzle of the conglomerate corporation."[44] This puzzle has not, however, deterred those who most rely on received microtheory from venturing the opinion that the conglomerate is innocent of anticompetitive purpose or potential and ought not to be an object of antitrust prosecution. But an affirmative rationale for the conglomerate, based on received microtheory, has yet to appear.[45]

The populist critics of the conglomerate have not allowed this lapse to go unnoticed. Robert Solo's views are perhaps representative. He contends that "when faced with a truly dangerous phenomenon, such as the conglomerate mergers of the 1960's, produced by financial manipulators making grist for their security mills, the professional antitrust economists were silent. Like other realities of a modern enterprise, this phenomenon, which will probably subvert management effectiveness and

[43] For a somewhat similar interpretation of the conglomerate, see A. A. Alchian and H. Demsetz, "Production, Information Costs, and Economic Organization," *American Economic Review* 62 (Dec., 1972): 777–795. For a cross-sectional study of conglomerates (which, however, does not make organizational form distinctions), see J. F. Weston and S. K. Mansinghka, "Tests of the Efficiency Performance of Conglomerate Firms," *Journal of Finance* 26 (Sept., 1971): 919–936.

[44] R. A. Posner, "The Appropriate Scope of Regulation in the Cable Television Industry," *Bell Journal of Economics and Management Science* 3 (Spring, 1972): 204.

[45] Some contend that reciprocity has attractive efficiency properties, in that it facilitates price shading in otherwise rigid price circumstances. While I concede that reciprocity can be used in this way, I do not find it an especially compelling economic rationale for the conglomerate. Surely the entire conglomerate movement is not to be explained in these terms. Also, I think it useful to appreciate that reciprocity can have inefficiency consequences. Once begun, perhaps as a price shading technique, it may be continued because it suits the bureaucratic preferences of the sales staff.

organizational rationale for generations, is outside their conceptual framework."[46]

Several things should be said in this connection. First, in defense of antitrust economists I would point out that financial manipulation is not their main concern. This is the principal business of the Securities and Exchange Commission rather than the Antitrust Division. Although Solo might object, with cause, that economists are excessively narrow, nevertheless, as matters are divided up currently, it is the security specialists who are presumably at fault. Second, and more important, Solo's sweeping charges leave the particular dangers of the conglomerate phenomenon completely unspecified. Third, I agree that an understanding of the conglomerate requires an extension of the conventional framework. Nevertheless, I think it noteworthy that populist critics of the conglomerate and received microtheorists alike pay little heed to the resource allocation consequences, in the form of capital market substitution effects, of internal organization. Finally, conglomerates come in a variety of forms and have a variety of purposes. Accordingly, any attack on conglomerates should be selective rather than broadside.

Responses to organizational innovations vary. The initial response of rival firms and financial analysts is typically to disregard such changes. Partly this is because "reorganization" is a common reaction by firms that are experiencing adversity. Discerning whether the response is intended to eliminate accumulated bureaucratic deadwood or to buy time from the stockholders by giving the impression that corrective action has been taken or whether (instead of in addition) it represents a really fundamental change in structure that warrants more widespread attention is initially quite difficult. Expressed in transaction cost terms, the problem is that opportunistic structural changes cannot easily be distinguished from fundamental ones on account of information impactedness and bounded rationality. Given the incapacity (or high costs) of communicating about and abstractly assessing the importance of organizational changes, the tendency is to wait and see how organizational changes manifest themselves in performance consequences. Inasmuch as performance is a function of many factors other than organizational structure alone, sorting out the effect of organizational changes is difficult. Therefore, a long recognition lag between fundamental innovation and widespread imitation is common.

[46] R. A. Solo, "New Maths and Old Sterilities," *Saturday Review*, Jan. 22, 1972, pp. 47–48.

Public policy analysts of populist persuasions are prone to regard organizational innovations as having anticompetitive purposes. Rarely are such innovations thought to have possible efficiency consequences, mainly because efficiency is thought to reside in technological rather than transactional factors. Harlan Blake's widely admired assessment of the conglomerate and its policy implications is in this technological tradition. Like Solo's, his treatment tends to be global rather than selective. References to "mergers whose anticompetitive potential is so widespread that it might appropriately be described as having an effect upon the economic system as a whole—in every line of commerce in every section of the country"—are unguarded.[47] An understanding of the conglomerate phenomenon will be better promoted by delimiting the attack.

For one thing, organization form distinctions, of which Blake makes none, ought to be made. Size considerations aside, he treats all conglomerates as an undifferentiated group. But there are indications that even some courts may be more discriminating than this.[48] More generally, the point is this: just as the structure of markets influences the performance of markets, so likewise allowance ought to be made for the possibility that internal organization influences firm performance.

Although Blake recognizes that the conglomerate may have had invigorating effects on the market for corporate control,[49] he does not regard its ability to reallocate assets internally from lower-yield to higher-yield uses as an affirmative factor. If anything, he seems to suggest that internal resource reallocations are undesirable as compared to reallocations in the capital market.[50] In an economy, however, where returning funds to and reallocating funds by the capital market incurs nontrivial

[47] H. M. Blake, "Conglomerate Mergers and the Antitrust Laws," *Columbia Law Review* 73 (Mar., 1973): 555–592.

[48] Thus, the district court in the *ITT–Hartford Insurance* case was prepared to dismiss reciprocity arguments by the government because of organization form considerations. United States *v.* International Tel. & Tel. Corp., 306 F. Supp. 766, 779, 782–783, 790, 795 (D. Conn. 1969) (hold separate order); United States *v.* International Tel. & Tel. Corp., 324 F. Supp. 19, 45 (D. Conn. 1970) (judgment for defendant).

[49] Blake, "Conglomerate Mergers," pp. 562–563, 572–573.

[50] Blake observes in this connection that "one objective of antitrust policy is to preserve a competitive system—a structure of the economy in which all economic units in the unregulated sector are subject to the continuing discipline of competitive market forces. The creation of vast conglomerate enclaves in which decisions with respect to resource use are insulated from these forces is inconsistent with the basic tenets of antitrust policy" (ibid., p. 574).

transaction costs and/or where managers of specialized firms have an opportunistic preference to retain earnings, the internal reallocation of resources to uses returning a higher yield is what most commends the conglomerate as compared with similarly constituted specialized firms. The conglomerate in these circumstances assumes miniature capital market responsibilities of an energizing kind. That Blake is unimpressed with such consequences is explained by his assessment (which he shares with conventional microtheory) that only economies having technological origins are deserving of consideration and his conviction that the supplanting of "competitive market forces," however feeble these forces may be, by internal organization is anticompetitive.[51]

Blake also finds conglomerates objectionable because of "hard evidence to support the no longer novel theory—and widely held belief in the business community—that large conglomerates facing each other in several markets tend to be less competitive in price than regional or smaller firms."[52] There are two problems with the argument. First, I would scarcely characterize the evidence on which Blake relies as "hard." Part of the evidence cited by Blake is Scherer's discussion of the "spheres of influence hypothesis." But Scherer is very careful to characterize the evidence quite differently, noting that even with respect to the prewar international chemical industry, which aside from marine cartels is his only Western example, the evidence is fragmentary. With respect to other industries he concludes that "there is a dearth of evidence on spheres of influence accords."[53]

Second, the definition of a conglomerate requires attention. Are all specialized firms (such as National Tea, to which Blake earlier refers) that operate similar plants or stores in geographically dispersed markets really to be regarded as conglomerates? Stretching the definition of a conglomerate to include geographically dispersed, but otherwise specialized, enterprises shrinks the number of nonconglomerate large firms to insignificance. If "conglomerate" is defined in terms of product diversification, Blake (and the Federal Trade Commission) ought to be expected to generate examples of abuse of conglomerate structure from the universe of product-diversified firms. If instead all large multimarket firms, whatever their product specialization ratios, are the objectionable

[51] Ibid., pp. 574–579.
[52] Ibid., p. 570.
[53] F. M. Scherer, *Industrial Market Structure and Economic Performance* (Chicago: Rand-McNally, 1970), pp. 278–280.

subset, the suspect firms ought to be expressly identified in this way rather than by designating them as "conglomerates."

Although I share Blake's suspicions with respect to the behavior of *very* large product-diversified firms (which is the narrower definition of the conglomerate), the facts have yet to be assembled. As things stand now, the price competitiveness of such firms can not be adversely distinguished from that of other large multimarket organizations.

The data are somewhat better with respect to reciprocity. Blake conjectures in this connection that "empirical research, if it could be carried out, would show that reciprocity is as inevitable a result of widespread conglomerate structure as price rigidity is a consequence of oligopoly structure"[54]—where, apparently, the latter, and hence the former, is believed to be extensive. Jesse Markham's recent study of conglomerates, which was unavailable to Blake, suggests otherwise: "highly diversified companies are no more, and may be even less, given to reciprocity than large corporations generally."[55]

The upshot is that subject to the qualifications about organization form, which I have repeatedly emphasized, the conglomerate is neither an anomaly nor an anticompetitive structure. To the contrary, it has attractive properties both because it makes the market for corporate control more credible, thereby inducing self-policing among otherwise opportunistic managements, and because it promotes the reallocation of resources to high-yield uses. Except, therefore, among giant-sized firms, where the risk of offsetting political distortions is seriously posed and economic gains are more dubious, a more sympathetic posture on the part of the antitrust enforcement agencies toward conglomerates would seem warranted.

The work of William Hamilton and Michael Moses on corporate financial planning within the International Utilities Corporation illustrates the strategic resource allocation process in a diversified firm.[56] As will be apparent, the effort to model the strategic resource allocation process at IUC has been an ambitious and costly undertaking. As compared, however, with the alternative of operating the large, complex,

---

[54] Blake, "Conglomerate Mergers," p. 569.

[55] J. Markham, *Conglomerate Enterprise and Public Policy* (Boston: Harvard Graduate School, Division of Research, 1973), p. 176.

[56] W. F. Hamilton and M. A. Moses, "An Optimization Model for Corporate Financial Planning," *Operations Research* 21 (May–June, 1973): 677–692.

diversified firm as a holding company, with attempts at strategic resource allocation very limited, it appears to have much to commend it.

The firm in question is described as one with more than fifty wholly and partially owned subsidiaries with operations in many different countries. The objective of the corporate financial planning model was to permit the headquarters unit better to evaluate proposed subsidiary strategies and assess their financial implications. The optimizing program was designed to maximize "total corporate performance over the multi-period planning horizon without violating important financial, legal, and operating constraints."[57]

The subsidiaries propose plans of two types: those which involve a continuation of current activities and those which involve new initiatives, where the latter include acquisitions, divestments, and market and product extensions.[58] The complex computer model which they devised contained approximately 1,000 variables and 750 constraints. Among the specific applications or results of the model that seem notable are the following:

1. The financial implications of alternative acquisitions are more fully and systematically exposed.

2. Profiles of "desirable" acquisition candidates, given the objectives and prospective financial flows within the firm, are generated to help guide acquisition search.

3. The merits of consciously considering divestment as a part of financial planning were made evident. Indeed, the optimization model was prepared to divest existing business lines in "amounts up to 40 percent of the total [continuation] business." Although divestments of this magnitude were managerially impracticable, and hence divestment constraints were introduced, the model had the property of highlighting divestment as an important attribute of an overall optimizing strategy.

4. The implicit prices associated with traditional rules of thumb were revealed, and in some instances the rules were revised where the implied sacrifices were thought by the management to be excessive.[59]

At best the above is suggestive of what strategic resource allocation entails. To be fully effective, follow-on controls (including *ex post* auditing and selective use of the incentive machinery) are also needed.

[57] Ibid., p. 678.
[58] Ibid., p. 680.
[59] Ibid., pp. 690–691.

My point, however, is that internal resource allocation can be performed in a strategic manner and that, subject to the condition that it does not exceed size and complexity limits (which is a manifestation of bounded rationality), conglomerate organizations that exercise self-discipline in internal control respects (and thus qualify as M-form types) can have, and some do have, attractive properties in miniature capital market respects.

CONCLUDING REMARKS

CONTRASTS WITH ALTERNATIVE APPROACHES

Strong technological assumptions are imbedded in each of the alternative approaches to the firm that is mentioned in my opening remarks. Models of firm behavior of the neoclassical kind ignore the comparative institutional study of transactional efficiency altogether. The assignment of transactions as between firms and markets is taken as given rather than as something to be investigated and, in some crude sense, derived. Although treating the firm as a production function to which a profit-maximizing objective has been assigned is useful for the purpose of deriving equilibrium and comparative statics results, this does not exhaust the range of interesting questions with which economics is concerned. To engage, however, in the study of transactional efficiency requires that a much more microanalytic orientation be adopted and that the properties of hierarchies be expressly examined. This moves outside the neoclassical paradigm.

The Galbraithian view of the firm is likewise technological, but in quite a different way. The study of economics in which the market is prominently featured is regarded as anachronistic, since internal organization has supplanted the market in virtually all significant respects. Conformably, competition in both product and capital markets is held to be dead or dying. The largest five or six hundred corporations purportedly dominate economic activity, and, within each, the preferences of a technological elite (unhappily referred to as the technostructure) prevail. Inasmuch as the firm has effectively pre-empted the market in all significant transactional respects, interesting questions of firm versus market modes of organization are ignored. A healthy regard for the limits of hierarchical organization in opportunistic and bounded rationality respects is nowhere evident.

The views of the New Left are that technology has relatively little to do with the efficient organization of production but that it can be and is used by capitalists to help impose hierarchical modes of organization upon workers when in fact egalitarian modes would be equally efficacious.[60] As contrasted with Galbraith, who fails to acknowledge the limits of hierarchies as size and complexity increase, the New Left is unwilling to concede that hierarchies have any advantages over peer groups whatsoever. Rather, hierarchy is a pernicious mode of organization, the origins for which are to be traced not to transactional economies but to the class struggle instead. My reasons for regarding hierarchies more affirmatively turn on transaction cost considerations which the New Left ignores. As compared with peer groups, simple hierarchy economizes on bounded rationality and serves to attenuate opportunism.[61]

RESEARCH IMPLICATIONS

The comparative institutional study of transactions in the micro-analytic way proposed requires refinement. Although a focus on transactions as the ultimate unit of analysis serves to raise a number of interesting issues and permits these issues to be addressed in a relatively systematic way, a considerable burden of self-discipline must be borne by the analyst. He has, in a sense, too many degrees of freedom at his disposal. If transaction costs of a frivolous kind are blown up out of proportion, the resulting "conclusions" are of dubious weight.

Experience with the paradigm should help to delimit it. Applications of three kinds would appear useful. For one thing, the interpretation of specific historical events in transactional terms will be instructive—both for purposes of developing a deeper understanding of the institutional fabric of society and for purposes of refining the paradigm. Additional case studies of the kinds examined in this chapter would thus be instructive. Second, abstract studies of specific contractual relations can be performed. One with which I am currently involved entails an assessment of the feasibility of franchise bidding for natural monopolies of the kind advocated by Harold Demsetz and Richard Posner.[62] But this

---

[60] S. A. Marglin, "What Do Bosses Do? The Origins and Functions of Hierarchy in Capitalist Production," *Review of Radical Political Economics*, Summer, 1974, pp. 33–60; Stone, "Origins of Job Structures," pp. 61–97; Gordon, "Recession is Capitalism as Usual," pp. 18ff.

[61] Williamson, *Markets and Hierarchies*, chap. 3.

[62] H. Demsetz, "Why Regulate Utilities?" *Journal of Law and Economics* 11 (Apr., 1968): 55–66; Posner, "Regulation in Cable Television."

is merely illustrative. A number of mixed law and economics issues can be usefully examined in this way. This would presumably entail re-examining a large number of issues that Posner studies in his "economic analysis of law" by reformulating these instead in what Arthur Leff has referred to as a "legal approach to economics," in which transaction costs and contractual issues are more prominently featured.[63]

Finally, it should be possible to do empirical work of a more traditional kind in which tests are run to detect whether internal efficiency and economic performance are systematically related to organizational structure. Probably the best tests for such effects will be within a firm in which organizational changes are observed to take place over time. Has reorganization of firms along M-form lines arrested or reversed performance difficulties that were developing and prospectively would have become worse? Is M-form reorganization superior to other organizational alternatives in this respect? The available evidence is consistent with the hypothesis,[64] but it is hardly dispositive.

A more ambitious variant of this approach is to conduct pooled time-series, cross-section tests on a much larger number of firms. It is important, if such were to be attempted, to partial out differences in product characteristics and rivalry, including the extent to which rivals have made prior organizational changes of the M-form kind. In consideration of the difficulty of adjusting for such interfirm differences, it may be more judicious at the outset to make the comparisons within firms or between only small numbers of firms that can be regarded, in competitive respects, as comparable.

[63] R. A. Posner, *Economic Analysis of Law* (New York: Little, Brown, 1972); A. A. Leff, "Teams, Firms, and the Aesthetics of Antitrust," unpublished manuscript, Feb., 1975.

[64] A. D. Chandler, Jr., *Strategy and Structure* (New York: Doubleday, 1966).

Chapter 8

Worker Alienation and the
Structure of the Firm

Eirik G. Furubotn

OVER the last decade, the socialist critique of capitalism has been given new emphasis by the writings of an emerging school of radical political economists.[1] While the members of this dissident group reflect various shades of opinion, and differ somewhat in their interpretations of contemporary social and economic problems, most adhere to what may be termed a neo-Marxist approach.[2] In particular, the radical writers reassert the traditional Marxist claim that virtually all major difficulties arising in a capitalist society derive from the fundamental structure of capitalist institutions. Institutions are regarded as crucial because they are thought to determine the nature of social relations and, thus, to explain the way in which power is exercised by the ruling capitalist class to secure gains at the expense of the mass of workers.

The radical analysis of capitalist society purports to be scientific and dispassionate, but in fact the arguments advanced are usually quite emotional in tone and one-sided in their presentation of problems. Sweeping condemnation is the rule; the apparent objective is to show that all of the real or imagined evils of contemporary America are attributable to the operation of the capitalist system.[3] Legitimate issues may be touched on, but the criticism is almost always greatly exaggerated and distorted. As Gerhart Niemeyer says of this approach: "Its basic orientation is to-

[1] A useful survey of this literature is found in M. Bronfenbrenner, "Radical Economics in America: A 1970 Survey," *Journal of Economic Literature* 8 (Sept. 1970): 747–766.

[2] See T. Parsons, "Commentary on Herbert Gintis, 'A Radical Analysis of Welfare Economics and Individual Development,'" *Quarterly Journal of Economics* 89 (May, 1975): 280–290.

[3] A good example of this type of commentary is R. C. Edwards, M. Reich, and T. B. Weisskopf, *The Capitalist System: A Radical Analysis of American Society* (Englewood Cliffs, N.J.: Prentice-Hall, 1972).

ward the defective, the absurd, the sin in life, which makes it easy to draw forth an endless string of indictments and condemnations, with a resulting wonderful sense of self-justification."[4]

Although the radical school may show a disturbing lack of objectivity and a naïve faith in utopian solutions, its activities cannot be disregarded. The revival of interest in socialist economics means that these ideas will tend to have an impact on the socioeconomic policies of the 1970's. Indeed, the socialist challenge has to be taken seriously for at least two reasons. American society does face some significant and distressing problems, and, at the same time, there is widespread ignorance on the part of the public regarding the true nature of capitalism, its objectives, and its performance. In the interventionist climate that has developed progressively during the postwar period, public confidence in the operation of a free economy has been undermined. And, clearly, if administrative controls have gained acceptance, it is not difficult to believe that there may be some predisposition to experiment with more basic socialist policies.

Radical criticism extends to all of the economic arrangements under capitalism, but the capitalist organization of production comes in for special denunciation by the neo-Marxists; this is one important area where future domestic policy may be influenced by socialist ideology. Ostensibly, the total character of social and economic life is at issue. Capitalist performance is said to be completely unsatisfactory because the very structure of the industrial system forces workers to lead fragmented, unfulfilling lives and to waste their resources acquiring products they neither need nor truly want. Workers are, in short, *alienated*, and, according to Marxist dogma, alienation is inevitable under capitalism since laborers do not own or control the means of production, do not participate in decision making, do not determine what products will be produced, but are, nevertheless, compelled to perform uninteresting, repetitive and often unpleasant work to secure income. From the radical standpoint, market institutions and capitalist control of production give rise to false or misleading standards of efficiency. Thus, instead of using labor and other economic inputs optimally, capitalism generates an inappropriate mix of commodities and reaches what amounts to a second-best solution for the system.

---

[4] G. Niemeyer, "What Will Poor Robin Do Then?" *National Review* 27 (June 20, 1975): 670.

To eliminate or lessen the problem of alienation, institutions have to be restructured so that workers can *control production and determine both the technological and social organization of the work process*. Professor Gintis makes the radical position on this question quite clear:

> I would argue that in this historical period only an expansion of the degree of democratic and participatory control that individuals have over their lives is compatible with full personal development, rewarding social activity, the elimination of class, racial, and sexual antagonisms, and material equality. The contribution of political democracy to this end is vitiated by the totalitarian organization of production. Only democracy and participation in production—i.e., the replacement of the capitalist class by the working class (white collar and blue, black and white, male and female) as the architects of production, and the accountability of managers and technicians to the will of workers—is compatible with equality and full individual development.[5]

In more concrete terms, what seems to be called for is a productive organization akin to the socialist labor-managed firm. That is, to attain the stated democratic ideals, the new structure should permit workers to have virtually unlimited powers in management and decision making and assure labor of a definite share of the firm's profits. Labor management is generally consistent with such requirements and is, moreover, an organizational form with which the world has had a certain amount of practical experience. After the economic reform of 1965, Yugoslavia established as its basic production unit something very close to the pure model of a self-managed firm, and this action was taken at least partly for ideological reasons analogous to those mentioned by Gintis. Thus, for example, in explaining Yugoslav motivations, Professor Horvat is at pains to stress the official line that "without self-government socialism is impossible."[6]

There may be sharp limits to democracy in Yugoslavia, but government rejection of monolithic state control of resources does appear to be genuine. Presumably, most Yugoslav thinkers now believe that state ownership can be a useful device to *initiate* socialist reconstruction, but

---

[5] H. Gintis, "Welfare Economics and Individual Development: A Reply to Talcott Parsons," *Quarterly Journal of Economics* 89 (May, 1975): 301–302.

[6] B. Horvat, "Yugoslav Economic Policy in the Post-War Period: Problems, Ideas, Institutional Developments," *American Economic Review* 61, supp. (June, 1971): 99.

that it is otherwise as alien to socialism as is private ownership.[7] The general position has been summarized by Djordjević as follows:

> . . . state ownership of the means of production creates a monopoly of economic and political power and . . . makes possible the unification of economic and political power under the control of a social group personifying the state. Thus, . . . the essence of classical [class] ownership is not changed. . . . As the holder of the title to property, the state disposes the producers' labor and its results, on the basis of which surplus labor is appropriated by groups which have their own interests in keeping their commanding functions, and thus retaining power and their social status and prestige.[8]

If these statements are taken at face value, the labor-managed firm emerges as an ideal mode of business organization and the vehicle through which the objectives of democratic socialism can be realized. The suggestion is that the alienating effects of capitalism, on the one hand, and those of state socialism, on the other, can be avoided by a clever reconstruction of the firm, which places control of production in the hands of the workers. Moreover, even when there is no desire to go all the way to social ownership of capital, the promise of greater industrial democracy and greater physical productivity gives worker participation schemes some appeal. In the United States, and in many countries of Western Europe, serious efforts are being made to discover a "less authoritarian" alternative to the conventional capitalist firm. The ideas of Anthony Wedgwood Benn in Great Britain have, perhaps, attracted the greatest publicity, and the greatest opposition, but the search for new organizational forms is real and pervasive.

What may be asked, then, is whether the neo-Marxists are fundamentally correct in claiming that both democracy and true economic efficiency require the end of hierarchically organized production. Does the so-called alienation of labor constitute a central problem for advanced industrial nations like the United States? Is some type of worker control of the firm essential, or, alternately, is the traditional capitalist approach based on contracts and markets capable of dealing with the alienation problem? These are important questions for the 1970's and for the future of capitalism itself. While they cannot be answered con-

---

[7] Ibid., p. 107.

[8] J. Djordjević, "A Contribution to the Theory of Social Property," *Socialist Thought and Practice* 24 (1966): 81.

clusively through theoretical reasoning, it is essential to subject the radical analysis of alienation to close scrutiny. By determining the empirical premises on which the radical case rests, and by exposing the logic of the argument, a more balanced perspective can be obtained on the need for industrial reorganization.

As it turns out, capitalism has more vitality and flexibility than its critics suggest; without exaggeration, one can say that the radical interpretation of alienation reflects a profound misunderstanding of how an enterprise economy functions and, more significantly, presents a completely distorted view of the basic economic choices open to society. Workers can have less arduous jobs and more attractive working conditions only at the expense of other goods. A competitive market system is considered valuable precisely because it permits each worker to select the particular product mix he most desires, and it permits this selection while a Pareto-efficient allocation of resources is achieved in the economy as a whole. By contrast, socialist labor management produces less attractive results. It can be shown that when each firm is controlled by its employees, resource allocation is virtually certain to be inefficient and the output of the system less than its potential. Ironically, it is also true that a labor-managed system is, on balance, less likely than a capitalist economy to allow a worker to obtain the combination of working conditions and income he finds most attractive. If the conclusions of economic logic are to be believed, there is no scientific reason why labor management should be the wave of the future.

I

The deficiencies of the radical analysis of alienation can best be revealed by a careful examination of the neo-Marxist case. Actually, the latter is developed at various levels of sophistication, but absolutely basic to any version is the idea that conventional marginal analysis can be of no use in considering alienation because the theory is tied rigidly to the capitalist status quo.[9] The point made is that marginalism already pre-

---

[9] On this interpretation marginalism is incapable of considering the real problems of modern society and has a useful role only if "existing social relations are taken as a datum and the problem is one of administering the system by adjustments around the edges" (R. C. Edwards, A. Mac Ewan, and the Staff of Social Science 125 [Harvard University], "A Radical Approach to Economics: Basis for a New Curriculum," *American Economic Review* 60, [May, 1970]: 352).

supposes the existence and inevitability of alienation: "The leisure-labor dichotomy characteristic of neoclassical analysis reflects an acceptance of the notion that, in general, labor or work activities will be nonfulfilling drudgery undertaken to secure an income, and that creative activities leading to individual development must necessarily be nonwork ('leisure') activities."[10]

The capitalist's control of the work process is central to the difficulties here, and, inescapably, workers find themselves alienated in a system where work activities are neither creative nor self-developmental. According to this interpretation, the nature of capitalism insures that the quality of the work process will always be sacrificed in the interest of capitalist dominance and greater profits. The situation is illustrated in Figure 1.[11] Assuming that a continuous trade-off relation exists between process quality (or the production environment, E) and profits (Π), various potential operating positions are open on curve TT'. However, capitalists' preferences, represented by the indifference curve U_c, imply

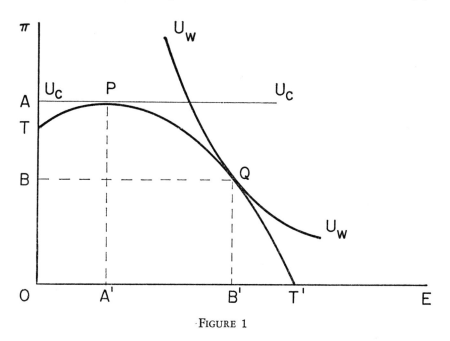

·FIGURE 1

[10] Ibid., p. 354.

[11] The diagram in the present paper follows the one used by the Harvard group in explaining the concept of alienation. See Edwards et al., "A Radical Approach," p. 354.

that the ideal operating point is at P, where the work environment is of relatively low quality (A'). This choice will rule even though workers' preferences, shown by curve U_w, would require operation at Q and the realization of a superior production environment (B').

The reason why capitalists are able to determine the level of E unilaterally is not made clear. But if this presumption is accepted, the fundamental conclusion to be drawn from the radical analysis is that workers must be frustrated in their attempts to achieve a more humane and meaningful work environment. The capitalist system has no way of responding to labor's desire for creative, self-developmental work activities and, therefore, workers can find no interest in their jobs as such. Motivation for work is extrinsic and provided largely by wage payments. Alienation becomes a normal way of life, a special burden that workers must endure without compensation.

Radical economists emphasize the point that while alienation represents a "cost" to workers, it is not a cost that can be recouped through a higher supply price for labor.[12] Ultimately, the institutional arrangements under capitalism are responsible for this "inequity." More immediately, however, the explanation of why workers are unable to extract higher wages as compensation for alienation is found in terms of the alternatives available in the system. As the radical argument has it, alienating conditions are pervasive throughout the capitalist economy. Thus, workers cannot transfer away from a few unpleasant industrial sectors and drive the wage rate up in these areas; characteristically, workers have no superior locations to which they can move because there are few if any nonalienating alternatives in existence. Moreover, even if certain employments do offer relatively attractive work environments, the stratification of the labor force insures that most workers will be unable to shift to such desirable positions. Quite simply, individuals find it impossible to move to fundamentally different types of jobs (and work environments) because of labor specialization and the difficulties of retraining.

Alienation is unavoidable; yet, as the radicals explain events, the interesting result is that *laborers will show no tendency to demand improved conditions of work*. The argument here turns on the dynamics of preference formation. Presumably, worker preferences are determined by the general socioconomic environment, and since there are virtually

[12] Ibid., p. 355.

no nonalienating jobs available in the system, workers have no basis on which to change their preferences. They adjust their desires and aspirations to the alternatives the capitalist status quo makes possible.

The neo-Marxist explanation of alienation has, perhaps, some superficial plausibility, but it certainly does not stand up to close analysis. There are serious difficulties at each stage of the argument, and the construction as a whole rests on a fundamental misunderstanding of how a capitalistic economy operates. In addition, much confusion arises because of the unwillingness, or the inability, of socialist theorists to define the precise nature of the system that is to replace capitalism. No doubt the problem of alienation would vanish if all goods were free and all work were purely voluntary, but such a solution is hardly a serious possibility, and thus the question remains of what practical changes are needed to reduce the presumed discontent of modern workers. Even to moderate alienation, as it has been discussed in the radical literature, would require a massive reorganization of the productive process. That is, to meet the many criticisms currently raised against capitalism, major movement would have to be made toward some new type of socialist "handicraft" system that would allow workers wide managerial powers and create an environment in which labor would take greater responsibility for and interest in the final product produced.

Such a prescription calls for a good deal more than the mere replacement of capitalist management by worker management. To achieve the reforms desired, the general character of existing capitalist firms would have to be changed profoundly. In particular, the reorganization would seem to require lesser specialization in production and reduced use of modern technological methods and organization, relaxation of labor discipline and lesser reliance on managerial authority, increased flexibility in the determination of the hours and conditions of work, imposition of special limitations on the types of products that can be produced and regulation of the sale of the products to approved consumers, and so on. Not all of these and other possible changes in the structure of production need lead to reduced efficiency; nevertheless, there can be little doubt that the net effect of the proposed changes in industrial and technical organization would be to *lower labor productivity as measured in terms of marketable output*. By adopting a productive system based more on "handicraft" technology, and by introducing a horizontal rather than a vertical structure of decision making, workers may be able to attain higher levels of satisfaction (utility). But there should be no mistaking the fact that the reorganization involves the substitution of nonpecuniary income for money wages. In practice, the work environment can be improved only by sacrificing marketable output.

This understanding is important in evaluating the radical assertion that workers receive no compensation for enduring unpleasant and unfulfilling work conditions. In a competitive economy, the "cost" implied by "alienation" is, in fact, fully offset by a higher supply price for labor. What cannot be extracted is additional "compensation" beyond the market wage. Since attainable wages would be much lower than the normal market levels if a major reorganization of productive activities were carried out along the lines demanded by the radical reformers, market wages must already reflect compensation for alienating effects, and in general no further reward is either justified or possible.

Radical economists are also wrong in assuming that workers in a capitalistic system will neither demand nor have the opportunity to choose improved (or less "alienating") work environments. No convincing evidence exists to show that workers are insensitive to the psychic and other fringe benefits and costs attaching to different occupations or jobs. However, whether these benefits and costs loom large in decision making is another matter. As Professor Domar has pointed out, the actions of labor unions in the United States do not lend much support to the idea that workers are greatly dissatisfied with existing production environments.[13] In any case, there is nothing in capitalist market structure that would prevent workers from obtaining jobs yielding either greater or lesser nonpecuniary returns. Neoclassical theory has long recognized that wage differences may arise precisely because of the relative subjective advantages or disadvantages of the work done,[14] and this theory applies, *mutatis mutandis*, to newly created positions.

Of course, even if it is accepted that workers never *demand* improved work environments, it does not follow that less alienating environments will not be offered by entrepreneurs. To suggest that no changes in working conditions can come about unless workers actively campaign for them is like saying that no new commodities are ever intro-

---

[13] E. D. Domar, "Poor Old Capitalism: A Review Article," *Journal of Political Economy* 82 (Nov.–Dec., 1974): 1304–1305.

[14] Opportunity cost doctrine has to be modified to take account of subjective effects. Thus, "the cost of productive service X in making A is equal to the amount of B that X could produce plus (or minus) the nonpecuniary returns (or costs) attached to producing B. The notion of objective cost must then be abandoned" (G. J. Stigler, *The Theory of Price* [New York: Macmillan, 1947], p. 108).

duced into the economy unless consumers conceive of the products first and insist that they be produced. The profit motive and competition insure that new or modified products will be offered to the public; similarly, entrepreneurs seeking profit will tend to experiment with new forms of business organization based on changed production environments. Whether less alienating productive arrangements can be sustained depends, quite simply, on the willingness of workers to trade wage income for nonpecuniary benefits.

The neo-Marxist discussion insinuates that profit maximization by capitalists necessarily leads to work environments of low quality. Figure 1 gives the diagrammatic statement of this case; presumably, decent conditions of work are neglected so that capitalists can reap large profits. But such a conclusion has no real justification. Profit maximization is consistent with many different outcomes and may, in fact, demand that the firm's environment be of very high quality. Capitalist organization per se does not rule out creative, self-developmental work activities.

II

Not only can a capitalist system respond to workers' desires for improved conditions of labor but, in principle at least, the competitive firm is able to provide an *optimal* environment for its employees. That is, the production environment will be optimal in the sense that the "quality" of the work process will be as high as it can be, given technology, the structure of market prices, and the willingness of workers to substitute nonpecuniary for pecuniary rewards. In explaining the nature of the optimization process and the equilibrium position to which the firm is drawn by market forces, it will be convenient to assume the existence of an idealized competitive economy that is free of externalities, nonconvexities and other difficulties capable of disturbing the normal functioning of markets. What has to be shown is how the behavior of profit-maximizing entrepreneurs and utility-maximizing workers leads to a wage-environment-profit solution that leaves all parties in positions from which no further advantageous moves can be made.

For our purposes here, the firm's profit function can be defined as follows:

$$\Pi = pq - wL - rK. \tag{1}$$

Profit (Π) is to be maximized under conditions where the commodity price (p) and the capital charge (r) are market parameters. These prices are, of course, accepted as data by the competitive firm. The wage rate, w, that will ultimately enter equation (1) is also given to the firm by way of the market, but precisely how w is established requires more discussion, and this variable will be discussed at greater length below.

The firm's output, q, depends on the inputs of labor, L, and capital, K, services employed and on the general working environment, E, maintained within the production unit:

$$q = f(L, K, E). \tag{2}$$

In the model, the magnitude of the environmental variable E is supposed to define the general character of the firm's technological and social organization. Although somewhat artificial, it is possible to think of E as being continuously variable. Then a full range of organizational forms exists, and we assume that as E grows larger the work environment becomes less alienating. Unfortunately, however, it is also true that as the work environment becomes less strongly hierarchical and controlled and as the technology becomes more primitive, the productive efficiency of the firm drops.[15] From a formal standpoint, the marginal products of labor and capital are assumed to diminish as the level of E is increased.

If, as the neo-Marxists suggest, alienation is a major problem for capitalism, workers must be concerned with both pecuniary returns (w) and nonpecuniary rewards (E). It seems reasonable to hypothesize, then, that there is not one supply schedule of labor facing an industry but many different schedules based on different possible work environments. In other words, for every wage-environment pair (w, E), there is a corresponding supply of labor potentially forthcoming. Perfect competition rules, and thus, from the standpoint of each *firm* in the industry, the conditions of labor supply are reflected as a set of horizontal curves. There is a completely elastic supply of labor available at each of many different wage rates, but at each rate a definite type of production environment must be provided. Figure 2 illustrates this situation. As the wage rate is increased, the environment can become more alienating, and conversely. The firm, of course, is free to secure any volume of labor

---

[15] The production function is usually defined in such way that it precludes variation in E. The organizational form (say E^*) consistent with the greatest output of the commodity for any input pair (L, K) is taken as "the" form to be used. Then, the function is given as $q = f(L, K; E^*)$, where E^* is a parameter. The latter tends to be regarded as fixed except insofar as technological change occurs. See E. G. Furubotn, "The Adaptability of Fixed Productive Services in the Short-Run," *Southern Economic Journal* 28 (Apr., 1962): 329–339.

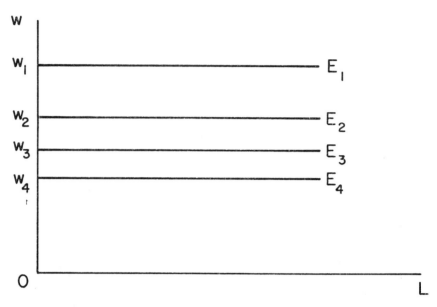

FIGURE 2

services it desires by paying the appropriate reward vector (w, E) to the workers.

When viewed collectively, the various labor markets based on different reward vectors reveal a general trade-off between money wages and the work environment. In effect, a trade-off curve can be drawn, as in Figure 3, that reflects the subjective preferences of workers regarding the balance to be maintained between pecuniary and nonpecuniary income. Presumably, labor will insist on extremely high wages when the quality of the work process approaches some lower limit E_0, and will resist dropping below a minimum money wage w_0. Individual workers, however, have different objectives and will sort themselves out into the different markets that are available. At any time, then, the trade-off curve can be expressed as a definite mathematical relation:

$$w = g(E). \qquad (3)$$

Of course, the curve in Figure 3 would be displaced to the right or left, or its shape would change, if the general attitude toward working in alienating environments were to be revised. For example, the lower limit E_0 could shift to the right under conditions where material goods were valued less highly.

With this background established, the way is open to consider how

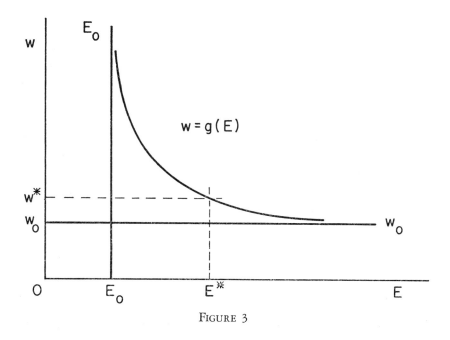

the profit-maximizing firm will determine the quality of the production environment. Two preliminary steps are required. First, equations (2) and (3) must be substituted into (1) so that the firm's profit function can be rewritten as

$$\Pi = p \cdot f(L, K, E) - g(E)L - rK. \tag{4}$$

Then, the problem is to maximize (4). For the simple system being studied, the procedure is straightforward, and the first-order conditions for the maximum emerge as

$$\frac{\partial \Pi}{\partial L} = p \frac{\partial q}{\partial L} - g(E) = 0, \tag{5a}$$

$$\frac{\partial \Pi}{\partial K} = p \frac{\partial q}{\partial K} - r = 0, \tag{5b}$$

$$\frac{\partial \Pi}{\partial E} = p \frac{\partial q}{\partial E} - \frac{\partial w}{\partial E} L = 0. \tag{5c}$$

It can also be shown that when plausible assumptions are made about the "shapes" of the functions in equations (2) and (3), the second-order conditions hold. Essentially, what is needed for the maximum when $\partial f/\partial E < 0$, $\partial g/\partial E < 0$, is $\partial^2 f/\partial E^2 < 0$, $\partial^2 g/\partial E^2 > 0$; or, in geometric terms, the slope of function f must become steeper as E is made larger, and the slope of function g must become less steep as E is increased. From the economic standpoint, these mathematical properties imply that continuing efforts to improve the work environment exert an increasingly adverse effect on physical productivity and cause output to fall more and more rapidly while, as far as the workers are concerned, improvements in the environment are valued less and less highly relative to money wages. Certainly the preceding interpretations seem consistent with a priori understanding of the alienation problem.

As can be seen, the first-order conditions of equations (5a) and (5b) are quite standard and merely require the efficient use of resources. Specifically, equation (5a) states that the value of the marginal product of labor must equal the wage rate (whatever it turns out to be), and (5b) demands that the value of the marginal product of capital services equal the given capital charge, r. The condition of equation (5c) is less familiar, but its meaning is easily grasped when it is put in the form $p(\partial q/\partial E) = (\partial w/\partial E)L$ and there is recognition that $\partial q/\partial E < 0$, $\partial w/\partial E < 0$. The implication here is that at equilibrium the decrement in value product $p(\partial q/\partial E)$ equals the decrement in the wage bill $(\partial w/\partial E)L$. As E is increased, the wage rate falls (Figure 3), and the new lower rate applies to all units of labor used by the firm. At the same time, as E is increased, productivity is reduced and so, with a constant commodity price p, the marginal value product of the firm falls. Moreover, it should also be noted that since the second-order conditions require, among other things, that the absolute magnitude of the value product fall more rapidly than that of the wage bill as E is made larger, there is always a limit beyond which E cannot be increased by the firm.[16] In other words, an alienating work environment will not normally be banished entirely, but conditions will be improved consistent with technology and the willingness of the workers to forgo money income in favor of other amenities.

Assuming that a unique maximum position can be reached by the system, simultaneous solution of conditions (5a)–(5c) will yield the *optimal*, or profit-maximizing, values for the factor inputs (L^*, K^*), the work environment (E^*), and commodity output (q^*). The firm will

[16] There is no obvious *natural* limit to the value of E; presumably, "improvement" in the conditions of work could continue to be made until no marketable output whatsoever became the norm. Indeed, even negative productivity is conceivable.

also be operating in a particular labor market where the given wage rate
(w^*) is regarded as acceptable because the workers understand that the
firm's production environment will be maintained at a certain quality
(E^*).

It is clear from equation (4) that the equilibrium values L^*, K^*,
and E^* lead to a definite level of profit for the firm, π^*. In the short run,
profit can be positive or negative. In the long run, however, self-interest
insures that the firm will not operate unless profit is nonnegative ($\pi^* \geq$
0). Of course, it is also true that, in the long run, competition and the
entry of new firms will tend to shift the commodity price and factor
prices to positions such that $\pi^* = 0$ for all firms in the industry. This
zero-profit equilibrium is important because by understanding its properties, one can judge the long-term capacity of a capitalist economy to provide less alienating work environments for labor.

As Figure 4 reveals, there is a maximum feasible value for the
work environment consistent with long-run equilibrium. Any attempt to
improve the environment beyond level E^* must bring about the dissolu-

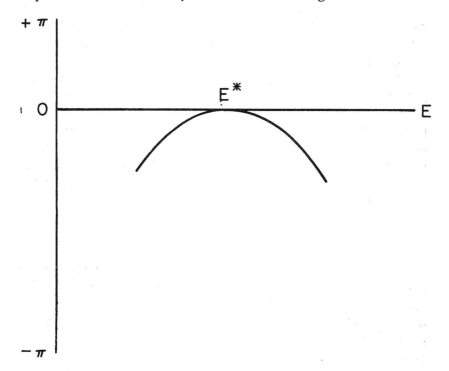

FIGURE 4

tion of the firm. The reason is simple. When E^* is exceeded, productivity is so reduced (relative to the concurrent wage reduction) that at the effective price structure $(p, r, g(E))$, the revenue from the sale of output cannot cover the costs of the factors involved in production. The firm is unable to go beyond E^*, but, equally, it has no incentive to provide a less attractive environment than E^*. If it were to do so, profits that could be made would be sacrificed, the realized profit would be negative, and, again, the ultimate result would be the failure of the firm.

What this simple competitive model suggests is that scarcity and human preferences dominate the outcome; it is the nature of the world, and not the nature of the capitalist system, that sets limits to the type of work environment that is attainable. Opportunity costs cannot be neglected, whatever the form of economic organization—including the socialist form. Thus, in the case sketched above, if the level of E were pushed beyond E^* in arbitrary fashion, the welfare of the system would become less than its potential. That is, assuming no special distributional problems have to be considered, the gain from increased nonpecuniary income, as valued by worker-consumers, would be less than the loss from diminished commodity output, as valued by the same group. Presumably, this adverse effect of reorganization would have to be taken into account even in a socialist state.

No doubt workers would like to secure constant or greater wages and, at the same time, enjoy improved working conditions, but realistically a trade-off is always necessary; wages must be reduced sufficiently to justify inferior techniques of production. Of course, depending on the actual technological alternatives open, some industries may be able to go further than others in establishing attractive work environments. This fact, however, does not change the basic requirement that an economic choice be made.

III

The idealized competitive model discussed in the preceding section is useful not because it presents an accurate picture of reality, but because it suggests the general direction events take in an enterprise economy. The fundamental theme is simple: The quality of the work environment is determined by the interplay of market forces in a system where individual decision makers are free to seek their own interests. This market explanation is, of course, denied vigorously by the neo-Marxists;

the radical position is that the quality of the work environment is not an economic choice but, rather, a socially dictated one based on the nature of capitalist institutions. What should be expected under this oppressive system is depicted in Figure 1; the variable E is held at some very low value in order to increase the firm's profits or to achieve long-term political objectives. Thus, no response is possible by capitalism to the workers' desires for an improved environment.

The trouble with Figure 1 is that among other things it fails to offer any convincing explanation of how the entrepreneur is able to reduce E to such a low level without simultaneously causing a sharp increase in the wage rate and a *reduction* in profit. After all, if workers object so strongly to the poor environment, why do they not insist on appropriate compensation (via pecuniary income) or transfer their labor services to other sectors where working conditions are superior? One radical answer to this question, such as it is, asserts that a paucity of nonalienating employment alternatives forces workers to accept unsatisfactory work activities. But it is difficult to believe that no suitable alternatives exist in the general conditions described. If there is, in fact, great desire to substitute nonpecuniary for pecuniary income, the wage-environment trade-off curve (Figure 3) will reflect this desire, and substantial incentive will be created for profit-seeking entrepreneurs to offer superior environments to their workers. Note that profit, not altruism, justifies the substitution of more E in the reward vector. Moreover, if existing technology tends to prevent the transition to less alienating environments (because productivity declines rapidly as E is made larger), incentive will also be created to discover efficient new productive processes consistent with higher E levels.

What has to be recognized is that the capitalist entrepreneur does not dictate the quality of the work environment. Rather, he responds to worker preferences concerning the mix of pecuniary and nonpecuniary rewards in much the same way that he responds to the prevailing conditions of technology. Insofar as he is interested in profits, he must adjust to both these classes of data optimally. Figure 1 is misleading because it suggests that the entrepreneur is able to follow an independent policy and reach equilibrium at P even though workers desire equilibrium at Q. But if workers genuinely wish to be at Q, they can always take steps that alter market conditions and made it advantageous for the capitalist to move to Q. In other words, under competition, workers can always insure that the firm's maximum profit position will occur at the E level the workers most desire.[17] Relative to the diagram, profits would not be lower at Q than at P if workers were willing to reduce the wage rate sufficiently. The fact that such willingness does not exist implies, however, that the worker-consumers value money income (commodities) more than additional E. In effect, the "price" of purchasing the improvement in the work environment (measured in terms of the value of forgone commodity output) is too high, given current preferences.

Granting the preceding argument, point P in Figure 1 must be interpreted as the operating point that *both* the workers and the capitalist find most satisfactory. The environment represented by $E = A'$ is the *optimal* environment, and in general Figure 1 can be regarded as analogous to Figure 4. It is true, however, that if positive profits are maintained in the long run, some revision must be made in the previous explanation. Sustained positive profits would indicate the presence of imperfect competition, and under such circumstances the solution reached by the firm would not normally be optimal. Departure from the ideal level of E could be expected. Indeed, in this case the neo-Marxist criticism would have some substance; workers would be offered a less attractive work environment than they would desire and be willing to pay for. Market forces would still push in the general directions described in the competitive situation, but the fine optimizing solution would be lost. Of course, the inferior outcome under monopoly comes as no surprise; it is a commonplace that departures from the conditions of perfect competition destroy the optimality characteristics of the idealized capitalist model.

Since the neo-Marxist attack on capitalism goes much beyond a mere objection to monopoly power, it is important to understand the basis on which more sophisticated radical writers attempt to discredit the general type of market model discussed in the preceding section. The approach taken by these critics is to disarm the opposition by suggesting that while market analysis is correct within its own limited set of assumptions, its results are trivial. Conventional theory neither applies to nor explains the dynamic capitalist world of contending social classes. Thus, the production environment and the pattern of work activities within the firm are said to be shaped by the overriding requirement that capitalist control of society be preserved. Marginalism is, simply, beside the point: "Note that it is *not* an objection to neoclassical theory that it

---

[17] Of course, if no sacrifice were involved, the "most desired" operating position from the workers' standpoint might be at T' in Figure 1.

overlooks 'work activities' as unit-objects in instrumental and relational modality. Neoclassical theory, as propounded by modern exponents, assumes each worker is able to choose from a wide array the particular activity that maximizes his (exogeneous) utility function, a utility function that depends on the quality of work, its intensity and duration, and the material reward that it offers. Thus in neoclassical theory the issue of who *controls* production does not arise."[18]

The last statement is the crucial one. Alienation is inevitable, according to this argument, because of the capitalist need to maintain effective control over the evolving system: "Capitalist development, through bureaucratic order and hierarchical authority in production, limits work activities to those that (a) permit an essential role for capitalists and their managerial representatives; (b) facilitate supervision and discipline of workers; (c) allow for flexible control from the top; and (d) limit through the division of tasks, the initiative of workers to 'safe' levels."[19] Profit maximization, then, is not the *sole* goal of the firm; the capitalist owners, by virtue of their class position, must also be concerned with other objectives. Specifically, points (a) through (d) have to be met so that the attitudes of labor can be manipulated appropriately and dominant roles in society be assured for capitalists. There is no mistaking the meaning, or the significance, of this dynamic interpretation of the theory of the firm:

> . . . radical theorists emphasize that worker sovereignty fails to obtain because the enterprise responds to the prices at which workers will supply their services in alternative types of work only insofar as the resulting work-organization is compatible with secure control by capitalists or managers. There are several aspects to this argument. First, it is held that the motivational basis of those in control of the production process is not profit making per se, but maintenance of their class position in production. While profit making is a crucial instrument toward this end, when the two come into conflict, their option is for maintenance of control.[20]

The idea that class position must be protected and sustained at all cost has some interesting implications for the model of the firm consid-

[18] H. Gintis, "A Radical Analysis of Welfare Economics and Individual Development," *Quarterly Journal of Economics* 86 (Nov., 1972): 591.

[19] Ibid., p. 591.

[20] H. Gintis, "Consumer Behavior and the Concept of Sovereignty: Explanations of Social Decay," *American Economic Review* 62 (May, 1972): 270.

ered in section II above. That is, if certain types of (less alienating) work environments are absolutely ruled out because of their long-term consequences for the economic and political organization of society, a maximum E level must exist. Assuming the most attractive environment that can be permitted is $\hat{E}$, the firm's problem translates into one of constrained maximization. The profit function

$$\Pi = p \cdot f(L, K, E) - g(E)L - rK \qquad (6)$$

has to be maximized subject to the constraint

$$E \leq \hat{E}. \qquad (7)$$

This new formulation is, of course, quite consistent with an outcome where the solution values E^*, L^*, and K^* are not ideal in the sense previously described. In general, the firm operating subject to (7) will not be earning as much profit as it would in the absence of the constraint, and workers will be forced to accept a more alienating environment than they desire.

A logical question at this point is whether the revised model established by (6) and (7) justifies the neo-Marxist position on the inevitability of alienation. Superficially, the results produced by the new construction seem to bear out the radical presumptions, but the real issue concerns the legitimacy of assuming a limit to E. From the standpoint of rational behavior, there is no reason whatsoever to believe that every capitalist entrepreneur will adhere to a uniform absolute limit such as $\hat{E}$, regardless of the "cost" of this policy in terms of forgone profits. What the radical writers have failed to recognize is the fact that interfirm competition exerts a powerful influence on entreprenurial choices and business organization. Assume for the moment that all of the firms in an industry do accept the constraint $\hat{E}$, and that costs of production are, therefore, relatively high.[21] But if costs are high and the commodity price is correspondingly high, substantial profits must await any firm that becomes a low-cost producer by relaxing the constraint $\hat{E}$ and adopting a less alienating (cost-reducing) work environment. Moreover, given competition, there is no serious obstacle to such a policy on the part of an individual firm. In an industry where many firms exist, it is difficult for the group to detect individual departures from $\hat{E}$, and in any event the group has no effective means for *enforcing* adherence to the desired environmental limit. Thus, any aggressive firm can "cheat" on the agreement with impunity and gain.

---

[21] That is, the constraint $\hat{E}$ is binding and the Lagrangian multiplier is greater than zero.

Certainly there are reasons why firms will wish to avoid the artificial restraint on the quality of the work environment and secure more profits in the short run. Even if all entrepreneurs are convinced that departure from $\hat{E}$ will weaken capitalist control of the system in the future and diminish long-run profits, individual decision makers may still not want to accept $\hat{E}$. Individuals, by definition, have different initial positions, different planning horizons, and different objectives; thus, it is reasonable to suppose that they can come to different opinions about the ideal time shape of the income stream. More important, once a movement to lower-cost production (higher E levels) begins, the pressures of competition will force reorganization on the industry as a whole. Each firm must recognize that as others change policy, there is less and less likelihood that long-term gains can be appropriated. The only course open is for the firm to follow the trend and secure profits while it can; the $\hat{E}$ policy is seen as obsolete and will be abandoned. In the end, therefore, each firm shifts to a genuine least-cost operating position. The work environment is optimal, and we are, in effect, back to the model discussed in the previous section.

Again, the existence of monopoly elements can frustrate the smooth working of this adjustment mechanism. The environmental situation faced under oligopoly is analogous to the more familiar case that arises when a few firms possess information on new technology but enter into collusive agreements in order to slow down or prevent the implementation of the improved methods of production. Actually, the analogy is precisely parallel when, as some radical theorists claim, an increase in the quality of the work environment enhances, rather than detracts from, the physical productivity of the firm.[22] In any case, collusion may retard the use of new technology or retard the improvement of the work environment, but collusive agreements normally break down and, certainly, there is no reason to believe that the work environment cannot improve over the long term.

The radical theory of capitalist development requires, among other things, that businessmen carry on a *perpetual* campaign to restrict the quality of the work environment and the initiative of the workers. Ostensibly, this is a condition for capitalist survival. The difficulty with the

---

[22] In the model it has been assumed that $\partial q/\partial E < 0$, but it is possible to assert that $\partial q/\partial E > 0$. For the latter case, the general arguments concerning the firm's behavior developed above hold a fortiori. That is, the capitalist entrepreneur has even more incentive to improve the work environment when $\partial q/\partial E > 0$.

concept, however, is that it presupposes an intense and passionate class loyalty on the part of capitalists. Not only are individuals able to identify themselves unambiguously as members of the elite class, but they are always quite willing to make major sacrifices of income and wealth in order to insure the preservation of the status quo. Such behavior, while perhaps not impossible, certainly seems much more in keeping with the attitudes of a feudal aristocracy than with the ideas of a modern business community. It is also interesting to note that this radical interpretation places entrepreneurs in a rather flattering new light; instead of being mere moneygrubbers, they are now idealists of a sort committed to a lofty mission promising rewards not to them but to their class.

As a practical matter, there is little doubt that the radical explanation of capitalist behavior is wrong. In general, profits will not be sacrificed in a political cause, more costly labor-alienating methods of production will not be used in an effort to keep workers in their place. If equilibrium E levels are low, it is not because of the politicoeconomic strategy of capitalists but because existing technology and the preference of workers concerning the mix of pecuniary and nonpecuniary income require low E levels.[23]

Whatever judgment is reached concerning the true basis of capitalist motivations, radical theorists would argue that the solutions produced by competitive markets are necessarily suboptimal. If this is so, it follows, of course, that any determination of the "optimal" level of the work environment (E^*) by way of markets is a sham, and, accordingly, the model given in the previous section can be nothing more than a futile analytical exercise. The criticism here is grounded in the idea that because worker and consumer preferences are formed largely through the results generated by markets, *these results are self-justifying.* Preferences are, in short, endogenous rather than exogenous. The character of the productive process,[24] the expected structure of availabilities, and the general capitalist milieu develop the capacities of people to derive satisfaction from particular types of goods and activities.[25] As the neo-Marxists

---

[23] Instead of reducing the efficiency and profitability of the firm by imposing an upper limit on E, capitalists might well consider the possibility of using more direct political means to insure the survival of the capitalist system. Even accepting some of the neo-Marxist premises, it would seem cheaper and more expedient for entrepreneurs to use economically efficient production methods but make lump-sum contributions each period to a general political fund dedicated to the advancement of capitalist interests.

[24] Gintis, "Radical Analysis," pp. 594–599.

[25] Gintis, "Consumer Behavior," pp. 273–277.

put it: exchange values, by influencing the process of capacity development, become essential determinants of use values.[26]

It is certainly plausible to say that people adjust to, and come to prefer, things that are familiar and products that are abundant. But the use to which the radicals put this reasonable proposition is something again. In effect, the assertion is made that worker-consumers possess the wrong preferences. These rank-and-file decision makers, having been conditioned by the capitalist system, are said to place too high a value on pecuniary income and market commodities while showing too little interest in social and creative activities. In terms of the model given earlier in this chapter, the (supposed) difficulty might be exemplified by the placement of the wage-environment trade-off curve. The curve, $w = g(E)$, would, presumably, be positioned sufficiently far to the left so that market solutions would show the optimal environment, E^*, to be of rather low quality.

The radical economist would insist that this type of outcome shows clearly that market solutions, even under competition, are inconsistent with the true welfare of the workers. Such solutions are not at all "optimal." A low value for E^* carries benefits for capitalist investors because such an equilibrium implies that the $\hat{E}$ constraint will not be binding; in other words, firms are free to seek the highest profit possible without any fear of creating production environments that will endanger capitalist survival. There is no nasty choice to be made between profits and class loyalty. But the workers are the losers. Capitalism perpetuates itself by distorting the preferences of those who would benefit enormously by an improvement in the character and conditions of work.[27] There is hope, however; it lies in the appearance of some contradiction or problem in the capitalist process that will break the low-level equilibrium trap and threaten further reproduction of the system.

To accept this line of argument is to accept the view that there is scientific meaning in the statement that workers would be happier if they had different preferences. Perhaps they would, perhaps not. There is no way to approach the issue on the basis of positive economic theory; the statement represents the ultimate in untestable propositions. What can be said, however, is that a convincing scientific case for the existence of pervasive worker alienation has not been made by the neo-Marxists.

[26] Ibid., p. 275.

[27] Ibid., pp. 276–277. If workers had the "correct" preferences, the wage-environment trade-off curve would be located far to the right of the curve shown in Figure 3.

IV

While radical reformers enter into lengthy discussions concerning the inadequacies of the capitalist system, they have relatively little to say about the scheme that is to replace capitalism and put an end to labor alienation. Certainly no detailed blueprint is provided for the ideal institutional structure; at best, only a few general characteristics of a nonalienating economy are suggested. By broad agreement, the new system must be socialistic, it must lead to an essentially egalitarian income distribution, and it must permit workers very wide powers in shaping the policies of the firm. As noted earlier, what seems to be called for is an economic system based on pervasive industrial democracy and labor management. The central idea is, of course, that if alienation is to be reduced or eliminated, each firm's actions have to be determined through democratic processes in which all current employees take part.

It is not implausible to suggest that the labor-managed firm may have some value in countering the problem of worker alienation. The question that arises, however, is whether this productive organization represents as flexible and effective an instrument for promoting human welfare as the capitalist firm. In particular, we should like to know whether the operation of the labor-managed firm is likely to bring about an efficient allocation of resources in the economy and whether labor management permits each worker to secure the mix of pecuniary and nonpecuniary income that he desires most. The answers to these questions are not obvious. Practical experience with a modern labor-managed system is still quite limited,[28] and the theory of the labor-managed economy remains in the process of development.[29] Nevertheless, there do exist theoretical grounds on which to believe that the labor-managed firm will not

[28] Following the economic reform of 1965, many features of an idealized labor-managed system were incorporated into the legal and institutional structure of Yugoslavia.

[29] The standard theory of the labor-managed firm has been developed by Ward, Domar, and Vanek. Dissenting views have been offered by Furubotn and Pejovich. See B. Ward, "The Firm in Illyria: Market Syndicalism," *American Economic Review* 58 (Sept., 1953): 566–589; E. Domar, "The Soviet Collective Farm as a Producer Cooperative," *American Economic Review* 56 (Sept., 1966): 734–757; J. Vanek, *The General Theory of Labor-Managed Market Economies* (Ithaca, N.Y.: Cornell University Press, 1970); E. G. Furubotn and S. Pejovich, "Property Rights and the Behavior of the Firm in a Socialist State: The Example of Yugoslavia," *Zeitschrift für Nationalökonomie* 30 (1970): 431–454; E. G. Furubotn, "The Long-Run Analysis of the Labor-Managed Firm: An Alternative Interpretation," *American Economic Review* 66, no. 1 (Mar., 1976), pp. 104–123.

function as successfully as some of its proponents suggest.[30] Fundamentally, difficulties appear because the structure of property rights inherent in the new system tends to produce conflict between the interests of certain workers attached to the firm and the interests of society as a whole.

In order to make predictions concerning the probable behavior of an economic system, it is essential to have information on the set of legally sanctioned property rights in existence and to establish the effective pattern of incentives in the system. At the level of the firm, we must know (1) the particular individuals or agencies that are empowered to determine the firm's policies, (2) the objectives and planning horizons of these decision makers, and (3) the specific penalty-reward structure facing the decision makers. Under labor management, of course, the focus is on the individual production unit and the ideal is to allow workers the widest latitude for decision making as long as they are actively employed by the firm. In a socialist state, the new organization differs from the traditional capitalist firm in several crucial respects. First, capital goods and other nonhuman means of production are socially owned rather than individually owned. However, the workers constituting the collective possess definite, if limited, rights in the income stream yielded by the capital goods. Moreover, the firm's policy choices are made through an internal political process in which all employees are expected to participate.

As socialist labor management is envisioned, a democratic voting process decides control of the firm and leads, ultimately, to the establishment of the firm's objectives with respect to wages, employment, output, investment, the work environment, and the like. At first thought, this type of institutional arrangement may seem both simple and desirable, but in fact the political process called for implies certain grave difficulties. If the firm's policy at each period of time is determined on the basis of a simple majority vote, it follows that the interests of the whole collective need not be served—either in the short run or the long run. The initial majority group controlling the firm will have incentive to perpetuate its domination of policy and, in such a way, insure the mainte-

30 Professor Vanek, in particular, has shown great confidence in the future of labor-management: "In brief, the labor-managed system appears to me to be superior by far, judged on strictly economic criteria, to any other economic system in existence" (J. Vanek, "Decentralization Under Workers' Management: A Theoretical Appraisal," *American Economic Review* 59 (Dec., 1969): 1006–1014.

nance of the best possible economic and social environment for its members. Assuming that this initial group can coalesce into a permanent interest bloc, and remain politically invincible over time, the basis of decision-making behavior by the collective is clear. The firm will be guided by the community welfare function reflecting the preferences of the employees forming the politically successful "original majority."[31]

The situation of the labor-managed firm reduces to this. At any moment of time, particular individuals are members of the group that holds effective political power in the collective; it is this group that decides the firm's actions for the next time period. Policies will, presumably, be evaluated in light of their probable consequences for the dominant majority group. Moreover, the worker-voters who actually determine the firm's behavior are not likely to be concerned with the position of labor in general, but with their own individual welfare. Under the voting process, the members of the majority group are able to appropriate special rights over socially owned capital, and they can be expected to act to preserve these rights.

Given the crucial significance of voting blocs within the firm, the original majority must consider employment policy with the greatest care. Any movement from the initial employment level is important because change in the size of the collective produces simultaneous effects in three distinct areas of concern. That is, for each potential change in employment, the original majority has to estimate the costs and benefits associated with (1) a production effect, (2) an environmental effect, and (3) a political effect. In the case of expansion, for example, the majority decision makers must predict not only the physical productivity of any additional labor hired but also the impact the labor increment will have on the firm's work environment and on the firm's internal political structure. It is obvious, of course, that any new workers coming into the collective are not just factors of production; they are potential policy makers as well. New workers, therefore, always imply some danger to the interests of the ruling majority. Offers of additional employment tend to open the way for transfers of power. Quite simply, voting patterns can be shifted by the appearance of added workers, and new policy directions can be established for the firm that are contrary to the desires of the original majority.

---

[31] The political process taking place within the firm may be much more complex than is suggested here. For example, the firm may be controlled by shifting coalitions of workers.

Since it is difficult for the original majority to estimate accurately the magnitudes of the three effects generated by change in the labor force, the best strategy for risk-averse decision makers is to avoid any major variation in employment. Thus, for example, while some hiring may be permitted to achieve greater output, the original majority is likely to guard against an unfavorable outcome by placing definite restrictions on employment. In particular, an overall upper limit ($\hat{L}$) can be expected on the total size of the working collective. The magnitude of the parameter $\hat{L}$ will reflect the majority group's judgment on how large a work force can be tolerated if effective political control is to be maintained. Given the upper limit on employment, the firm's labor input is free to vary from period to period, but in no instance will the number of workers exceed the critical value indicated by $\hat{L}$.

Insofar as workers shun altruism and actively seek their own interests, the employment policy of the labor-managed firm will be decided on the basis of the *net advantage* that labor change promises the majority group. It follows from this condition, however, that allocative efficiency will not be realized under labor management. In general, the labor-managed economy will *not* be Pareto optimal.[32] Competition, free entry, and the use of identical technology by all firms in an industry will not be sufficient to insure that the marginal-value product of labor will be the same for all firms. For, depending on the political situation within a given firm, there will be greater or lesser reluctance at each point to increase the firm's labor force. Even when circumstances are such that the limit $\hat{L}$ is not closely approached, concern for the quality of the firm's work environment may prevent employment from being carried as far as the usual marginal logic would demand.

A simple illustration suggests the forces at work here. Assume that the firm's existing capital/labor ratio is larger than the equilibrium ratio required to maximize the average wage rate. It follows from this that an increase in the firm's labor input can lead to a higher average wage per worker, and, in the limit, the maximum (average) wage w^* can be achieved. From the standpoint of the original majority, though, the desirability of greater employment cannot be judged on the basis of productivity alone. The impact of added labor on the environmental and political conditions of the firm must also be considered by the majority decision makers. If the latter believe that, on balance, their satisfaction

32 Compare Vanek, "Decentralization," p. 1007.

level will be diminished by the hiring of additional workers, they will vote against the policy. Then, instead of attaining the ideal solution $p\,(\partial q/\partial L) = w^*$, employment will be limited so that: $p\,(\partial q/\partial L) < w^*$. At equilibrium, the value of the marginal product of labor is less than the potentially realizable maximum wage rate (w^*). It should be emphasized that the choice of this restrictionist policy is perfectly understandable when the role of *appropriability* is recognized. The rewards that are meaningful to the decision makers are the pecuniary and non-pecuniary returns that they can actually capture during their period of tenure with the firm.

The fact that the policy decisions of the labor-managed firm are made on the basis of political power and voting blocs implies the possibility that a minority of workers within the collective will be forced to accept policies that run counter to their interests. In general, conditions in a labor-managed system will not insure that only workers having the same preferences and planning horizons will join a given firm; rather, diversity must be expected. Although many problems would disappear if all of the employees of the firm did possess identical views concerning what policies should be followed, there is little chance for this unanimity of opinion to occur. It is costly to screen potential employees carefully about attitudes and objectives. Moreover, there need not be any compelling reasons for the firm to do so. As long as the members of the original majority feel convinced that they can retain power, they have no particular concern for the welfare position of the minority within the collective. Fundamentally, the problem confronting the decision makers is one of evaluating costs and benefits. That is, the costs associated with determining the "political reliability" of an incremental group of workers, and the costs of maintaining these additional workers in the firm, have to be considered in relation to the advantages that flow from using the increment to the labor force.

The firm may not screen out potential minority members because of the relatively high costs of "quality control," but it is still true, of course, that the individuals constituting the minority within a collective are free to leave the firm and seek employment in more congenial and rewarding environments elsewhere. Each individual has strong incentive to find a firm controlled by people with objectives similar to his own. Nevertheless, freedom of movement and individual incentives are not sufficient to create a system in which the membership of each firm is homogeneous with respect to preferences and planning horizon. As a practical matter, it is both difficult and costly for the individual worker to obtain adequate information about any firm he is contemplating joining.

Since the labor-managed firm is an ongoing and changing organization, the worker seeking a different job must consider not only the current wage rate and conditions of work offered but the time stream of pecuniary and nonpecuniary income he is likely to secure over his planning horizon if he joins a new collective. In other words, the prospective employee is required to make a very complex estimate of future rewards, or he must be prepared to change jobs at frequent intervals and suffer the costs of such a strategy. Thus, from the standpoint of the job seeker, any change of position represents something of a leap in the dark, and the individual worker may well decide that the best plan is to remain where he is.

Workers must be concerned particularly with the future prospects and performance of the labor-managed firm because of the special nature of the organization. When an individual joins a collective, his situation is analogous to that of a person entering into a partnership. To some extent, at least, he is "locked in," and his welfare depends on the character and the timing of the policies followed by the group—or, more accurately, by the ruling majority.[33] These decision makers, however, are virtually certain to alter their objectives and policies over time, because as time elapses, changes tend to occur within the firm in such crucial areas as the age distribution of the labor force, the political alignments of the voter workers, the technology used in production, the structure of fixed capital, the commodity mix produced, and so on. The general result is that while changes can be expected to take place that will affect the reward stream the firm will offer, the precise composition of future reward vectors is extremely hard to estimate. And, as noted earlier, such uncertainty about pecuniary and nonpecuniary returns leads to a sluggish labor market.

If labor-managed firms tend to restrict offers of employment (because of the existence of the upper limit $\hat{L}$) and if individual workers are not easily induced to move from one firm to another (because com-

---

[33] Among other things, the majority decides on the allocation of the firm's net income and can elect to keep wages low in order to undertake collective consumption or self-financed investment in the firm. As long as a worker remains in the employ of the firm, he has a right to a share of the firm's net product. Nevertheless, he has no permanent or transferable claims on the firm's income stream, and this condition holds even if the worker has previously sacrificed current income (wages) to invest in the firm.

parisons of reward are difficult to make), misallocation of labor in the economy as a whole is not only possible but probable.[34] Moreover, with workers either frozen in their initial location or unable to discriminate finely among existing employment opportunities, there can be no assurance that each individual will find his way to the ideal work environment. What can be anticipated is that dissident minority groups—groups of employees who oppose the policies followed but who are unable to change these policies and secure the combinations of pecuniary and nonpecuniary income they most desire—will exist in most labor-managed firms. In short, a system of labor-managed socialist firms does not promise an end to worker alienation.

No small part of the attraction of labor management rests on the emotional response the term evokes. The presumption seems to be that democratic decision making by workers in an economy free of capitalist "exploitation" *must* be conducive to the public welfare. Systematic analysis, however, reaches different conclusions; in practice, the labor-managed firm's internal voting process can be expected to lead to serious problems. As has been suggested above, the new organization produces neither efficient factor allocation nor a nonalienating work environment. Even under idealized assumptions, a Pareto-optimal solution will appear only as a special and unlikely outcome. Indeed, the case against socialist labor management can be extended substantially beyond the basic arguments presented in this section. For example, it can be shown that labor management is consistent with chronic unemployment of labor and the misallocation of capital.[35] In general, both the rate and direction of investment are distorted by the special pattern of incentives generated in the system; capital accumulation, therefore, fails to conform to the preferences of the voter-workers despite the elaborate structure for democratic decision making. It is also true that labor management, per se, does not guarantee (and does not normally lead to) an egalitarian distribution of income.[36] Still other difficulties exist, but without going fur-

---

[34] For various reasons it is not easy for unemployed workers to find jobs in existing firms or to form new firms. See E. G. Furubotn and S. Pejovich, "Property Rights, Economic Decentralization, and the Evolution of the Yugoslav Firm, 1965–1972," *Journal of Law and Economics* 16 (Oct., 1973): 277–286.

[35] See Furubotn, "Long-Run Analysis of the Labor-Managed Firm," and E. G. Furubotn, "Bank Credit and the Labor-Managed Firm: The Yugoslav Case," reprinted in E. G. Furubotn and S. Pejovich, eds., *The Economics of Property Rights* (Cambridge: Ballinger, 1974), pp. 257–276.

[36] The question of income distribution is particularly important to socialist gov-

ther the preceding objections to labor management would seem to be sufficiently weighty to give pause to even the most ardent radical reformers.

Whatever the importance of labor alienation in the contemporary American economy, it is far from clear that market capitalism cannot deal with the problem. The inherent flexibility of the system lends support to the idea that any amenity seriously demanded will soon be forthcoming. To say this is not to argue that the search for alternative and improved forms of economic organization should not proceed. What is necessary, however, is a rational approach to the criticism of capitalist institutions. Standard scientific procedure should be followed. For, as Professor Domar states: "An analysis of capitalism, like any analysis, can be expected to consist of two parts: first, a logical formulation of a hypothesis showing how this or that evil is caused by capitalism; and, second, an empirical testing of the hypothesis against the reality of capitalist and noncapitalist systems."[37] It must be emphasized in this connection that a clear specification of the noncapitalist system being considered as an alternative is essential. To talk in terms of a vague ideal such as "democratic socialism" is not enough; rather, a relatively detailed blueprint of the new scheme is needed.

The difficulty that arises when broad utopian prescriptions are substituted for concrete proposals is well illustrated by the case of labor management. Certainly the concept of democratic decision making by independent voter-workers has appeal; but the arrangement is seen in less favorable light when the actual mechanics of the system are considered closely. While it is true that the theory of socialist labor management requires further development, preliminary study does suggest that the labor-managed firm is much less effective in reducing worker alienation than its capitalist counterpart, and less efficient in the use of scarce resources to boot. At the very least, then, second thoughts about the desirability of labor management seem to be in order. And the moral here is simple: one should look where he is leaping before he leaps. This idea is hardly very profound, but the point should be pondered by those who would destroy an effective economic system in the blind pursuit of an illusion.

---

ernments. See Furubotn and Pejovich, "Property Rights, Economic Decentralization, and Evolution," pp. 286–302.

[37] Domar, "Poor Old Capitalism," p. 1302.